Summary of Contents

D0473958

THE ART & SCIENCE OF JAVASCRIPT

BY **CAMERON ADAMS**
JAMES EDWARDS
CHRISTIAN HEILMANN
MICHAEL MAHEMOFF
ARA PEHLIVANIAN
DAN WEBB
SIMON WILLISON

The Art & Science Of JavaScript

by Cameron Adams, James Edwards, Christian Heilmann, Michael Mahemoff, Ara Pehlivanian, Dan Webb, and Simon Willison

Copyright © 2007 SitePoint Pty. Ltd.

Expert Reviewer: Robert Otani

Managing Editor: Simon Mackie

Technical Editor: Matthew Magain

Technical Director: Kevin Yank

Printing History:
   First Edition: January 2008

Editor: Georgina Laidlaw

Index Editor: Fred Brown

Cover Design: Alex Walker

Latest Update: March 2008

Notice of Rights

Notice of Liability

Trademark Notice

Reprint Permissions

Published by SitePoint Pty. Ltd.

48 Cambridge Street Collingwood
VIC Australia 3066.
Web: www.sitepoint.com
Email: business@sitepoint.com

ISBN 978-0-9802858-4-0
Printed and bound in Canada

About the Authors

Cameron Adams—The Man in Blue[1]—melds a background in computer science with over eight years' experience in graphic design to create a unique approach to interface design. Using the latest technologies, he likes to play in the intersection between design and code to produce innovative but usable sites and applications. In addition to the projects he's currently tinkering with, Cameron has taught numerous workshops and spoken at conferences worldwide, including @media, Web Directions, and South by South West. Every now and then he likes to sneak into bookshops and take pictures of his own books, which have been written on topics ranging from JavaScript to CSS and design. His latest publication, *Simply JavaScript*, takes a bottom-up, quirky-down approach to the basics of JavaScript coding.

James Edwards says of himself:

In spring, writes, and builds
Standards and access matters
Hopes for sun, and rain

Chris Heilmann has been a web developer for ten years, after dabbling in radio journalism. He works for Yahoo in the UK as trainer and lead developer, and oversees the code quality on the front end for Europe and Asia. He blogs at http://wait-till-i.com and is available on many a social network as "codepo8."[2]

Michael Mahemoff[3] is a hands-on software architect with 23 years of programming experience, 12 years commercially. Building on psychology and software engineering degrees, he completed a PhD in design patterns for usability at the University of Melbourne.[4] He documented 70 Ajax patterns—spanning technical design, usability, and debugging techniques—in the aptly-named *Ajax Design Patterns* (published by O'Reilly) and is the founder of the popular AjaxPatterns.org wiki. Michael is a recovering Java developer, with his programming efforts these days based mostly on Ruby/Rails, PHP and, of course, JavaScript. Lots of JavaScript. You can look up his blog and podcast, where he covers Ajax, software development, and usability, at http://softwareas.com/.

Ara Pehlivanian has been working on the Web since 1997. He's been a freelancer, a webmaster, and most recently, a front-end architect and team lead for Nurun, a global interactive communications agency. Ara's experience comes from having worked on every aspect of web development throughout his career, but he's now following his passion for web standards-based front-end development. When he isn't teaching about best practices or writing code professionally, he's maintaining his personal site at http://arapehlivanian.com/.

Dan Webb is a freelance web application developer whose recent work includes developing Event Wax, a web-based event management system, and Fridaycities, a thriving community site for Londoners. He maintains several open source projects including Low Pro and its predecessor, the Unobtrusive JavaScript Plugin for Rails, and is also a member of the Prototype core team. He's been a JavaScript programmer for seven years and has spoken at previous @media conferences, RailsConf, and The Ajax Experience. He's also and written for A List Apart, HTML Dog, SitePoint and *.NET Magazine*. He blogs regularly about Ruby, Rails and JavaScript at his site, danwebb.net, and wastes all his cash on hip hop records and rare sneakers.

---

[1] http://www.themaninblue.com
[2] Christian Heilmann photo credit: Philip Tellis [http://www.flickr.com/photos/bluesmoon/1545636474/]
[3] http://mahemoff.com/
[4] http://mahemoff.com/paper/patternLanguages.shtml

Simon Willison is a seasoned web developer from the UK. He is the co-creator of the Django web framework[5] and a long-time proponent of unobtrusive scripting.

About the Expert Reviewer

Robert Otani enjoys working with brilliant people who make products that enhance the way people think, see, and communicate. While pursuing a graduate degree in physics, Robert caught onto web development as a career, starting with game developer Psygnosis, and has held software design and engineering positions at Vitria, AvantGo, and Sybase. He is currently working with the very talented crew at IMVU,[6] where people can express their creativity and socialize by building their own virtual worlds in 3D, and on the Web. He enjoys his time away from the keyboard with his wife Alicia and their two dogs, Zeus and Stella. His personal web site can be found at http://www.otanistudio.com.

About the Technical Editor

Before joining the SitePoint team as a technical editor, Matthew Magain worked as a software developer for IBM and also spent several years teaching English in Japan. He is the organizer for Melbourne's Web Standards Group,[7] and enjoys candlelit dinners and long walks on the beach. He also enjoys writing bios that sound like they belong in the personals column. Matthew lives with his wife Kimberley and daughter Sophia.

About the Technical Director

As Technical Director for SitePoint, Kevin Yank oversees all of its technical publications—books, articles, newsletters, and blogs. He has written over 50 articles for SitePoint, but is best known for his book, *Build Your Own Database Driven Website Using PHP & MySQL*. Kevin lives in Melbourne, Australia, and enjoys performing improvised comedy theater and flying light aircraft.

About SitePoint

SitePoint specializes in publishing fun, practical, and easy-to-understand content for web professionals. Visit http://www.sitepoint.com/ to access our books, newsletters, articles, and community forums.

---

[5] http://www.djangoproject.com/

[6] http://www.imvu.com

[7] http://webstandardsgroup.org/

Table of Contents

Chapter 5   **Metaprogramming with JavaScript** 149

Preface

Once upon a time, JavaScript was a dirty word.

It got its bad name from being misused and abused—in the early days of the Web, developers only ever used JavaScript to create annoying animations or unnecessary, flashy distractions.

Thankfully, those days are well behind us, and this book will show you just how far we've come. It reflects something of a turning point in JavaScript development—many of the effects and techniques described in these pages were thought impossible only a few years ago.

Because it has matured as a language, JavaScript has become enormously trendy, and a plethora of frameworks have evolved around many of the best practice techniques that have emerged with renewed interest in the language. As long-time JavaScript enthusiasts, we've always known that the language had huge potential, and nowadays, much of the polish that makes a modern web application really stand out is usually implemented with JavaScript. If CSS was the darling of the early 2000s, JavaScript has since well and truly taken over the throne.

In this book, we've assembled a team of experts in their field—a veritable who's who of JavaScript developers—to help you take your JavaScript skills to the next level. From creating impressive mashups and stunning, dynamic graphics to more subtle user-experience enhancements, you're about to open Pandora's box. At a bare minimum, once you've seen what's possible with the new JavaScript, you'll likely use the code in this book to create amazing user experiences for your users. Of course, if you have the inclination, you may well use your new-found knowledge to change the world.

We look forward to buying a round of drinks at your site's launch party!

Who Should Read This Book?

This book is targeted at intermediate JavaScript developers who want to take their JavaScript skills to the next level without sacrificing web accessibility or best practice. If you've never written a line of JavaScript before, this probably isn't the right book for you—some of the logic in the later chapters can get a little hairy.

If you have only a small amount of experience with JavaScript, but are comfortable enough programming in another language such as PHP or Java, you'll be just fine—we'll hold your hand along the way, and all of the code is available for you to download and experiment with on your own. And if you're an experienced JavaScript developer, we would be very, *very* surprised if you didn't learn a thing or two. In fact, if you *only* learn a thing or two, you should contact us here at SitePoint—we may have a book project for you to tackle!

What's Covered in This Book?

Chapter 1: Fun with Tables

HTML tables get a bad rap among web developers, either because of their years of misuse in page layouts, or because they can be just plain boring. In this chapter, Ara Pehlivanian sets out to prove that not only are properly used tables *not* boring, but they can, in fact, be a lot of fun—especially when they're combined with some JavaScript. He introduces you to the DOM, then shows how to make table columns sortable and draggable with either the mouse or the keyboard.

Chapter 2: Creating Client-side Badges

Badges are snippets of third-party data (image thumbnails, links, and so on) that you can add to your blog to give it some extra personality. Christian Heilmann walks us through the task of creating one for your own site from scratch, using JSON and allowing for a plan B if the connection to the third-party server dies.

Chapter 3: Creating Vector Graphics with `canvas`

In this chapter, Cameron Adams introduces the `canvas` element, and shows how you can use it to create vector graphics—from static illustrations, to database driven graphs and pie charts—that work across all modern browsers. After you've read this chapter, you'll never look at graphics on the Web the same way again!

Chapter 4: Debugging and Profiling with Firebug

Firebug is a plugin for the Firefox browser, but calling it a plugin doesn't do it justice—Firebug is a full-blown editing, debugging, and profiling tool. It takes the traditionally awkward task of JavaScript debugging and optimization, and makes it intuitive and fun. Here, Michael Mahemoff reveals tons of pro-level tips and hidden treasures to give you new insight into this indispensable development tool.

Chapter 5: Metaprogramming with JavaScript

Here, Dan Webb takes us on a journey into the mechanics of the JavaScript language. By understanding a little about the theory of metaprogramming, he shows how we can use JavaScript to extend the language itself, improving its object oriented capabilities, improving support for older browsers, and adding methods and operators that make JavaScript development more convenient.

Chapter 6: Building a 3D Maze with CSS and JavaScript

Just when you thought you'd seen everything, James Edwards shows you how to push the technologies of CSS and JavaScript to their limits, as he creates a real game in which the player must navigate around a 3D maze! Complete with a floor-plan generator and accessibility features like keyboard navigation and captions, this chapter highlights the fact that JavaScript's potential is limited only by one's imagination.

Chapter 7: Flickr and Google Maps Mashups

Ever wished you could combine the Web's best photo-management site, Flickr, with the Web's best mapping service, Google Maps, to create your own über-application? Well, you can! Simon Willison shows that, by utilizing the power of JavaScript APIs, creating a mashup from two third-party web sites is easier than you might have thought.

The Book's Web Site

Located at http://www.sitepoint.com/books/jsdesign1/, the web site that supports this book will give you access to the following facilities.

The Code Archive

As you progress through this book, you'll note file names above many of the code listings. These refer to files in the code archive—a downloadable ZIP file that contains all of the finished examples presented in this book. Simply click the **Code Archive** link on the book's web site to download it.

Updates and Errata

No book is error-free, and attentive readers will no doubt spot at least one or two mistakes in this one. The Corrections and Typos page on the book's web site will provide the latest information about known typographical and code errors, and will offer necessary updates for new releases of browsers and related standards.[1]

The SitePoint Forums

If you'd like to communicate with other web developers about this book, you should join SitePoint's online community.[2] The JavaScript forum,[3] in particular, offers an abundance of information above and beyond the solutions in this book, and a lot of fun and experienced JavaScript developers hang out there. It's a good way to learn new tricks, get questions answered in a hurry, and just have a good time.

The SitePoint Newsletters

In addition to books like this one, SitePoint publishes free email newsletters including *The SitePoint Tribune*, *The SitePoint Tech Times*, and *The SitePoint Design View*. Reading them will keep you up to date on the latest news, product releases, trends, tips, and techniques for all aspects of web development. Sign up to one or more SitePoint newsletters at http://www.sitepoint.com/newsletter/.

---

[1] http://www.sitepoint.com/books/jsdesign1/errata.php
[2] http://www.sitepoint.com/forums/
[3] http://www.sitepoint.com/launch/jsforum/

Your Feedback

If you can't find an answer through the forums, or if you wish to contact us for any other reason, the best place to write is books@sitepoint.com. We have an email support system set up to track your inquiries, and friendly support staff members who can answer your questions. Suggestions for improvements as well as notices of any mistakes you may find are especially welcome.

Conventions Used in This Book

You'll notice that we've used certain typographic and layout styles throughout this book to signify different types of information. Look out for the following items.

Code Samples

Code in this book will be displayed using a fixed-width font, like so:

```
<h1>A perfect summer's day</h1> <p>It
    was a lovely day for a walk in the park. The birds were
    singing and the kids were all back at school.</p>
```

If the code may be found in the book's code archive, the name of the file will appear at the top of the program listing, like this:

example.css

```
.footer { background-color: #CCC; border-top: 1px
        solid #333; }
```

If only part of the file is displayed, this is indicated by the word *excerpt*:

example.css *(excerpt)*

```
border-top: 1px solid #333;
```

Some lines of code are intended to be entered on one line, but we've had to wrap them because of page constraints. A ➡ indicates a page-break that exists for formatting purposes only, and should be ignored. A vertical ellipsis (:) refers to code that has been omitted from the example listing to conserve space.

```
if (a == b) {
    ⋮
}
URL.open.("http://www.sitepoint.com/blogs/2007/11/01/the-php-anthology-101-essent
    ➡ial-tips-tricks-hacks-2nd-edition");
```

Tips, Notes, and Warnings

 Hey, You!

Tips will give you helpful little pointers.

 Ahem, Excuse Me ...

Notes are useful asides that are related—but not critical—to the topic at hand. Think of them as extra tidbits of information.

 Make Sure You Always ...

... pay attention to these important points.

 Watch Out!

Warnings will highlight any gotchas that are likely to trip you up along the way.

Fun with Tables

For the longest time, tables were the tool of choice for web designers who needed a non-linear way to lay out a web page's contents. While they were never intended to be used for this purpose, the row-and-column structure of tables provided a natural grid system that was too tempting for designers to ignore. This misuse of tables has shifted many designers' attention away from the original purpose for which they were intended: the marking up of tabular data.

Though the life of a table begins in HTML, it doesn't have to end there. JavaScript allows us to add interactivity to an otherwise static HTML table. The aim of this chapter is to give you a solid understanding of how to work with tables in JavaScript, so that once you've got a grip on the fundamentals, you'll be comfortable enough to go well beyond the examples provided here, to do some wild and crazy things of your own.

If you're new to working with the DOM, you'll also find that this chapter doubles as a good introduction to DOM manipulation techniques, which I'll explain in as much detail as possible.

Anatomy of a Table

Before we can have fun with tables, it's important to cover some of the basics. Once we have a good understanding of a table's structure in HTML, we'll be able to manipulate it more easily and effectively with JavaScript.

In the introduction I mentioned a table's row-and-column structure. In fact, there's no such thing as columns in a table—at least, not in an HTML table. The columns are an illusion. Structurally, a table is a collection of rows, which in turn are collections of cells. There is no tangible HTML element that represents a column of cells—the only elements that come close are `colgroup` and `col`, but they serve only as aids in styling the table. In terms of actual structure, there are no columns.

Let's take a closer look at the simple table shown in Figure 1.1.

Figure 1.1. A simple table

I've styled the table with some CSS in order to make it a little easier on the eyes. The markup looks like this:

simple.html *(excerpt)*

```
<table id="sales" summary="Quarterly sales figures for competing
companies. The figures are stated in millions of dollars.">
  <caption>Quarterly Sales*</caption>
  <thead>
    <tr>
      <th scope="col">Companies</th>
      <th scope="col">Q1</th>
      <th scope="col">Q2</th>
      <th scope="col">Q3</th>
      <th scope="col">Q4</th>
    </tr>
  </thead>
  <tbody>
    <tr>
      <th scope="row">Company A</th>
      <td>$621</td>
```

```
          <td>$942</td>
          <td>$224</td>
          <td>$486</td>
        </tr>
        <tr>
          <th scope="row">Company B</th>
          <td>$147</td>
          <td>$1,325</td>
          <td>$683</td>
          <td>$524</td>
        </tr>
        <tr>
          <th scope="row">Company C</th>
          <td>$135</td>
          <td>$2,342</td>
          <td>$33</td>
          <td>$464</td>
        </tr>
        <tr>
          <th scope="row">Company D</th>
          <td>$164</td>
          <td>$332</td>
          <td>$331</td>
          <td>$438</td>
        </tr>
        <tr>
          <th scope="row">Company E</th>
          <td>$199</td>
          <td>$902</td>
          <td>$336</td>
          <td>$1,427</td>
        </tr>
      </tbody>
    </table>
    <p class="footnote">*Stated in millions of dollars</p>
```

Each set of <tr></tr> tags tells the browser to begin a new row in our table. The <th> and <td> tags inside them represent header and data cells, respectively. Though the cells are arranged vertically in HTML, and almost look like columns of data, they're actually rendered horizontally as part of a row.

Notice also that the rows are grouped within either <thead> or a <tbody> tags. This not only provides a clearer semantic structure, but it makes life easier when we're working with the table using JavaScript, as we'll see in a moment.

Accessing Table Elements with `getElementById`

When our browser renders a page, it constructs a DOM tree of that page. Once this DOM tree has been created, we're able to access elements of our table using a range of native DOM methods.

The `getElementById` method is one that you'll see in most of the chapters of this book. Here's an example of how we'd use it to access a table's rows:

```
var sales = document.getElementById("sales");
var rows = sales.rows;
```

In the above code, we first obtain a reference to our table using the DOM method `getElementById`, and place it into a variable named `sales`. We then use this variable to obtain a reference to the collection of table rows. We place this reference into a variable named, quite aptly, `rows`.

The example above is all very well, but what if we only wanted the row inside the `thead` element? Or maybe just the ones located inside the `tbody`? Well, those different groups of rows are also reflected in the DOM tree, and we can access them with the following code:

```
var sales = document.getElementById("sales");
var headRow = sales.tHead.rows;
var bodyRows = sales.tBodies[0].rows;
```

As the above code demonstrates, accessing the row inside the `thead` is fairly straightforward. You'll notice that getting at the `tbody` rows is a little different, however, because a table can have more than one `tbody`. What we're doing here is specifying that we want the collection of rows for the first `tbody` in the `tBodies` collection. As collections begin counting at zero, just like arrays, the first item in the collection is actually item `0`, and can be accessed using `tBodies[0]`.

Who's This DOM Guy, Anyway?

The **Document Object Model (DOM)** is a standardized API for programmatically working with markup languages such as HTML and XML.

The DOM is basically an object oriented representation of our document. Every element in our HTML document is represented by an object in that document's DOM tree. These objects—referred to as **nodes**—are organized in a structure that mirrors the nested HTML elements that they represent, much like a tree.

The DOM tree also contains objects whose job is to help make working with our document easier; one example is the following code's `rows` object, which doesn't exist in our source HTML document. And each object in the DOM tree contains supplementary information regarding, among other things, its position, contents, and physical dimensions.

We follow the same principle to access a particular row. Let's get our hands on the first row inside the first `tbody`:

```javascript
var sales = document.getElementById("sales");
var bodyRows = sales.tBodies[0].rows;
var row = bodyRows[0];
```

Of course, JavaScript offers us many ways to achieve the same goal. Take a look at this example:

```javascript
var sales = document.getElementById("sales");
var tBody = sales.tBodies[0];
var rows = tBody.rows;
var row = rows[0];
```

The result of that code could also be represented by just one line:

```javascript
var row = document.getElementById("sales").tBodies[0].rows[0];
```

In the end, the approach you choose should strike the right balance between efficiency and legibility. Four lines of code may be considered too verbose for accessing a row, but a one-line execution may be difficult to read. The single line above is also more error prone than the four-row example, as that code doesn't allow us to check for the existence of a collection before accessing its children.

Of course, you could go to the other extreme:

```javascript
var sales = document.getElementById("sales");
if (sales) {
  var tBody = sales.tBodies[0];
  if (tBody) {
    var rows = tBody.rows;
    if (rows) {
      var row = rows[0];
    }
  }
}
```

This code checks your results every step of the way before it proceeds, making it the most robust of the above three code snippets. After all, it's possible that the table you're accessing doesn't contain a `tbody` element—or any rows at all! In general, I favor robustness over terseness—racing towards the first row without checking for the existence of a `tbody` , as we've done in our one-line example, is likely to result in an uncaught error for at least some users. We'll discuss some guidelines for deciding on an appropriate coding strategy in the coming sections.

We follow the same principles to access the cells in a table: each row contains a `cells` collection which, as you might have guessed, contains references to all of the cells in that row. So, to access the first cell in the first row of a table, we can write something like this:

```
var sales = document.getElementById("sales");
var cell = sales.rows[0].cells[0];
```

Here, we've ignored the fact that there may be a `tHead` or a `tBodies` collection, so the row whose cells we're accessing is the first row in the table—which, as it turns out, is the row in the `thead`.

Accessing Table Elements with `getElementsByTagName`

We have at our disposal a number of ways to access table information—we aren't restricted to using collections. For example, you might use the general-purpose DOM method `getElementsByTagName`, which returns the children of a given element. Using it, we can grab all of the `td`s in a table, like this:

```
var sales = document.getElementById("sales");
var tds = sales.getElementsByTagName("td");
```

Those two lines of code make a convenient alternative to this much slower and bulkier option:

```
var sales = document.getElementById("sales");
var tds = [];
for (var i=0; i<sales.rows.length; i++) {
  for (var j=0; j<sales.rows[i].cells.length; j++) {
    if (sales.rows[i].cells[j].nodeName == "TD") {
      tds.push(sales.rows[i].cells[j]);
    }
  }
}
```

Of course, choosing which technique you'll use is a question of using the right tool for the job. One factor you'll need to consider is performance; another is how maintainable and legible your code needs to be. Sometimes, though, the choice isn't obvious. Take a look at the following examples. Here's the first:

```
var sales = document.getElementById("sales");
var cells = sales.rows[1].cells;
```

And here's the second:

```
var sales = document.getElementById("sales");
var cells = sales.rows[1].getElementsByTagName("*");
```

Both of these code snippets produce the same results. Neither uses any for loops; they're both two lines long; and they both reach the cells collection through sales.rows[1]. But one references the cells collection directly, while the other uses getElementsByTagName.

Now if speed was our main concern, the first technique would be the right choice. Why? Well, because getElementsByTagName is a generic function that needs to crawl the DOM to fetch our cells. The cells collection, on the other hand, is specifically tailored for the task.

However, if flexibility was our main concern (for example, if you only wanted to access the td elements, not the surrounding elements that form part of the table's hierarchy), getElementsByTagName would be much more convenient. Otherwise, we'd need to loop over the cells collection to filter out all of the th elements it returned along with the td elements.

Sortable Columns

Now that we know how to work with our table through the DOM, let's add to it some column sorting functionality that's similar to what you might find in a spreadsheet application. We'll implement this feature so that clicking on a column's heading will cause its contents to be sorted in either ascending or descending order. We'll also make this behavior as accessible as possible by ensuring that it works with and without a mouse. Additionally, instead of limiting the functionality to one specific table, we'll implement it so that it works with as many of a page's tables as we like. Finally, we'll make our code as easy to add to a page as possible—we'll be able to apply the sorting functionality to any table on the page by including a single line of code.

Making Our Tables Sortable

First, in order to apply our sort code to as many tables as we want, we need to write a function that we can instantiate for each table that we want to make sortable:

tablesort.js (excerpt)

```
function TableSort(id) {
  this.tbl = document.getElementById(id);
  if (this.tbl && this.tbl.nodeName == "TABLE") {
    this.makeSortable();
  }
}
```

In the code above, we've created a function named TableSort. When it's called, TableSort takes the value in the id parameter, and fetches a reference to an element on the page using the getElementById DOM method. We store this reference in the variable this.tbl. If we find a valid element with that id, and that element is a table, we can make it sortable by calling the makeSortable function.

Making the Sort Functionality Accessible

I mentioned that we'd make our sorting functionality accessible to both mouse and keyboard users. Here's the code that will help us achieve this:

tablesort.js (excerpt)

```
TableSort.prototype.makeSortable = function () { ❶
  var headings = this.tbl.tHead.rows[0].cells;
  for (var i=0; headings[i]; i++) { ❷
    headings[i].cIdx = i; ❸
    var a = document.createElement("a");
    a.href = "#";
    a.innerHTML = headings[i].innerHTML; ❹
    a.onclick = function (that) { ❺
      return function () {
        that.sortCol(this);
        return false;
      }
    }(this);
    headings[i].innerHTML = ""; ❻
    headings[i].appendChild(a);
  }
}
```

We wrap anchors (a elements) around the contents of each of the th elements. This enables our users to tab to an anchor, and to trigger an onclick event by pressing the **Enter** key—thereby allowing the sort to be activated without a mouse. And, since we're adding these anchors dynamically, we don't need to worry about them cluttering up our markup.

Here are the details:

❶ We're assigning our function to the object's prototype object. The prototype object simplifies the process of adding custom properties or methods to all instances of an object. It's a powerful feature of JavaScript that's used heavily throughout the rest of this book, particularly in the field of metaprogramming (see Chapter 5).

❷ We iterate over the cells in the headings collection with a for loop. This loop is slightly different from those we've seen in previous examples in that the condition that's checked on each pass is headings[i], rather than the traditional i<headings.length. This is an optimization technique: the for loop checks to see if there's an item in the headings collection at position i, and avoids having to calculate the length of the array on each pass.

Avoiding length can save valuable milliseconds if you're dealing with large datasets, though in our case—with only five items in our array—this approach is just shorter (and quicker to write).

③ Because of a bug in Safari 2.0.4 that causes the browser to always return a value of 0 for cellIndex, we need to emulate the cellIndex value for each heading. We do so by assigning the value of i to a new property that we've created, called cIdx.

④ Inside the loop, we create a new anchor, and copy the contents of the th into it.

⑤ We also add an onclick event to the anchor, the reason for which I'll explain in a moment.

⑥ Finally, we clear the original contents of the th and insert the new anchor in place of the original contents.

Using innerHTML

I'm using the innerHTML property here; even though it isn't part of the W3C recommendation, it's widely supported and operates faster (as well as being much simpler to use) than the myriad DOM methods I'd have to use to achieve the same outcome.

Making Assumptions is Okay … Sometimes

You'll note that we're grabbing the th cells in the table's thead with only one line of code, taking for granted that a thead exists, and that it contains at least one row. I've done so for brevity—in this example, we can be certain of the contents of the table that we're working with. If we didn't have the same control over the table on which we were operating, we'd have to use more verbose code to check each step along the way, as demonstrated earlier.

Handling Events and Scope Issues

You'll notice that we assigned an onclick event to the anchor just before we added it to the page.

The reason why we've used nested functions here is to fix a scope problem with the this keyword. In a function that's called by an event such as onclick, the this keyword refers to the calling element. However, in this case, we need this to point to our instance of TableSort—not the anchor that was just clicked—so that our onclick code can access the this.tbl property.

Normally, we'd assign an anonymous function directly to our anchor's onclick event handler like this:

```
a.onclick = function () {
  alert(this);
}
```

But if we were to take this approach, the this keyword would return a reference to the anchor element that was just clicked. Instead, we replace it with a self-executing function that returns another anonymous function to the `onclick` handler. The outer function forms a **closure**, a concept that's discussed in more detail in Chapter 5. Here's the revised code:

```
a.onclick = function (that) {
  return function () {
  }
} (this);
```

The brackets at the end of the main function cause it to be executed as soon as it is loaded by the browser (rather than when the click event is triggered); the parameter passed to the function is the current `this` keyword, which refers to our `TableSort` instance.

Inside the function, we receive the `TableSort` reference in a variable named `that`. Then, in the scope of the actual `onclick` event, all we have to do is call our `sortCol` function and pass *it* the reference to the anchor element, like so:

```
a.onclick = function (that) {
  return function () {
    that.sortCol(this);
    return false;
  }
} (this);
```

Here, `return false;` ensures that the anchor doesn't try to follow its `href` value—the default behavior for an anchor element. The use of `return false;` is important here, because if our `href` value was #, it would add the click to our browser's history, and return users to the top of the page if they weren't there already.

Adding Some Class

Now that we've wrapped our `th` elements with anchors and added a few more lines of CSS, we have a table that looks like the one in Figure 1.2.

 Be Careful when Assigning Events

In this example, I've assigned functions directly to our event handlers as a way to minimize the size of the script. However, this can be a dangerous practice! Our use of code like `a.onclick = function () { … }` creates a one-to-one relationship between our event and the function. So if, previously, a function had been assigned to the event handler, this code would overwrite it. To make your scripts more robust, consider using one of the many `addEvent` functions available online. I'm a big fan of the Yahoo! User Interface Library's `addListener` function.[1]

---

[1] http://developer.yahoo.com/yui/event/

Figure 1.2. A table ready to be sorted

The arrows next to the column headings signify that each column can be used as a basis to sort the table's data. The active column's arrow is darkened; the inactive columns' arrows are dimmed to show that, though they're clickable, they aren't currently being used to sort the table's content. The arrows are inserted as CSS background images on the newly inserted a elements, and are managed with two class names: asc for ascending and dsc for descending. Heading cells without an asc or dsc class name receive an inactive arrow.

These class names aren't included just for decorative purposes. We'll be using them in our code to identify the direction in which a column is being sorted, and to toggle the sort direction when a user clicks on a heading. Here's how our table begins:

tablesort.html *(excerpt)*

```
<thead>
  <tr>
    <th class="asc" scope="col">Companies</th>
    <th scope="col">Q1</th>
    <th scope="col">Q2</th>
    <th scope="col">Q3</th>
    <th scope="col">Q4</th>
  </tr>
</thead>
```

In this code, we've added the class name asc to the first column heading because we know that the companies are sorted alphabetically in the markup.

Performing the Sort

Once the users click on a heading (technically speaking, they click on the anchor surrounding the heading), the sortCol function is called, and is passed a reference to the calling (clicked) element. This process is important, as it identifies to us the column that we need to sort.

Our first order of business is to set up a few important variables:

tablesort.js (excerpt)

```
TableSort.prototype.sortCol = function (el) {
  var rows = this.tbl.rows;
  var alpha = [], numeric = [];
  var aIdx = 0, nIdx = 0;
  var th = el.parentNode;
  var cellIndex = th.cIdx;
  ⋮
}
```

Here's a description of each of these variables:

rows

This variable is a shortcut to the table's rows; it lets us avoid having to type this.tbl.rows each time we want to refer to them.

alpha, numeric

These arrays will allow us to store the alphanumeric and numeric contents of the cells in our column.

aIdx, nIdx

These two variables are indices to be used with our two arrays. We'll increment them individually every time we add an item to one of the arrays.

th

This is a reference to the clicked anchor's parent, which is a th. The anchor's reference is el, which is passed as a parameter to the sortCol function.

cellIndex

This variable stores the th element's index within its parent row. Using the cellIndex value, we'll be able to skip to the correct cell in each row, effectively traversing a column of cells.

Parsing the Content

Now let's loop over the table's rows and process each cell that falls beneath the heading that was clicked. The first thing we're going to have to do is retrieve the cell's contents—regardless of whether that data is found inside nested <span> or <strong> tags, for example:

tablesort.js (excerpt)

```
for (var i=1; rows[i]; i++) {
  var cell = rows[i].cells[cellIndex];
  var content =
    cell.textContent ? cell.textContent : cell.innerText;
    ⋮
```

We're after the final data value of the cell, regardless of whether that value is simply $150, <strong>$</strong>150, or <p><strong>$</strong><em>150</em></p>. The simplest way to achieve this goal is to use either the `textContent` or `innerText` properties of the element. Firefox supports only `textContent`, and Internet Explorer supports only `innerText`, while Safari and Opera support both. So in order to make the code work across the board, we'll use a ternary operator that uses one property or the other, depending on what's available in the browser executing the script.

Now that we've grabbed the cell's contents, we need to determine whether the data we retrieved is alphanumeric or numeric. We need to do this because we need to sort the two types of data separately—alphanumeric data should come *after* numeric data in our output.[2]

Using the Ternary Operator to Normalize Browser Inconsistencies

Sometimes you'll encounter situations where browser makers have decided not to follow the W3C spec, or for whatever reason, have implement proprietary functionality. Either way, the resulting inconsistencies can be a headache when you're trying to support multiple browsers.

Using a traditional `if/else` statement can be a bit bulky when all you want is to assign a value to your variable from two potentially different sources, depending on which is available. Enter: the **ternary operator**, a compressed `if/else` statement with the syntax `condition ? true : false;` Let's consider its application in terms of this code:

```
if (cell.textContent) {
  var content = cell.textContent;
} else {
  var content = cell.innerText ;
}
```

We can use the ternary operator to replace the above with this single line of code (well, it would be a single line if we could fit it on this page!):

```
var content = cell.textContent ?
  cell.textContent : cell.innerText;
```

---

[2] If we were to expand our table sort to accommodate other types of data—such as dates—we'd need to separate our data even further. For this demo, however, we'll restrict our sort functionality to include only alphabetic and numeric data.

Here's the code:

```
var num = content.replace(/(\$|\,|\s)/g, ""); 
if (parseFloat(num) == num) { 
  numeric[nIdx++] = {
    value: Number(num),
    row: rows[i]
  }
} else {
  alpha[aIdx++] = { 
    value: content,
    row: rows[i]
  }
}
```

❶ Before we check the data type, we need to strip the cell's contents of any characters that could be used in a numerical context—dollar signs, commas, spaces, and so on—but which might cause numeric data to be interpreted as alphanumeric data. We use a regular expression and the `replace` method to achieve this result.

❷ Once we've stripped out the characters, we use JavaScript's `parseFloat` function to see whether or not the remaining cell value is a number. If it is, we store the stripped-down version of it in the `numeric` array.

❸ If it isn't a number, we store the untouched cell value in the `alpha` array.

You'll note that we're storing the value in an object literal, which allows us also to store a reference to the row in which the cell was originally found. This row reference will be crucial later, when we reorder the table according to our sort outcome.

Implementing a Bubble Sort

Now that our column's contents are parsed and ready to be sorted, let's take a look at our sort algorithm. If we wanted to, we could use JavaScript's built in `sort` method, which looks like this:

```
var arr = [19, 2, 77, 111, 33, 8];
var sorted = arr.sort();
```

This approach would produce the array [111, 19, 2, 33, 77, 8], which isn't good enough, since the items have been sorted as if they were strings. Luckily, the `sort` method allows us to pass it a comparison function. This function accepts two parameters, and returns either a negative number, a positive number, or zero. If the returned value is negative, it means that the first parameter is smaller than the second. If the returned value is a positive number, the first parameter is greater than the second. And if the returned value is zero, they're both the same.

Here's how we'd write such a comparison function:

```
function compare(a, b) {
  return a-b;
}
var sorted = unsorted.sort(compare);
```

The trouble with `sort` is that the algorithm itself (that is, the logic it uses to loop over the data) is hard-coded into the browser—the comparison part of the function is the only part you can tweak. Also, `sort` was introduced in JavaScript 1.1—it's not available in older browsers. Of course, supporting outdated browsers isn't a major issue, but if you're a control freak like me, you might want to write your own sort algorithm from scratch, so that it does support older browsers. Let me walk you through an example that shows how to do just this.

We don't need to reinvent the wheel here; we have many different kinds of sort algorithms to choose from—every possible type seems already to have been worked out.[3] Even though it's not the quickest algorithm, I've chosen to use a bubble sort[4] here because it's simple to understand and describe.

A bubble sort works by executing two loops—an inner loop and an outer loop. The inner loop goes over our dataset once and checks the current item against the next item. If the current item is bigger than the next one, it swaps them; if it isn't, the loop moves on to the next item. The outer loop keeps running the inner loop until there are no more items to swap. Figure 1.3 illustrates our table's Q3 data being bubble sorted.

Each iteration of the outer loop is labeled as a "pass," and each column of data within a pass represents one step forward in the inner loop. The black arrow next to the numbers shows the progress of the inner loop (as does the "i=0" on top of each column). The red, curved arrows represent a swap that has taken place between the current item and the next one. Note how the outer loop goes over the entire dataset once more at the end, to make sure that there aren't any more swaps to perform.

We'd like our function to be able to perform both ascending and descending sorts. Since we don't want to write the same function twice—the two sort algorithms would perform the same operations, only in reverse—we'll write just one `bubbleSort` function, and have it accept a direction parameter as well as the array to be sorted.

---

[3] http://en.wikipedia.org/wiki/Sorting_algorithm
[4] http://en.wikipedia.org/wiki/Bubble_sort

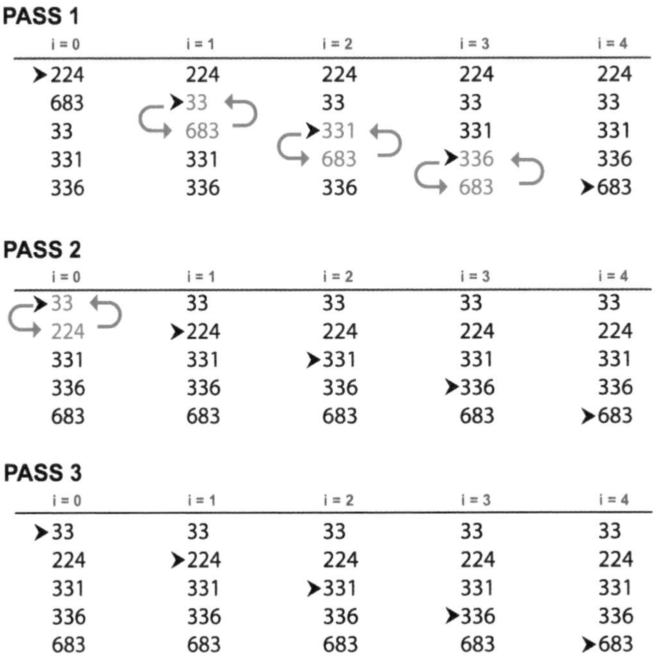

PASS 1

i = 0	i = 1	i = 2	i = 3	i = 4
➤224	224	224	224	224
683	➤33 ↰	33	33	33
33	↳ 683 ↱	➤331 ↰	331	331
331	331	↳ 683 ↱	➤336 ↰	336
336	336	336	↳ 683 ↱	➤683

PASS 2

i = 0	i = 1	i = 2	i = 3	i = 4
➤33 ↰	33	33	33	33
↳ 224 ↱	➤224	224	224	224
331	331	➤331	331	331
336	336	336	➤336	336
683	683	683	683	➤683

PASS 3

i = 0	i = 1	i = 2	i = 3	i = 4
➤33	33	33	33	33
224	➤224	224	224	224
331	331	➤331	331	331
336	336	336	➤336	336
683	683	683	683	➤683

Figure 1.3. A bubble sort in action

There are a couple of things to note here. First, `bubbleSort` is a standalone function and doesn't need to be added to `TableSort` with a `prototype` object—after all, there's no need to make copies of the function every time a new `TableSort` instance is made. Second, since we'll be using the `dir` parameter to make `bubbleSort` bidirectional, this code may be a little harder to follow than the code we've looked at so far.

Take a deep breath, and let's dive in:

tablesort.js *(excerpt)*

```
function bubbleSort(arr, dir) {
  var start, end;
  if (dir === 1) {     ❶
    start = 0;
    end = arr.length;
  } else if (dir === -1) {
    start = arr.length-1;
    end = -1;
  }
  var unsorted = true;
  while (unsorted) {     ❷
    unsorted = false;     ❸
    for (var i=start; i!=end; i=i+dir) {     ❹
      if (arr[i+dir] && arr[i].value > arr[i+dir].value) {     ❺
        var a = arr[i];
        var b = arr[i+dir];
```

```
            var c = a;
            arr[i] = b;
            arr[i+dir] = c;
            unsorted = true;
        }
      }
    }
    return arr;
}
```

Let's take a look at what's going on here:

 Before we start looping over our data, we need to set up a couple of variables. The dir parameter's only valid values, 1 and -1, represent ascending and descending order respectively. Checking for the value of dir, we set the start and end points for our inner loop accordingly. When dir is ascending, we'll start at zero and end at the array's length; when it's descending, we'll start at the array's length minus one, and end at negative one.

❷ I've used a while loop for our outer loop, and set it to continue executing until the value for unsorted is equal to false.

❸ For each iteration, we immediately set unsorted to false, and only set it to true in the inner loop if a sort needs to be made.

❹ I've used a for loop for our inner loop. A for loop has three parts to it: an **initialization**, a **condition**, and an **update**:

```
for (initialization; condition; update) {
  // do something
}
```

Our loop criterion looks like this:

```
for (var i=start; i!=end; i=i+dir) {
```

The initialization is set to our start value. Our condition returns true as long as the counter i is not equal to our end value, and we updated our counter by adding the value of dir to it.

In the case of an ascending loop, our counter is initialized to zero. The loop continues executing as long as the counter's value does not equal the array's length; the counter is incremented by one with each iteration.

In a descending loop, the counter is initialized to a value that's equal to the array's length minus one, since the array's index counts from zero. The counter is decremented by a value of one on each iteration, and the loop continues until the counter's value equals -1. This might seem confusing, but this criterion works because dir is a negative value, so 1 is subtracted from our counter on each pass.

 Now that we've got our loop working in both directions, we need to check whether the next item in the list is larger than the current one. If it is, we'll swap them:

```
if (arr[i+dir] && arr[i].value > arr[i+dir].value) {
   var a = arr[i];
   var b = arr[i+dir];
   var c = a;
   arr[i] = b;
   arr[i+dir] = c;
   unsorted = true;
}
```

Our if statement is made up of two parts. First, to make sure that there is a neighboring item to check against, we try to access arr[i+dir]. Since dir can be a negative or positive number, this statement will check the item either before or after the current item in the array. If there's an item in that position, our attempt will return true. This will allow us to check whether the value of the current item is greater than that of its neighbor. If it is, we need to swap the two.

We also set the variable unsorted to true, as we've just made a change in the order of our dataset, and ensure that the item's new position doesn't put it in conflict with its new neighbors.

Now we've got a sorting algorithm, let's use it:

tablesort.js (excerpt)

```
var col = [], top, bottom;

if (th.className.match("asc")) { ❶
  top = bubbleSort(alpha, -1);
  bottom = bubbleSort(numeric, -1);
  th.className = th.className.replace(/asc/, "dsc");
} else { ❷
  top = bubbleSort(numeric, 1);
  bottom = bubbleSort(alpha, 1);
  if (th.className.match("dsc")) {
    th.className = th.className.replace(/dsc/, "asc");
    } else {
    th.className += "asc";
  }
}
```

First, we check to see the current state of our column. Is it sorted in ascending order? If it is, we'll call our bubble sort algorithm, requesting that it sort our array in descending order.

❷ Otherwise, if the column's data is already sorted in descending order (or is unsorted), we request that it be sorted in ascending order.

We call `bubbleSort` twice because we've split our column data into two separate arrays, `alpha` and `numeric`. The results of the sort are then placed into two generic arrays, `top` and `bottom`. We use this approach because we can't be sure in advance whether we're going to be sorting in ascending or descending order. If the sort order is ascending, the `top` array will contain numeric data and the `bottom` array will contain alphanumeric data; when we're sorting in descending order, this assignment of array to data type is reversed. This approach should be fairly intuitive, given that once they're assigned, the contents of `top` will always appear at the top, and the contents of `bottom` will always appear at the bottom of our column.

Managing Heading States

Once the data's sorted, we set the `th` element's class name to either `asc` or `dsc` to reflect the column's current state. This will allow us to toggle the sort order back and forth if ever the user clicks on the same heading twice. Figure 1.4 shows the first column of our table in each of its toggle states.

Figure 1.4. Heading states

Before we modify any headings, we need to make sure that the only column to have an `asc` or `dsc` class name is the one that was clicked. Each of the other columns needs to be reverted to its original, unsorted order—we do so by removing any `asc` or `dsc` class names that may previously have been assigned to those columns. In order to do this, we'll need a `TableSort`-level variable that will always remember the `th` element that belongs to the column that was last sorted. Let's go back and add a variable declaration called `this.lastSortedTh` to our `TableSort` function. We'll also write a small loop that will seek out any `asc` or `dsc` class names present in our HTML, and will store the last occurrence in `this.lastSortedTh`:

tablesort.js *(excerpt)*

```
function TableSort(id) {
  this.tbl = document.getElementById(id);
  this.lastSortedTh = null;
  if (this.tbl && this.tbl.nodeName == "TABLE") {
```

```
      var headings = this.tbl.tHead.rows[0].cells;
      for (var i=0; headings[i]; i++) {
        if (headings[i].className.match(/asc|dsc/)) {
          this.lastSortedTh = headings[i];
        }
      }
      this.makeSortable();
    }
}
```

The variable `this.lastSortedTh` will now reflect any columns that are naturally sorted in the HTML; the `for` loop above sees to this by simply by reading the class names of the headings in the `thead`. In our example, even if the first click to sort a column occurred on a column other than the "Companies" column, our code would still be able to remove the "Companies" column's `asc` value, because a reference to that column's `th` is now held in `this.lastSortedTh`.

Here's how we'll clear the class names for previously sorted `th` elements:

tablesort.js *(excerpt)*

```
      if (this.lastSortedTh && th != this.lastSortedTh) {
        this.lastSortedTh.className =
          this.lastSortedTh.className.replace(/dsc|asc/g, "");
      }
      this.lastSortedTh = th;
```

In the above code, we check to see whether a value is assigned to `this.lastSortedTh`. Then we verify that any value it *does* have is not simply a reference to the current column (we don't want to clear the class names for the column we're in the process of sorting!). Once we're sure that this is indeed a valid column heading (and not the current one), we can go ahead and clear it using a simple regular expression.

Rearranging the Table

At this point in our script, we have two sorted arrays (named `top` and `bottom`), and a bunch of column headings that properly reflect the new sort state. All that's left to do is to actually reorder the table's contents:

tablesort.js *(excerpt)*

```
      col = top.concat(bottom);
      var tBody = this.tbl.tBodies[0];
      for (var i=0; col[i]; i++) {
        tBody.appendChild(col[i].row);
      }
```

The first thing we do is build a single array, col, from the two that contain our sorted data. We do this by concatenating the contents of bottom to top, and placing the whole thing into the variable col. Next, we loop over the contents of the col array, taking each item's parent row and moving it to the bottom of the table's tbody. By doing this, we order the column's cells while keeping their relationships with the cells in other columns intact. Figure 1.5 demonstrates this process in action.

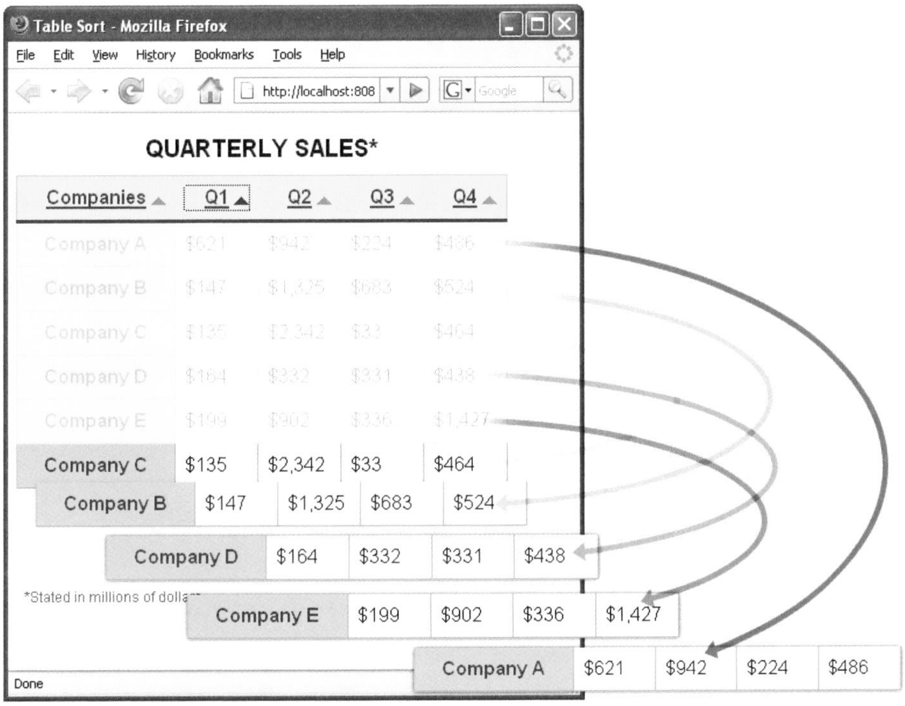

Figure 1.5. Rearranging the table

And with that final step, our script is complete! All that's left for us to do is to call TableSort. We do this by adding the following code to our document's head:

tablesort.html *(excerpt)*

```
<script type="text/javascript" src="tablesort.js"></script>
<script type="text/javascript">
window.onload = function () {
  var sales = new TableSort("sales");
} </script>
```

Though there are more optimal ways of doing it, for the sake of brevity I've used window.onload to call TableSort when the page loads. Remember that to make multiple tables sortable, all you need to do is create another instance of TableSort using a different table's ID. Here's our final script, in all its glory:

```javascript
function TableSort(id) {
  this.tbl = document.getElementById(id);
  this.lastSortedTh = null;
  if (this.tbl && this.tbl.nodeName == "TABLE") {
    var headings = this.tbl.tHead.rows[0].cells;
    for (var i=0; headings[i]; i++) {
      if (headings[i].className.match(/asc|dsc/)) {
        this.lastSortedTh = headings[i];
      }
    }
    this.makeSortable();
  }
}

TableSort.prototype.makeSortable = function () {
  var headings = this.tbl.tHead.rows[0].cells;
  for (var i=0; headings[i]; i++) {
    headings[i].cIdx = i;
    var a = document.createElement("a");
    a.href = "#";
    a.innerHTML = headings[i].innerHTML;
    a.onclick = function (that) {
      return function () {
        that.sortCol(this);
        return false;
      }
    }(this);
    headings[i].innerHTML = "";
    headings[i].appendChild(a);
  }
}

TableSort.prototype.sortCol = function (el) {
  /*
   * Get cell data for column that is to be sorted from HTML table
   */
  var rows = this.tbl.rows;
  var alpha = [], numeric = [];
  var aIdx = 0, nIdx = 0;
  var th = el.parentNode;
  var cellIndex = th.cIdx;
  for (var i=1; rows[i]; i++) {
    var cell = rows[i].cells[cellIndex];
    var content =
      cell.textContent ? cell.textContent : cell.innerText;
    /*
     * Split data into two separate arrays, one for numeric content
     * and one for everything else (alphabetical). Store both the
```

```
   * actual data that will be used for comparison by the sort
   * algorithm (thus the need to parseFloat() the numeric data)
   * as well as a reference to the element's parent row. The row
   * reference will be used after the new order of content is
   * determined in order to actually reorder the HTML
   * table's rows.
   */
  var num = content.replace(/(\$|\,|\s)/g, "");
  if (parseFloat(num) == num) {
    numeric[nIdx++] = {
      value: Number(num),
      row: rows[i]
    }
  } else {
    alpha[aIdx++] = {
      value: content,
      row: rows[i]
    }
  }
}


/*
 * Sort according to direction (ascending or descending)
 */
var col = [], top, bottom;
if (th.className.match("asc")) {
  top = bubbleSort(alpha, -1);
  bottom = bubbleSort(numeric, -1);
  th.className = th.className.replace(/asc/, "dsc");
} else {
  top = bubbleSort(numeric, 1);
  bottom = bubbleSort(alpha, 1);
  if (th.className.match("dsc")) {
    th.className = th.className.replace(/dsc/, "asc");
  } else {
    th.className += "asc";
  }
}


/*
 * Clear asc/dsc class names from the last sorted column's th if
 * it isn't the same as the one that was just clicked
 */
if (this.lastSortedTh && th != this.lastSortedTh) {
  this.lastSortedTh.className =
    this.lastSortedTh.className.replace(/dsc|asc/g, "");
}
this.lastSortedTh = th;

/*
```

```
 *   Reorder HTML table based on new order of data found in the
 *   col array
 */
col = top.concat(bottom);
var tBody = this.tbl.tBodies[0];
for (var i=0; col[i]; i++) {
  tBody.appendChild(col[i].row);
}
}

function bubbleSort(arr, dir) {
  // Pre-calculate directional information
  var start, end;
  if (dir === 1) {
    start = 0;
    end = arr.length;
  } else if (dir === -1) {
    start = arr.length-1;
    end = -1;
  }

  // Bubble sort: http://en.wikipedia.org/wiki/Bubble_sort
  var unsorted = true;
  while (unsorted) {
    unsorted = false;
    for (var i=start; i!=end; i=i+dir) {
      if (arr[i+dir] && arr[i].value > arr[i+dir].value) {
        var a = arr[i];
        var b = arr[i+dir];
        var c = a;
        arr[i] = b;
        arr[i+dir] = c;
        unsorted = true;
      }
    }
  }
  return arr;
}
```

Creating Draggable Columns

A feature that's often desired by those working with tabular data in desktop applications is the ability to move a table's columns around in order to get a better look at its data. For example, you may want to compare the values in the first and last columns of a table. Being able to move those columns next to each other makes the task much easier.

But why should desktop applications have all the fun? We can create draggable columns on the Web too—Figure 1.6 shows an example of a simple HTML table that we'll add this functionality to.

As with our sorting script, let's make this functionality as accessible as possible by:

- ensuring it works with and without a mouse
- ensuring it works with multiple tables on the one page
- making it super-easy to implement

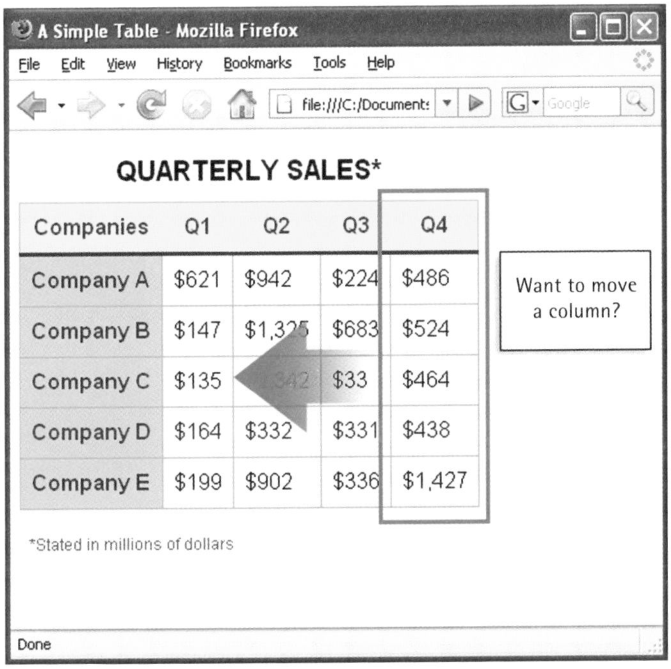

Figure 1.6. Want to move a column?

Let's address the third point in that list. All that will be required to implement the draggable column functionality is the addition of a single line of code to the page, as in our sorting example in the previous section:

```
window.onload = function () {
  var sales = new ColumnDrag("sales");
}
```

Making the Table's Columns Draggable

Taking the lead from our table sort example, we first need to create a JavaScript function that we can instantiate. We'll call this function ColumnDrag:

columndrag.js *(excerpt)*

```
function ColumnDrag(id) {
  this.tbl = document.getElementById(id);
  if (this.tbl && this.tbl.nodeName == "TABLE") {
    this.state = null;
    this.prevX = null;
    this.cols = this.tbl.getElementsByTagName("col");
    this.makeDraggable();
  }
}
```

In the code above, the first thing that we do is try to access the table whose columns are to be made draggable. If a `table` element with the `id` we've specified exists, we know that we're in business.

Next, we set a few variables that we'll be using later on. Note that unlike the `tBodies`, `rows`, and `cells` elements, there isn't a DOM reference for the `col` element. So instead of spending precious CPU cycles calling `getElementsByTagName` every time we want to access one of the newly added `col` elements below, we've used it here once, and stored the references that it returned for later use. Here's where the `col` elements fit into our markup:

columndrag.html *(excerpt)*

```
<table id="sales" summary="Quarterly sales figures for competing
companies. The figures are stated in millions of dollars.">
  <caption>Quarterly Sales*</caption>
  <col />
  <col />
  <col />
  <col />
  <col />
  <thead>
    ⋮
```

The `col` element is used as a convenient way to apply styles to columns of data in a table—you can add a class to a `col` instead of adding classes to each individual `td` in a column. We'll use the `col` element to highlight the column that's being dragged.

The Phantom Column

The approach we'll use to move our columns around is very similar to the one we used to reorganize our table in the table sort example. However, in this case we're not moving rows, but cells. We'll also be inserting them into their new positions, rather than always appending our cells to the end of the collection. To achieve this aim, we'll use the `insertBefore` method, which takes two parameters: the node that's to be inserted, and the node before which it will be inserted.

Now, normally this method is used to insert a newly created node, like so:

```
var para = document.getElementById("foo");
var newPara = document.createElement("p");
para.parentNode.insertBefore(newPara, para);
```

However, the `insertBefore` method isn't limited to just inserting new elements into the DOM—we can also use it to shuffle existing elements around within the DOM. For this example, we'll be doing something like this:

```
row.insertBefore(row.cells[a], row.cells[b]);
```

Suppose, for example, that we wanted to move the third cell in our row to the end of our collection of cells. How should we specify where the node is to be inserted? Some browsers, such as Firefox, allow us to refer to "the last cell plus one." Others (in particular, Internet Explorer) won't allow this, instead telling us that "the last cell plus one" doesn't exist.

To work around this problem, we'll insert a phantom column of cells at the end of the table. These cells will be hidden, and will serve only as a valid reference before which we can always insert cells:

columndrag.js (excerpt)

```
ColumnDrag.prototype.makeDraggable = function () {
  for (var i=0; this.tbl.rows[i]; i++) {
    var td = document.createElement("td");
    td.style.display = "none";
    this.tbl.rows[i].appendChild(td);
  }
  ⋮
```

Accessible Dragging

As before, we want to make this functionality as accessible as possible—and that means making it work without a mouse. So, once again, we'll introduce anchors in order to allow the user to tab from one `th` to the other:

columndrag.js (excerpt)

```
    var headings = this.tbl.tHead.rows[0].cells;
    for (var i=0; headings[i]; i++) {
      headings[i].cIdx = i;
      var a = document.createElement("a");
      a.href = "#";
      a.innerHTML = "&larr; "+headings[i].innerHTML+" &rarr;";
```

```
  a.onclick = function () {
    return false;
  }
  headings[i].className += " draggable";
  ⋮
```

This time, however, the anchor's `onclick` event handler does nothing but return `false`. This ensures that clicking an anchor won't cause a new entry to be added to our browser's history—an action that would scroll the browser window to the top of the page. In this particular example, we don't need to worry about this issue—we're only using a small table at the top of the page. However, if your table was located in the middle or at the bottom of a very long page, this behavior could be disastrous.

You'll notice that I've added a property named `cIdx` to our `<th>` tags. As with our table sort example, this property just numbers the cells—a task that we'd normally leave to the built-in property `cellIndex`. However, because Safari 2.0.4 always returns 0 for `cellIndex`, we'll emulate this behavior with our own `cIdx` property.

I've taken the liberty of adding left and right arrow characters (the `&larr;` and `&rarr;` entities, respectively) to either side of the `th` element's existing content. These characters act as a visual cue to the user that the arrow keys can be used to drag columns within the table.

I've also added a small graphic to the upper right-hand corner of each `th` cell—a "grip" that indicates to mouse users that the column is draggable. I've implemented this graphic as a background image via the `draggable` class name in the style sheet. Some may consider using both of these cues together to be overkill, but I think they work quite well—we'll let the usability experts argue over that one! Figure 1.7 shows our table with both of these visual flourishes in place.

Alternatives to the Arrow Keys

Under certain circumstances, you may find that the arrow keys behave unreliably in certain browsers. If you run into this problem, consider using keys other than the arrow keys—for example, **n** and **p** could be used for **Next** and **Previous**. If you follow such an approach, be sure to point out these keyboard shortcuts to your users, or your hard work may go unused!

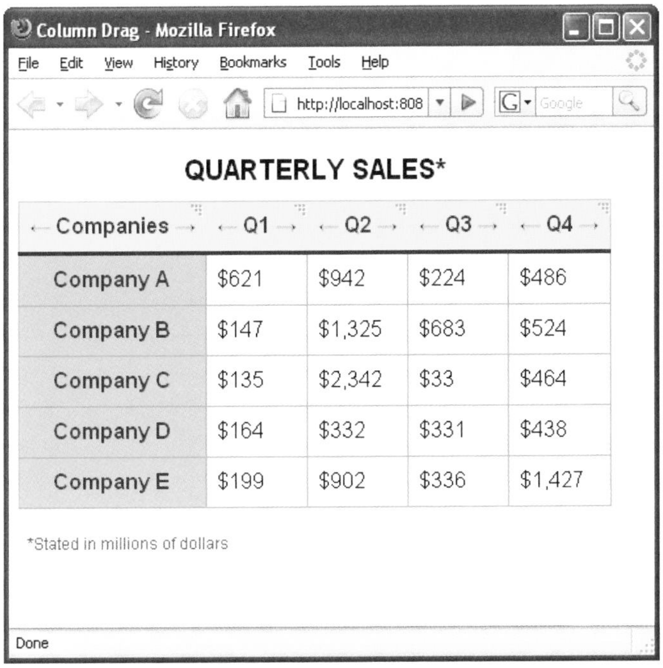

Figure 1.7. Providing visual cues for dragging

Event Handling

Our next step is to wire up the mousedown, mousemove, mouseup, and mouseout events. This is a relatively straightforward process—once again, we're using the scope correction technique that we employed in the table sort example, whereby we point the this keyword to our instance of ColumnDrag, rather than the element that triggered the event. We also pass the event object e to the functions that will be handling our events:

columndrag.js (excerpt)

```
headings[i].onmousedown = function (that) {
  return function (e) {
    that.mousedown(e);
    return false;
  }
}(this);
document.onmousemove = function (that) {
  return function (e) {
    that.mousemove(e);
    return false;
  }
}(this);
document.onmouseup = function (that) {
  return function () {
    var e = that.clearAllHeadings();
    if (e) that.mouseup(e);
```

```
        }
      }(this);
      document.onmouseout = function (that) {
        return function (e) {
          e = e ? e : window.event;
          related = e.relatedTarget ? e.relatedTarget : e.toElement;
          if (related == null) {
            var e = that.clearAllHeadings();
            if (e) that.mouseup(e);
          }
        }
      }(this);

      a.onkeyup = function (that) {
        return function (e) {
          that.keyup(e);
          return false;
        }
      }(this);
```

The onmousemove, onmouseup, and onmouseout event handlers are set up to trap the event no matter where it occurs in the document. We've taken this approach to ensure that the drag functionality isn't limited to the area that the th elements occupy. One drawback to this approach, however, is that neither the onmouseup or the onmouseout event handlers know which th is currently being dragged, so these event handlers can't reset the event if the user should drag the mouse out of the browser window or release it somewhere other than on a <th>. In order to fix that, we'll use a function that we've called clearAllHeadings. This function will cycle through all the headings, clear them of the down class name, and return a reference to the th so that we can pass it to the mouseup function. We'll flesh out the clearAllHeadings function in just a minute.

Earlier, we set our anchor's onclick event to do nothing but return false. Here, we're giving the anchor an onkeyup event handler—this will allow us to trap the left and right arrow key events for accessibility purposes.

We also add a hover class to, or remove it from, our th elements whenever a mouseover or a mouseout event is triggered on them, respectively. We do this because anchors are the only elements for which Internet Explorer 6 supports the CSS :hover pseudo-class:

columndrag.js *(excerpt)*

```
    headings[i].onmouseover = addHover;
    headings[i].onmouseout = removeHover;
    headings[i].innerHTML = "";
    headings[i].appendChild(a);
  }
}
```

Here's that `clearAllHeadings` function that I promised you earlier. After a heading has begun to be dragged, this function will be called if the mouse leaves the browser window, or if the mouse button is released:

```
ColumnDrag.prototype.clearAllHeadings = function (){
  var e = false;
    for (var i=0; this.cols[i]; i++) {
      var th = this.tbl.tHead.rows[0].cells[i];
      if (th.className.match(/down/)) {
        e = {target: th};
      }
    }
  return e;
}
```

Here are the `addHover` and `removeHover` functions:

columndrag.js *(excerpt)*

```
addHover = function () {
  this.className += " hover";
}
removeHover = function () {
  this.className = this.className.replace(/ hover/g, "");
}
```

The `addHover` function simply adds a `hover` class name, preceded by a space (to prevent a conflict with any existing class names). The `removeHover` function removes all occurrences of the `hover` class name from an element.

In both functions, we leave the `this` keyword alone and avoid trying to correct the scope. In this example, `this` behaves exactly the way we need it to: it refers to the element whose class name we want to modify. Also note that we don't need a reference to our instance of `ColumnDrag`, which is why we haven't bothered adding these functions to `ColumnDrag` via the `prototype` object.

The onmousedown Event Handler

Our onmousedown event handler reads as follows:

columndrag.js *(excerpt)*

```
ColumnDrag.prototype.mousedown = function (e) {
  e = e ? e : window.event;
  var elm = e.target? e.target : e.srcElement;
  elm = elm.nodeName == "A" ? elm.parentNode : elm;

  this.state = "drag";
```

```
    elm.className += " down";
    this.cols[elm.cIdx].className = "drag";
    this.from = elm;
    operaRefresh();
}
```

The event object that I mentioned earlier is an object created by the browser when an event is triggered. It contains information that's pertinent to the event, such as the element that triggered it, the mouse's x and y coordinates at the moment it was triggered, and so on. Unfortunately, while some browsers pass the event object as a parameter to the event handler, others provide access to this object differently. For example, in the code above, we anticipate receiving the event object as the argument e that's passed to the event handler. However, we also prepare a fallback approach whereby if the code finds that e has not been set, we set it via the global window.event object, which is how Internet Explorer delivers this event information. Once again, the ternary operator comes in handy—we use it here to set the object into our e variable regardless of where it comes from.

The cross-browser inconsistencies don't end there, though. Passed along inside the event object is a reference to the object that triggered it. Some browsers use the target property name to store this reference, while others (I'm looking at you, Internet Explorer!) call it srcElement. We normalize this behavior as well, using another ternary operator, and store the result in the elm variable.

If the user clicks on one of our wrapper anchors, the event for this mouse click will bubble up and trigger the parent th element's onmousedown event. When that occurs, elm will refer to an anchor, rather than the th we require. We need to correct this; otherwise, we risk having an incorrect reference passed to the mousedown function. So, if elm's nodeName value is A (meaning that it's an anchor element), we know that we need its parent. So we introduce yet another ternary operator to choose between elm and its parent node.

You'll also notice a call to the operaRefresh function in our code. This is an unfortunate but necessary evil, because the latest version of Opera (9.23 at the time of writing) doesn't refresh the affected cells of a table when a class name is added to or changed on a col element. All this function does is change the body element's position from the browser's default of static to relative and back again, forcing a refresh. Here's what the operaRefresh function looks like:

columndrag.js (excerpt)

```
operaRefresh = function () {
    document.body.style.position = "relative";
    document.body.style.position = "static";
}
```

Depending on the final value that you require for your style sheet, you may need to use different values here—it might seem odd, but the important thing is that the body's `position` changes between two different values in order for Opera to play ball.

All this function does is change the `body` element's position from the browser's default of `static` to `relative`, and back again, which forces a refresh. Depending on the position values that you've used in your style sheet, you may want the final value to be something else.

Figure 1.8 shows what our column looks like once the user has clicked on the "Q2" heading cell.

Figure 1.8. mousedown in action

The `onmousemove` Event Handler

As I mentioned earlier, the basic principle behind the column drag functionality is to take the currently selected column of cells and reinsert them elsewhere in the table. As we're using the `insertBefore` function, we don't need to worry about shifting the surrounding cells into their new positions.

The `mousemove` function is called every time the cursor moves over a `th` cell in the table's `thead`. Here's the first part of the code for this function:

columndrag.js *(excerpt)*

```
ColumnDrag.prototype.mousemove = function (e) {
  e = e ? e : window.event;
  var x = e.clientX ? e.clientX : e.pageX;
```

```
var elm = e.target? e.target : e.srcElement;
if (this.state == "drag" && elm != this.from) {
    ⋮
```

First, we normalize the event object, the mouse's current *x* coordinate, and the element that triggered the `onmousemove` event. Then we make sure that we're currently in `drag` mode—if the value of `this.state` isn't set to `drag`, then the user hasn't kept the mouse button pressed down and is simply hovering over the `th` elements. If that's the case, we don't need to do anything. But if the value of `this.state` *is* set to `drag`, we proceed with dragging the column:

columndrag.js *(excerpt)*

```
var from = this.from.cIdx; ❶
var to = elm.cIdx; ❷

if ((from > to && x < this.prevX)
    || (from < to && x > this.prevX)) { ❸
```

❶   In order to know where we're dragging *from*, we first grab the cell index value (`cIdx`) of the `th` element that we stored in the `this.from` variable back in our `onmousedown` function.

❷   In order to know where we're dragging *to*, we grab the `cIdx` value of the `th` we're currently hovering over.

❸   Now, because the columns in our table can have wildly different widths, we need to make sure that the direction in which we're moving the column and the direction in which the mouse is moving are synchronized. If we don't perform this check, the moment a wider `th` takes the place of the one we're dragging, it will *become* the cell we're dragging, as it will end up under the cursor, and will therefore replace the object stored in `elm`. Our code will then try and swap the original cell back, causing an unsightly flickering effect.

We therefore check the relationship between the `from` and `to` values and the cursor's current and previous *x* coordinates. If `from` is greater than `to`, and the mouse's current *x* coordinate is less than it was the previous time we called `mousemove`, we proceed with the drag. Likewise, if `from` is less than `to`, and the *x* coordinate is greater than the previous value, then again we have the green light to proceed.

Before we actually move the cells, we must alter the class names of the `col` elements representing the positions that we're dragging cells from and to. To achieve this, we use the `from` and `to` variables that we created a few lines earlier. Since we're not using the `col` elements for anything other than to signify whether a column is being dragged or not, we can safely clear the existing `drag` value from the `from` column by assigning it a value of `""`. We can then assign the `drag` class name to the `to` column:

columndrag.js (excerpt)

```
this.cols[from].className = "";
this.cols[to].className = "drag";
```

Highlighting the column in the style sheet as it moves, as pictured in Figure 1.8, helps users follow what's happening while they're dragging the column.

Since we're using `insertBefore` to move our cells around, we might need to make a slight adjustment to our `to` value. If we're moving forward (that is, from left to right) we need to increment the value of `to` by one, like so:

columndrag.js (excerpt)

```
if (from < to) to++;
```

This alteration is necessary because we need to insert our `from` cell before the cell that comes *after* the `to` cell, as Figure 1.9 reveals.

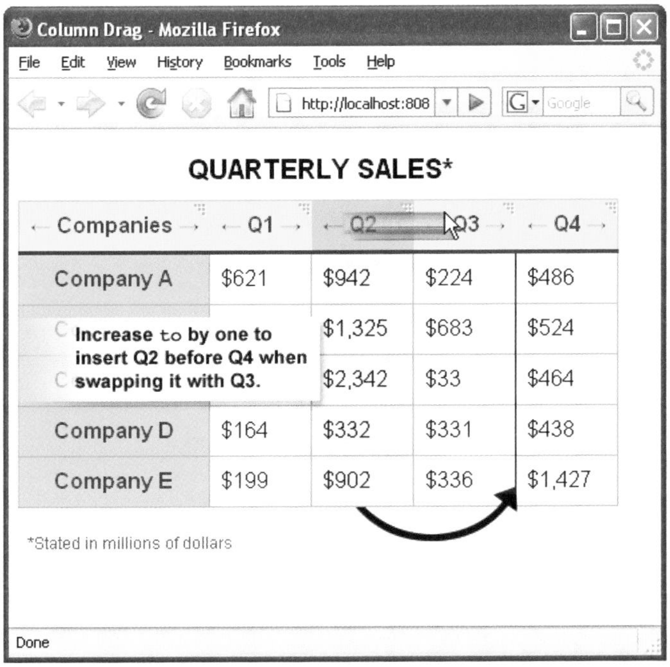

Figure 1.9. Increasing `to` by one

Now that we've worked out our references, all that's left to do is cycle through all of our cells and move them:

columndrag.js *(excerpt)*

```
      var rows = this.tbl.rows;
      for (var i=0; rows[i]; i++) {
        rows[i].insertBefore(rows[i].cells[from], rows[i].cells[to]);
```

Next, we update our `cIdx` values, as they'll be out of sync now that we've reordered our cells:

columndrag.js *(excerpt)*

```
        var headings  = this.tbl.tHead.rows[0].cells;
        for (var i=0; headings[i]; i++) {
          headings[i].cIdx = i;
        }
      }
    }
  }
}
this.prevX = x;
```

The last thing that we do before exiting `mousemove` is to register the current *x* coordinate as the previous one in `this.prevX`. That way, the next time we enter `mousemove`, we'll know in which direction the mouse is moving.

The `onmouseup` Event Handler

Once the users are happy with the position of the dragged column, they'll let go of the mouse button. That's when the `onmouseup` event will be triggered. Here's the `mouseup` function that's called by this event:

columndrag.js *(excerpt)*

```
ColumnDrag.prototype.mouseup = function (e) {
  e = e ? e : window.event;
  var elm = e.target? e.target : e.srcElement;
  elm = elm.nodeName == "A" ? elm.parentNode : elm;
  this.state = null; ❶
  var col = this.cols[elm.cellIndex];
  col.className = "dropped"; ❷
  operaRefresh();
  window.setTimeout(function (cols, el) {
    return function () {
      el.className = el.className.replace(/ down/g, "");
      for (var i=0; cols[i]; i++) {
        cols[i].className = "";
      }
      operaRefresh();
    }
  }(this.cols, this.from), 1000); ❸
}
```

onmouseup's purpose is to reset all of the variables that have to do with the drag.

 We set `this.state` to `null` right away. This tells any future call to `mousemove` functions not to drag anything (that is, of course, until the mouse button is pressed again).

 We then write the value `dropped` to the `col` element that represents the final resting place of our dragged column. This allows us to change the column's color, which indicates visually to the user that its state has changed.

3 We set up a one-second delay, using `window.setTimeout` to reset both the `col`'s and the `th`'s class names. This delay allows us to linger a little on the column that was dropped, making for a better user experience.

You'll notice our `operaRefresh` function pops up again in two places throughout this code. It ensures that the newly modified class names on the table's `col` elements are applied properly in the Opera browser.

Dragging Columns without a Mouse

Earlier, I wrapped the contents of our `th` elements with anchors for accessibility purposes. I also gave them an `onkeyup` event handler. Normally, we'd write code specifically to handle key releases, but in the spirit of reuse, let's write code that will convert left and right arrow button presses into left and right mouse drags. That way, we can reuse the column drag code that we just finished writing for the mouse. In short, we'll be using the keyboard to impersonate the mouse and the events that a mouse would trigger.

The only parameter that's ever passed to `mousedown`, `mousemove`, and `mouseup` is the event object. We can retrieve everything we need from it and a few variables that are set in our instance of `ColumnDrag`.

 onkeyup versus onkeydown

The reason I capture the `onkeyup` event, and not `onkeydown` or `onkeypress`, is because `onkeyup` only fires once, whereas the other events continue firing so long as the key is kept down. This can make it really difficulty to accurately move a column to the right position if the user presses the key for too long. Using `onkeyup` ensures that one action equals one move.

All we have to do now, in order to pretend we're the mouse when we're calling those functions, is to set those variables manually, and pass our own fake event object, like so:

columndrag.js (excerpt)

```
ColumnDrag.prototype.keyup = function (e) {
  e = e ? e : window.event;
  var elm = e.target ? e.target : e.srcElement;
  var a = elm;
  elm = elm.parentNode;
  var headings = this.tbl.tHead.rows[0].cells;
```

As always, our first step is to normalize our event object and the clicked element into e and elm, respectively. We then make a backup of elm in a and change elm to point to its parent node. This will change our elm variable from an anchor into a th element.

Next, we capture the events for the left and right key releases:

columndrag.js (excerpt)

```
switch (e.keyCode){ ❶
  case 37:
    this.mousedown({target:elm}); ❷
    var prevCellIdx = elm.cIdx==0 ? 0 : elm.cellIndex-1;
    this.prevX = 2;
    this.mousemove(
      {
        target: headings[prevCellIdx],
        clientX: 1
      }
    );
    this.mouseup({target: elm});
    a.focus();
    break;
  case 39:
    this.mousedown({target:elm});
    var nextCellIdx = elm.cellIndex==headings.length-2 ?
      headings.length-2 : elm.cellIndex+1;
    this.prevX = 0; ❸
    this.mousemove(
      {
        target: headings[nextCellIdx],
        clientX: 1
      }
    );
    this.mouseup({target: elm});
    a.focus();
```

```
        break;
    }
}
```

Let's look at what's going on in the above code:

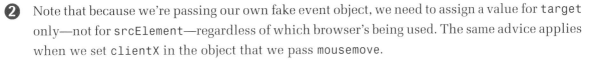

We create a `switch` block to compare the value of the event object's `keyCode` property with the key codes 37 and 39, which represent the left and right arrow keys respectively. In both cases, we call `mousedown` and pass it `elm` as the value for `target`.

Note that because we're passing our own fake event object, we need to assign a value for `target` only—not for `srcElement`—regardless of which browser's being used. The same advice applies when we set `clientX` in the object that we pass `mousemove`.

We need to set a few extra values when calling `mousemove`. Specifically, we need to set `this.prevX` and `clientX` so that one value is greater than the other, depending on which way we want to pretend the mouse is moving. If `clientX` is greater than `this.prevX`, for example, the mouse is moving to the right.

When we pass our event handler a value for `target`, we need to make sure we aren't out of bounds. This task is fairly simple when the column's moving left: all we need to do is make sure that our `cellIndex` value doesn't fall below zero. Moving the column right, however, means checking against the number of cells in the row minus two—one for the fact that `length` returns a one-based result (while the collection of cells is zero-based just like an array) and one extra, to account for the phantom cells we inserted earlier.

Object Literal Notation

We've just seen an example in which an object was created using **object literal** notation. A simple example of this is: `var myObj = {};`

Here's a slightly more complex example:

```
var groceryList = {
    bananas: 0.49,
    apples: 1.39,
    milk: 5.99
};
```

In the above example, the three variables that are declared are effectively public properties of the `groceryList` object. More details about the syntax that's available to those using an object oriented approach in JavaScript can be found in Chapter 5.

Lastly, we call mouseup and pass it our th, which is now in its new position. We finish off by setting focus on its anchor, which sets us up for the next key release.

Now, we add our instantiation of ColumnDrag to our document's head, and we're done:

columndrag.html *(excerpt)*

```html
<script type="text/javascript" src="columndrag.js"></script>
<script type="text/javascript">
window.onload = function () {
  var sales = new ColumnDrag("sales");
}
</script>
```

Here's our final code in full:

columndrag.js

```javascript
function ColumnDrag(id) {
  this.tbl = document.getElementById(id);
  if (this.tbl && this.tbl.nodeName == "TABLE") {
    this.state = null;
    this.prevX = null;
    this.cols = this.tbl.getElementsByTagName("col");
    this.makeDraggable();
  }
}

ColumnDrag.prototype.makeDraggable = function () {
  // Add trailing text node for IE
  for (var i=0; this.tbl.rows[i]; i++) {
    var td = document.createElement("td");
    td.style.display = "none";
    this.tbl.rows[i].appendChild(td);
  }

  // Wire up headings
  var headings = this.tbl.tHead.rows[0].cells;
  for (var i=0; headings[i]; i++) {
    headings[i].cIdx = i; // Safari 2.0.4 "cellIndex always equals 0" workaround

    var a = document.createElement("a");
    a.href = "#";
    a.innerHTML = "&larr; " + headings[i].innerHTML + " &rarr;";
    a.onclick = function () {
      return false;
    }

    headings[i].className += " draggable";
```

```
      headings[i].onmousedown = function (that) {
        return function (e) {
          that.mousedown(e);
          return false;
        }
      }(this);
      document.onmousemove = function (that) {
        return function (e) {
          that.mousemove(e);
          return false;
        }
      }(this);
      document.onmouseup = function (that) {
        return function () {
          var e = that.clearAllHeadings();
          if (e) that.mouseup(e);
        }
      }(this);
      document.onmouseout = function (that) {
        return function (e) {
          e = e ? e : window.event;
          related = e.relatedTarget ? e.relatedTarget : e.toElement;
          if (related == null) {
            var e = that.clearAllHeadings();
            if (e) that.mouseup(e);
          }
        }
      }(this);
      a.onkeyup = function (that) {
        return function (e) {
          that.keyup(e);
          return false;
        }
      }(this);
      headings[i].onmouseover = addHover;
      headings[i].onmouseout = removeHover;

      headings[i].innerHTML = "";
      headings[i].appendChild(a);

  }
}

ColumnDrag.prototype.clearAllHeadings = function (){
var e = false;
for (var i=0; this.cols[i]; i++) {
  var th = this.tbl.tHead.rows[0].cells[i];
  if (th.className.match(/down/)) {
    e = {target: th};
  }
```

```
    }
    return e;
}

ColumnDrag.prototype.mousedown = function (e) {
  e = e ? e : window.event;
  var elm = e.target? e.target : e.srcElement;
  elm = elm.nodeName == "A" ? elm.parentNode : elm;

  // set state and clicked "from" element
  this.state = "drag";
  elm.className += " down";
  this.cols[elm.cIdx].className = "drag";
  this.from = elm;
  operaRefresh();
}

ColumnDrag.prototype.mousemove = function (e) {
  e = e ? e : window.event;
  var x = e.clientX ? e.clientX : e.pageX;
  var elm = e.target? e.target : e.srcElement;

  if (this.state == "drag" && elm != this.from) {
    var from = this.from.cIdx;
    var to = elm.cIdx;

    // make sure that mouse is moving in same dir as swap (to avoid
    // swap flickering)
    if ((from > to && x < this.prevX) || (from < to && x > this.prevX)) {

      // highlight column
      this.cols[from].className = "";
      this.cols[to].className = "drag";

      // increase 'to' by one if direction is positive because we're inserting
      // 'before' and so we have to refer to the target columns neighbor
      if (from < to) to++;

      // shift all cells belonging to head
      var rows = this.tbl.rows;
      for (var i=0; rows[i]; i++) {
        rows[i].insertBefore(rows[i].cells[from], rows[i].cells[to]);
      }

      // update cIdx value (fix for Safari 2.0.4 "cellIndex always equals 0" bug)
      var headings  = this.tbl.tHead.rows[0].cells;
      for (var i=0; headings[i]; i++) {
        headings[i].cIdx = i;
      }
    }
```

```
    }
    this.prevX = x;
}

ColumnDrag.prototype.mouseup = function (e) {
  e = e ? e : window.event;
  var elm = e.target? e.target : e.srcElement;
  elm = elm.nodeName == "A" ? elm.parentNode : elm;

  this.state = null;
  var col = this.cols[elm.cIdx];
  col.className = "dropped";
  operaRefresh();
  window.setTimeout(function (that) {
    return function () {
      that.from.className = that.from.className.replace(/ down/g, "");
      for (var i=0; that.cols[i]; i++) {
        that.cols[i].className = ""; // loop over all cols to avoid odd sized
      }                              // column conflicts
      operaRefresh();
    }
  }(this), 1000);
}

ColumnDrag.prototype.keyup = function (e) {
  e = e ? e : window.event;
  var elm = e.target ? e.target : e.srcElement;
  var a = elm;
  elm = elm.parentNode;
  var headings = this.tbl.tHead.rows[0].cells;

  switch (e.keyCode){
    case 37: // left
      this.mousedown({target:elm});

      var prevCellIdx = elm.cIdx == 0 ? 0 : elm.cIdx - 1;
        this.prevX = 2;
        this.mousemove(
          {
            target: headings[prevCellIdx],
            clientX: 1
          }
        );

        this.mouseup({target: elm});

        a.focus();
        break;

    case 39: // right
```

```
        this.mousedown({target:elm});

        // -2 for IE fix phantom TDs
        var nextCellIdx =
            elm.cIdx == headings.length-2 ? headings.length-2 : elm.cIdx + 1;
        this.prevX = 0;

        this.mousemove(
          {
            target: headings[nextCellIdx],
            clientX: 1
          }
        );
        this.mouseup({target: elm});

        a.focus();
        break;
    }
}

addHover = function () {
  this.className += " hover";
}

removeHover = function () {
  this.className = this.className.replace(/ hover/, "");
}

operaRefresh = function () {
  document.body.style.position = "relative";
  document.body.style.position = "static";
}
```

Summary

I hope you've enjoyed reading this chapter as much as I've enjoyed writing it. In putting together these examples I've tried not only to show you how to manipulate tables through JavaScript, but also how to write efficient, optimized, and reusable JavaScript code.

In this chapter, we've learned how to access a table, its rows, cells, and various groups thereof. We've covered techniques for managing columns of data, even though sorting cells and dragging columns is not a native functionality of either HTML or JavaScript. And we've taken functionality that's traditionally considered to be "mouse only" and made it work with the keyboard as well.

I hope that at least some of the concepts I've shared here, such as regular expressions, sorting algorithms, event handlers, objects, and of course tables, will inspire you to dig deeper and build your own wild and crazy JavaScript apps!

Creating Client-side Badges

If you're an avid reader of weblogs, you might have noticed a recent trend for site authors to display a small, often animated collection of images or text in their sites' sidebars or footers. Site owners might display their latest photos, as illustrated in Figure 2.1, their latest updates on external sites such as Twitter[1] or Facebook,[2] or even a list of the most recent visitors to the site.

These snippets of information are called **badges**, and in this chapter I'll show you how to create your own without having to resort to a server-side language like PHP or Java. I'll also discuss the various file formats you can use when you're pulling together the information to display in the badge, and we'll look at ways to avoid a number of problems that arise when your page relies on data that's hosted on a server that's different from the one that hosts your own site.

---

[1] http://twitter.com/
[2] http://www.facebook.com/

Figure 2.1. An example of a badge (showing Flickr photos) on a blog

Before we start, however, let's spend a little time getting to know badges.

Badges—an Introduction

Badges haven't been around for that long—after all, the Web wasn't as social and distributed in the past as it is now.

With the boom of the social web, and the increase in popularity of sites like del.icio.us,[3] Flickr,[4] and YouTube,[5] now anyone can easily upload information and share it with the world without having to pay a fortune in server traffic. In this new, distributed environment, badges have evolved as a solution that allows people to pull their disparate content into a central location. By placing a badge on your site, you can reuse information that you have previously placed somewhere else—for example, your blog can display your latest photos and videos without sending people off to a third-party site.

Too Many Badges Spoil the Broth

Before we get too far into this chapter, I should point out that it is possible to go overboard with badges, regardless of how you implement them.

---

[3] http://del.icio.us/

[4] http://www.flickr.com/

[5] http://www.youtube.com/

Like everything, badges should be enjoyed in moderation. The primary reason to curb your badge enthusiasm is to prevent the badges from impacting on your site's performance. Another (and, arguably, equally important) reason to limit the number of badges you display is so that the user experience is not adversely affected.

Performance Issues

The performance of a site is most frequently measured by its speed.

We can determine how fast a site is by recording the time it takes for a page to load, or the time that elapses between successive actions performed by a user. Badges can introduce significant delays to a page's load time, especially if they're embedded on the server, because the server needs to contact each of the third-party servers individually before the page is sent to the client to be displayed in the browser.

Additionally, once the page has loaded, other delays associated with badges can impact the perceived performance of the site. The browser may slow down or—even worse—*appear* to have finished loading but still actually be loading data, thus locking up the user interface. This issue can arise for several reasons:

- Numerous embedded media files (images and videos) are referenced in the page.
- Too many HTTP requests are being executed while the page is loading.
- There are too many client-side scripts embedded in the document.

The first two of these points are actually related: every embedded video or image, if hosted on an external server, requires a separate HTTP request. As you embed more and more third-party content, the likelihood that the number of HTTP requests required will affect your page load time increases dramatically. For example, every call to an externally hosted **avatar** image (those little thumbnail graphics that identify individual users) will require the user's browser to: initiate a new HTTP request, negotiate with the DNS servers, and finally download the image. Videos can cause even bigger problems than static images, as a plugin is generally required before the browser can display them—this translates to yet another HTTP request while the plugin is loaded and initialized.

The third of the points above poses what is potentially a much bigger problem—when a browser encounters a client-side script in a document, it halts rendering until the script's execution has completed. If there are any problems during the execution of that script, some browsers may freeze and need to be restarted.

All of these elements have a large impact on the performance of a site, but we can avoid them by making badges a supplementary part of the page, rather than the majority of the content.

User Experience Issues

Another reason to limit the number of badges on your page is that too many badges can distract users from the main page content. The extra links or thumbnail images in a badge are not only additional content that your browser needs to load and render—they also take up screen real estate. If you overload your page with too many badges, not only will you increase your page size unnecessarily, but the badges will compete with your main content.

When you're planning which badges to display on your site, ask yourself whether the badge is something that your visitors would expect to see, and will really add value, or if it's just unnecessary noise.

To reiterate, a couple of badges can enhance a site, but adding too many badges is a bad approach. Now it's time we looked at the options available for implementing a badge.

Out-of-the-box Badges

Companies that run social web sites understand the allure of badges, and offer out-of-the-box badges and badge builders to allow users to display their data on another site. Figure 2.2 and Figure 2.3 show some examples.

These out-of-the-box badges enable users to add to their sites all sorts of external data—text, links, images, or multimedia—without having any knowledge of HTML or JavaScript. There are benefits to the owners of a site that provides such a badge, of course: the badge provides free advertising for the site, and all of the incoming links that result from badge usage fuel the social web site's search engine ranking.

These badges generally use client-side scripting to perform their magic. However, the providers of out-of-the-box badges have several issues to deal with:

- They have no knowledge about the environment in which the badge will be used. (MySpace,[6] for example, allows users to add Flash badges, but not JavaScript ones. Therefore, although a JavaScript badge might work fine on a user's self-built site, a badge that's intended to work on a MySpace page cannot be created in JavaScript.)
- They have no insight into how much the person implementing the badge knows about web development.
- There is no surefire way for the company creating the badge to protect its brand image or styles.
- There is no guarantee that other scripts on the page won't interfere with scripts that the badge relies upon.

---

[6] http://www.myspace.com/

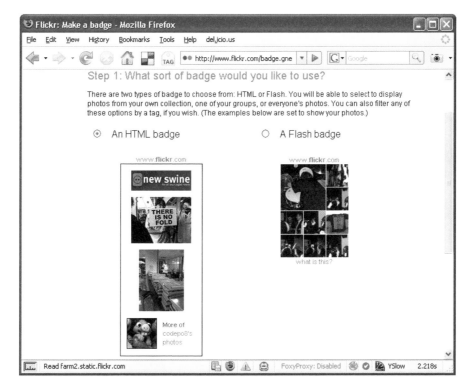

Figure 2.2. Flickr offering both HTML and Flash badges that can be created in several easy steps

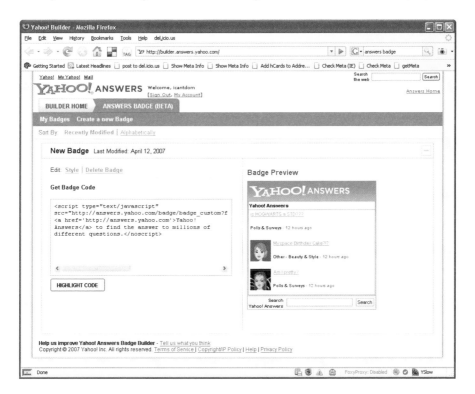

Figure 2.3. Using the Yahoo Answers badge builder to edit a badge, style it, and copy the code—all from one page

These last two points, especially, are real problems for any company producing badges for users to apply to other sites. Since CSS styles can easily be overridden, there's no bulletproof way to ensure that the style rules comprising the badge's design will be maintained when it's placed on someone's site. Although it's possible to minimize the chance that a rule will be overridden (either by applying lots of hooks to the badge's markup, or by adding the keyword `!important` to every style rule), doing so makes the badge's code unnecessarily large.

As with the badge's presentation, any scripts that control aspects of a badge's behavior are vulnerable—code embedded elsewhere in the document could potentially hijack events or interfere with the functionality of a badge. To address these points, many out-of-the-box badges are either built in Flash, or embedded in an `iframe` element. Both of these solutions avoid the problems listed above.

In essence, to provide a badge for the mass market, the badge creator needs to be sure that the badge works in the most obscure and flaky of environments. That's why an out-of-the-box badge will *never* be lean or state-of-the-art—it will always focus on being functional rather than elegant.

An alternative to using an out-of-the-box badge is to write your own custom badge, and embed it in your page on the server.

Server-side Badges

The *safest* way to embed information in your page from an external server is undoubtedly to do so on the server, using either server-side includes or a language like PHP, Python, or Ruby. The reasons for this are obvious:

■ The badge is not reliant upon any client-side scripting.
■ You gain control over the logic that retrieves data from the third-party server *before* your page is generated. This provides the advantage that, for example, should the data on the third-party server be unavailable, you can simply choose not to display anything.

It's not all roses, though: issues are associated with including your badges on the server. Earlier, we discussed the performance problems that server-side badges can introduce; in addition to those hurdles, server-side badges can cause a site's search engine optimization (or SEO) to suffer.

Embedding on a page a server-side badge that contains a large number of links, for example, can impact that page's ranking in a search engine. For example, if you were to embed your entire list of bookmarks on a page, search engines would follow those links when indexing your page, and your site's search rankings would probably suffer. Your site would be considered to have a very high external-links-to-content ratio, which a search engine like Google may interpret as one of two things:

1. Every link in the document is a recommendation for the site to which the link points.
2. The document is a sitemap.

Neither of these interpretations is a good thing for your site's SEO. The former creates the potential for your site to be tagged as spam, while the latter would cause the search engine's spider to revisit the page very infrequently.

Displaying a large number of links in your site's sidebar can also impact the owners of the sites to which you link: whenever an external site links to a blog, the blog's owner is notified via a **trackback**. Trackbacks are very handy—blog owners can follow the links to see what was said about their blogs on external sites. However, it can be very frustrating when those trackback notifications turn out to be nothing more than a blogger's bookmark lists.

There is a way to make the use of badges a lot less painful for your visitors, search engines, and other web users—delay the loading and display of third-party data until after the page has been loaded. We can achieve this goal by moving the badge functionality to the client.

Custom Client-side Badges

Implementing a badge using custom client-side scripting gives you the best of both worlds, which is why we'll dedicate the remainder of this chapter to the task of building this type of badge.

Benefits of Custom Client-side Badges

Building a custom badge using client-side scripting has many benefits, including:

- The badge can be lightweight (in terms of code).
- It can be infinitely styled using CSS.
- It doesn't interfere with the performance of your site.
- It doesn't affect your site's ability to be found by search engines.
- The impact upon your site's rendering speed is minimal.

In essence, a custom client-side badge isn't as bloated as an out-of-the-box solution, nor does it suffer from the performance or SEO issues sometimes introduced by server-side solutions.

Introducing the Example Badge

When you've completed this chapter, you'll be able to create a badge for your site that loads content from the social bookmarking site del.icio.us, and offers all the benefits listed above. The badge will be relatively unobtrusive to visitors, and when it's clicked, it will expand to display the site owner's ten most recently added bookmarks. These bookmarks are loaded as the user clicks the link, so this list will always be up to date.

We'll use JavaScript to display the badge through the del.icio.us **Application Programming Interface (API)**—the interface through which del.icio.us allows its data to be queried and manipulated—and we'll transfer the information from del.icio.us in **JavaScript Object Notation (JSON)**, a lightweight file format for transmitting text data. Though its final appearance will depend on how you choose to style it, the completed badge will look something like the one shown in Figure 2.4.

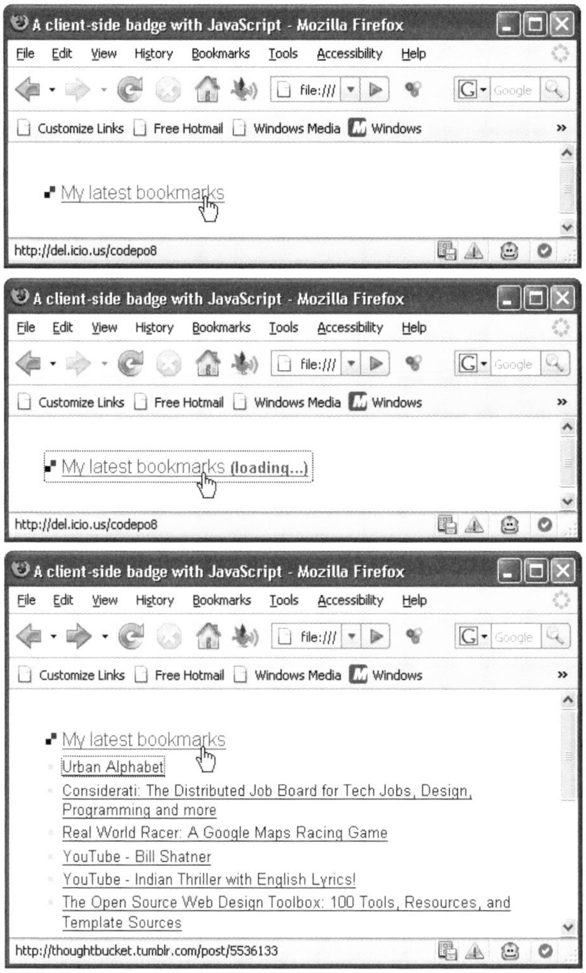

Figure 2.4. The final badge in its different states

The only changes that you'll need to make to your site in order to display the badge are:

1. Add a link to your bookmarks on del.icio.us.
2. Include a small JavaScript link in the head of your document.

For example, the URL for my bookmarks on del.icio.us is http://del.icio.us/codepo8/, so all I need to add to my site are the two lines shown in bold below:

badge_final.html

```
<!DOCTYPE HTML PUBLIC "-//W3C//DTD HTML 4.01//EN"
    "http://www.w3.org/TR/html4/strict.dtd">
<html dir="ltr" lang="en">
```

```
<head>
  <meta http-equiv="Content-Type" content="text/html; charset=utf-8">
  <title>A client-side badge with JavaScript</title>
  <script type="text/javascript" src="deliciousbadge.js"></script>
  <link rel="stylesheet" href="deliciousbadge.css">
</head>
<body>
  <a href="http://del.icio.us/codepo8/" id="delicious">My latest
    bookmarks</a>
</body>
</html>
```

You can see the badge in action by displaying the **badge_final.html** file from the code archive for this book in your browser, or on my personal site under the **My Latest Bookmarks** heading.[7]

Client-side Badge Options: Ajax and JSON

Just a few years ago, most web developers would have told you that there was no way to update part of a web page without either using frames or reloading the entire page. The advent of Ajax and the discovery (or more precisely, the rediscovery) of the XMLHttpRequest object changed all of that—in only a few short years Ajax has become the standard tool used in modern applications that need to perform partial updates to a page.

However, there's a catch!

The Problem with Ajax

From a developer's perspective, one of the downsides of Ajax requests is that it's impossible to use the XMLHttpRequest object to retrieve data from a domain other than the one on which the script is running. This limitation is in fact a security measure that was implemented to prevent malicious code from being injected into a user's page without the user realizing it.

If your application uses the XMLHttpRequest object, and you want to load information from another server, you'll need to make use of a **server-side proxy script** on your web server. The problem with this approach is that it eradicates the benefit of moving the badge functionality to the client.

So what alternative approaches can we use in cases where we want to retrieve data from an external server? Well, there is an alternative to Ajax, and it's called JSON.

---

[7] http://icant.co.uk/

JSON: the Lightweight Native Data Format

As I mentioned earlier, JSON is a lightweight file format for transmitting text data, and it's native to JavaScript.[8] If a site's API supports the JSON format, you can easily integrate that site's data in a pure client-side environment.

As an example, check out the del.icio.us site's JSON output demo.[9] It demonstrates how very easy it is to retrieve a list of your latest del.icio.us bookmarks as a JSON object—all you need to do is call the appropriate URL.

For example, my own bookmarks can be called up in JSON format via the URL http://del.icio.us/feeds/json/codepo8/. Here's what del.icio.us sends back:

```
if (typeof(Delicious) == 'undefined') Delicious = {};
Delicious.posts = [
   {
     "u":"http://www.considerati.com/",
     "d":"Considerati: The Distributed Job Board for Tech Jobs, Design, Programmi
       ➥ng and more",
     "t":["jobs","business","job","consulting","uk","programming"]
   },
   {
     "u":"http://www.thomasscott.net/realworldracer/",
     "d":"Real World Racer: A Google Maps Racing Game",
     "t":["game","google","mashup","maps","b3ta","funny"]
   },
   {
     "u":"http://www.youtube.com/watch?v=MVbv6r_tKnE",
     "d":"YouTube - Bill Shatner",
     "t":["video","music","funny","shatner","fun","rocketman"]
   }
 ]
```

The code above is perfectly valid—and useful—JavaScript. It checks whether the `Delicious` variable has already been defined, and creates a new `Object` by that name if it hasn't. It then defines a new property of this `Object` called `posts`. This property is an `Array` of `Object`s, each of which contains information about one of my bookmarks.

---

[8] http://json.org/
[9] http://del.icio.us/help/json/posts/

Strictly Speaking, This is Not Pure JSON

While the del.icio.us team refers to the output the API produces as JSON, what it delivers is not strictly valid JSON, as the data format does not allow for conditionals (it's a variant known as JSON with Padding, or JSONP). However, referring to the output as "a JavaScript fragment" or something similar would have been confusing—the goal of the del.icio.us API developers was to allow their users to easily display bookmarks in a browser using JavaScript.

If this situation bothers you, feel free to make use of the *raw* parameter—it returns plain, valid JSON.

Each of the `Objects` in the `Array` has three properties:

- `u`, the URL of the bookmark
- `d`, the description of the bookmark
- `t`, an array of tags associated with this bookmark

You can simply add a `script` element that points to this URL, and immediately afterwards, use the information returned by the URL to loop through the `Array` and write your bookmarks to the page:

display_json.html *(excerpt)*

```
<script src="http://del.icio.us/feeds/json/codepo8/"></script>
<script>
  var out = '<ul>';
  for(var i=0; Delicious.posts[i]; i++){
    out += '<li><a href="' + Delicious.posts[i].u + '">' +
           Delicious.posts[i].d + '</a></li>';
  }
  out += '</ul>';
  document.write(out);
</script>
```

The del.icio.us API provides additional parameters to the bare-bones URL that we've seen so far. For example, you can reduce the number of bookmarks that are returned by providing a *count* parameter—if you only wanted a single bookmark, you'd use the URL http://del.icio.us/feeds/json/codepo8/?count=1, which would return something like this:

```
if (typeof(Delicious) == 'undefined') Delicious = {};
Delicious.posts = [
   {
     "u":"http://www.considerati.com/",
     "d":"Considerati: The Distributed Job Board for Tech Jobs, Design, Programmi
       ➥ng and more",
```

```
      "t":["jobs","business","job","consulting","uk","programming"]
   }
]
```

This is all fine and dandy if you plan to use an object named `Delicious` to store your data before writing it to the page. But what if you don't want to have a global object with that name? Well, you can further tweak the returned information by adding another parameter, called *callback*, to the URL. This parameter defines a function name that will be wrapped around the object that's returned. For example, the URL http://del.icio.us/feeds/json/codepo8/?count=1&callback=show will return the following code:

```
show([
   {
     "u":"http://www.considerati.com/",
     "d":"Considerati: The Distributed Job Board for Tech Jobs, Design, Programmi
        ➥ng and more",
     "t":["jobs","business","job","consulting","uk","programming"]
   }
])
```

This kind of flexibility enables us to write a reusable function that displays different bookmark lists within the same document.

However, we're still required to add to our document inline `script` elements, which slow down the initial rendering. We can work around that problem by creating the `script` element on the fly, like this:

dynamicScriptElement.js

```
deliciousCall = {  ❶
  init:function(){  ❷
    var url = 'http://del.icio.us/feeds/json/codepo8/' +
              '?callback=deliciousCall.show';
    var s = document.createElement('script');  ❸
    s.setAttribute('src',url);
    document.getElementsByTagName('head')[0].appendChild(s);
  },
  show:function(o){  ❹
    var out = '<ul>';
    for(var i=0;o[i];i++){
      out += '<li><a href="' + o[i].u + '">' +
             o[i].d + '</a></li>';
    }
    out += '</ul>';
  document.getElementById('bookmarks').innerHTML = out;
```

```
    }
}
deliciousCall.init();
```

Let's take a closer look at that code.

 First, we create a new object, named `deliciousCall`, which will contain our methods. This syntax is referred to as an **object literal**, and it is an effective approach for preventing your variable and function names from overwriting others embedded in the same document. (Of course, this variable will still be overwritten if there is another variable, function, or object of exactly the same name, so choose the name of this variable wisely.)

② The `init` method defines the URL that calls the del.icio.us API.

③ We then create a new `script` element, set its `src` attribute to the URL that we defined earlier, and add the element as a new child node to the `head` element of the document. Once the element has been added, the browser initiates a connection to the del.icio.us server. Once that connection has successfully returned a JSON object, that object's `show` method is called (we've specified that this should happen via the `callback` parameter that we included in the URL).

④ In the `show` method, we retrieve the JSON data and assemble a string that contains all of our bookmarks and the surrounding HTML for displaying them. We then set the content of the element that has an `id` of `bookmarks` to this string.

⑤ Immediately after we close the object definition brackets, we call the `init` method.

With JSON, you can store all of the functionality that will retrieve and format your badge data in a single script, as long as it's executed after your document has loaded. By following this approach, we're effectively delaying the extra HTTP request and the display of the badge information until after the visitor can see the web page.

This is a fairly good solution, except for one small problem: you just cannot trust Internet connections.

 Don't Put the Script in the head

This script needs to be embedded at the end of the **body** of the document, not in the **head**! The reason is that the element it uses for displaying the information is only available when the document has loaded! Granted, adding JavaScript inline like we've done here isn't ideal, but it is the simplest way to address this issue. We will, however, look at a better approach to waiting for our page to load in the final version of the script that we write.

Providing a Fallback for Failed Connections

I've spent enough of my time on slow dial-up connections, and in hotels and airport lounges with flaky wireless, to know that network connections cannot be relied upon.

When we use the `XMLHttpRequest` object, we have full control over the connection process, so we can make decisions based on whether the data that we tried to access was available or not. When we generate a `script` element to retrieve information from a JSON API, however, we don't have the same luxury. If our page relies completely on JavaScript to function successfully, we risk losing the trust of visitors whose connections fail.

A good script should therefore offer a fallback option for failing connections. The most common reasons why a connection fails are:

- The connection times out.
- The server is not available.

You can cater for the event in which a connection fails by writing your script to *expect* the connection to fail, and allowing a grace period to pass before your script gives up on the connection. When this period has elapsed, you can inform your visitors that something went wrong.

In JavaScript, we create this functionality using the `window` object's `setTimeout` method—a method that allows you to tell the browser to execute JavaScript after a given amount of time. Here's how we'd do that for our del.icio.us badge example:

dynamicScriptElementTimeout.js

```
deliciousCall = {
  failed: false, ❶
  init: function() {
    var url = 'http://del.icio.us/feeds/json/codepo8/' +
              '?callback=deliciousCall.show';
    var s = document.createElement('script');
    s.setAttribute('src', url);
    document.getElementsByTagName('head')[0].appendChild(s);
    this.to = window.setTimeout('deliciousCall.failure()', 1000); ❷
  },
  show: function(o) {
    if(this.failed === false) { ❸
      window.clearTimeout(this.to); ❹
      var out = '<ul>';
      for(var i=0; o[i]; i++) {
        out += '<li><a href="' + o[i].u + '">' +
               o[i].d + '</a></li>';
      }
      out += '</ul>';
      document.getElementById('bookmarks').innerHTML = out;
```

```
    }
  },
  failure: function() { ⑤
    window.clearTimeout(this.to);
    this.failed = true;
    document.getElementById('bookmarks').innerHTML =
        'Connection Error';
  }
}
deliciousCall.init();
```

You'll notice that the above script differs slightly from the previous example.

① We've used a property named `failed`, which is preset to the value `false`.

② In the `init` method, we set a timeout that executes a new method named `failure` after one second (1000 milliseconds).

③ In the `show` method, we check whether `failed` is still `false`—if it is, we reset the timeout and commence displaying the links as before.

④ We clear the timeout in the `show` method to prevent the `failure` method from executing.

⑤ If the call has not returned successfully after our timeout reaches one second, the `failure` method kicks in. This method clears the timeout, sets `failed` to `true`, and displays a connection error. We need the `failed` property in case the connection happens to return successfully *after* we've waited a period of one second—this is outside our acceptable waiting period, and we're not interested in what our function call might return so late in the game.

Let's put these ideas together and create a script that delivers all of the features that I promised at the beginning of this chapter.

Planning the Badge Script

The first step to writing good JavaScript is not to jump immediately into the code. Instead, it's best to plan exactly what you're trying to achieve. In particular, you need to identify the user interactions you're looking to hijack and transform. You also need an idea of what kind of markup you'll be generating or manipulating.

In our badge example, rather than showing all of our bookmarks, we could instead display a link to our page on del.icio.us. That way, if the connection fails, or users have JavaScript turned off, site visitors can still follow the link to view our bookmarks. This is a good example of **progressive enhancement**—building a page by starting with solid markup, then adding extra functionality on top. Ideally, we want to show a list of bookmarks when the user clicks on that link. By using progressive enhancement, we can deliver the best of both worlds: a list of bookmarks if our JavaScript functions correctly, and a valid link that users can follow if it doesn't.

We need to add some hooks to our page so that we can insert our bookmarks in the correct place, and style the list of bookmarks once it's been inserted. We can apply both these hooks by adding `id` attributes to specific elements: one to the original link, so that we can find it from our script, and one to the newly created list. We add the first of these `id`s to the link in our markup, as shown in bold below:

badge_final.html (excerpt)

```html
<a href="http://del.icio.us/codepo8/" id="delicious">
My latest bookmarks
</a>
```

The script should execute once the document has finished loading, so that we can be certain that our script will successfully locate the element that we're looking for, should it exist on the page. Our script will then add the second `id` to the generated list of bookmarks.

Here are some other goals for our final script:

- The script's initialization method should test whether the browser supports the methods that we're using to traverse the page's DOM tree, and should also test for the existence of the link in the code listing above.

  Only after these two facts have been verified is it safe for us to override the default behavior of the link—we'll modify it to load our bookmark information as a JSON object, rather than sending the visitor to our page on the del.icio.us site. This type of defensive scripting ensures that our script will not attempt to execute functionality that's not supported by the user's environment.

- The method that's called when a user clicks the link should retrieve the user name from the link and dynamically inject a `script` element into the page. This element will use the del.icio.us API to request our bookmark data. As a small usability aid for the visitor, we'll display a message that reads "loading…" while the JSON call is executing.

- Our script will once again implement a timeout to provide a window of one second for the JSON request to execute. This time, should the connection fail, rather than display an error message, our script will simply forward the user to our page on the del.icio.us site as if the element that was clicked was a plain old link.

- If the JSON call is successful, our script should:
  1. Create a list of bookmarks.
  2. Remove the "loading…" message.
  3. Apply the document focus to the first bookmark in the list.

4. Reinstate the original link destination so that visitors can click it again to visit our page on del.icio.us.

Great—that takes care of the functionality of the script, but there are a couple of other issues we'll need to consider:

■ To aid the maintainability of our code, let's place all of the parameters that are likely to change in configuration variables at the beginning of the script.

■ We should ensure that our script plays well with others and that it doesn't override any variables or methods created by other scripts embedded in the document. We've seen the object literal approach, and this technique certainly does the trick. However, we'll take advantage of a much more versatile technique for writing scripts: the **module pattern**. This technique for writing JavaScript allows us to specify public methods, private methods, and properties, as do other "pure" object oriented programming languages like Java or C++. You can read more about the module pattern on the Yahoo User Interface Blog.[10]

The Complete Badge Script

Without further ado, here's the full, unabridged script that creates the functionality that we described at the start of this chapter. Don't worry if parts of the script aren't perfectly clear, as we'll step through it bit by bit in the coming pages:

deliciousbadge.js

```
deliciousbadge = function() {
  /* configuration */

  // link and output list IDs
  var badgeid = 'delicious';
  var outputid = 'deliciouslist';
  // message to add to the link whilst loading
  var loadingMessage = ' (loading...)';
  // amount of links
  var amount = 10;
  // timeout in milliseconds
  var timeoutdelay = 1000;
  // stores the link that was clicked
  var o = null;
  /* public methods */
  return {
    // addEvent by Scott Andrew LePera
    // http://www.scottandrew.com/weblog/articles/cbs-events
    addEvent:function(elm,evType,fn,useCapture) {
      if (elm.addEventListener) {
```

---

[10] http://yuiblog.com/blog/2007/06/12/module-pattern/

```javascript
      elm.addEventListener(evType, fn, useCapture);
      return true;
    } else if (elm.attachEvent) {
      var r = elm.attachEvent('on' + evType, fn);
      return r;
    } else {
      elm['on' + evType] = fn;
    }
  },
  // init - checks for DOM and element support
  init:function(){
    if (document.getElementById && document.createTextNode) {
      o = document.getElementById(badgeid);
      if(o && o.href){
        deliciousbadge.addEvent(o, 'click', callData, false);
      }
    }
  },
  // retrieveData - stops timeout and sends the JSON dataset
  retrieveData: function(dataset) {
    window.clearTimeout(deliciousbadge.to);
    displayData(dataset);
  },
  // failure - follows the link if there was a 404
  failure: function() {
    window.clearTimeout(deliciousbadge.to);
    window.location = o.getAttribute('href');
  }
};
/* private methods */
// callData - assembles the JSON call and initiates the timeout
function callData(e) {
  if(!document.getElementById(outputid)) {
    deliciousbadge.to = window.setTimeout('deliciousbadge.failure()',
        timeoutdelay)
    var user = o.href.replace(/.*\//g,'');
    var msg = document.createElement('span');
    msg.appendChild(document.createTextNode(loadingMessage));
    o.appendChild(msg);
    var seeder = document.createElement('script');
    var srcurl = 'http://del.icio.us/feeds/json/' +
                 user + '?count=' + amount +
                 '&callback=deliciousbadge.retrieveData';
    seeder.setAttribute('src', srcurl);
    document.getElementsByTagName('head')[0].appendChild(seeder);
    cancelClick(e);
  }
};
// displayData - assembles the list of links from the JSON dataset
function displayData(dataset) {
```

```
      var output = document.createElement('ul');
      output.id = outputid;
      for (var i=0; dataset[i]; i++) {
        var entry = document.createElement('li');
        var entryLink = document.createElement('a');
        entryLink.appendChild(document.createTextNode(dataset[i].d));
        entryLink.setAttribute('href',dataset[i].u);
        entry.appendChild(entryLink);
        output.appendChild(entry);
      }
      o.parentNode.insertBefore(output, o.nextSibling);
      o.removeChild(o.lastChild);
      output.getElementsByTagName('a')[0].focus();
    };
    // cancelClick - prevents the link from being followed
    function cancelClick(e) {
      if (window.event) {
        window.event.cancelBubble = true;
        window.event.returnValue = false;
        return;
      }
      if (e) {
        e.stopPropagation();
        e.preventDefault();
      }
    };
}();
/* initiate when the window has finished loading */
deliciousbadge.addEvent(window, 'load', deliciousbadge.init, false);
```

Let's break this script up into bite-size chunks.

Defining Configuration Variables

In the first few lines of our script, we define some configuration variables:

deliciousbadge.js *(excerpt)*

```
deliciousbadge = function() {
  /* configuration */

  // link and output list IDs
  var badgeid = 'delicious';
  var outputid = 'deliciouslist';
  // message to add to the link whilst loading
  var loadingMessage = ' (loading...)';
  // amount of links
```

```
var amount = 10;
// timeout in milliseconds
var timeoutdelay = 1000;
```

The first two variables allow us to change the values of the `id` attributes that we're adding to the initial link, and to the generated list of bookmarks, respectively, should we want to do so. We then define our "loading…" message—this will be added to the link text as a `span` element while the bookmarks are being retrieved from the del.icio.us server. We've also pulled a few other key values, which define the script's operation, into configuration variables; these values include the number of links that are to be shown, and the time (in milliseconds) that our script should wait before assuming that the server cannot be reached.

Next, we define a variable that will serve as a reference to the original link to our del.icio.us page:

deliciousbadge.js *(excerpt)*

```
// stores the link that was clicked
var o = null;
```

Although we've initially assigned it a value of `null`, this variable will provide us with a handy shortcut that'll prevent us from having to type `document.getElementById` every time a method needs to access the link.

Defining Public Methods

We'll only need a few public methods, most of which are helpers:

deliciousbadge.js *(excerpt)*

```
/* public methods */
return {
  // addEvent by Scott Andrew LePera
  // http://www.scottandrew.com/weblog/articles/cbs-events
  addEvent:function(elm, evType, fn, useCapture) {
    if(elm.addEventListener){
      elm.addEventListener(evType, fn, useCapture);
      return true;
    } else if (elm.attachEvent) {
      var r = elm.attachEvent('on' + evType, fn);
      return r;
    } else {
      elm['on' + evType] = fn;
    }
  },
```

The first method is Scott Andrew LePera's `addEvent`, which allows us to apply event handlers to elements on the page in a cross-browser fashion. This method will allow us to delay the running of our script's initialization method until after the window has finished loading, without having to resort to inline JavaScript.

In our initialization method, we have to check whether or not the DOM methods that we plan on calling are in fact supported:

deliciousbadge.js *(excerpt)*

```
// init - checks for DOM and element support
init:function(){
  if(document.getElementById && document.createTextNode){
    o = document.getElementById(badgeid);
```

If we get the green light to use these methods, we store our link element in the variable o. If we hadn't defined o in the main script beforehand, it would be a global variable (something to be avoided, if at all possible).

Next we need to confirm that our link really exists, and that it is indeed a link (that is, an anchor element):

deliciousbadge.js *(excerpt)*

```
    if(o && o.href) {
      deliciousbadge.addEvent(o, 'click', callData, false);
    }
  }
},
```

As the code above demonstrates, we perform this check by verifying that the object represented by o (the link) is present on the page, and that it has an attribute called `href`. Checking for the presence of the `href` attribute makes sure that the element with an `id` of `badgeid` really is a link and not something else (a `div` or a `p`, for example). Assuming that everything is in order, we can safely add to our link a `click` event handler that will execute the `callData` method when it's triggered.

Figure 2.5 shows the badge before it has been clicked. As you can see, the status bar displays the link destination when the user mouses over the link.

Figure 2.5. Clicking the link will run the `callData` method

The last two public methods deal with the JSON returned from the dynamically generated `script` element:

deliciousbadge.js *(excerpt)*

```javascript
// retrieveData - stops timeout and sends the JSON dataset
retrieveData:function(dataset){
  window.clearTimeout(deliciousbadge.to);
  displayData(dataset);
},
```

If the connection to the del.icio.us server was successful, the code we get back will execute the `retrieveData` method and send the object containing our bookmarks as a parameter. If this happens, we need to stop our timeout and call the `displayData` method to show the bookmarks.

If there was a problem with the connection, the fallback timeout will call the `failure` method:

deliciousbadge.js *(excerpt)*

```javascript
// failure - follows the link if there was a 404
failure: function() {
  window.clearTimeout(deliciousbadge.to);
  window.location = o.getAttribute('href');
  }
};
```

This method halts the timeout and instead sends the visitor to the del.icio.us web site by assigning the URL that's stored in our link's `href` attribute to the `window` object's `location` property.

That concludes all of the public methods that we need to expose to the world. In summary, we created a method to allow for event handling, one that handles initialization, and two that deal with the success or failure of the call to the third-party server.

Defining Private Methods

Next, we need to define the private methods that do the display and retrieval work.

First up is `callData`. This function will generate the `script` tag to retrieve the JSON object. It also contains the logic for giving users who click the link some visual feedback that indicates that something is indeed happening.

We need to ensure that our list of bookmarks has not yet been displayed. This is important because we've decided to send the user to the del.icio.us site, rather than display another copy of the list of bookmarks, should they click the link a second time. This task is easily completed—all we need to do is to check for the existence of an unordered list element that has an `id` with the value that we've defined in our configuration variables. If such an element doesn't exist, we can proceed with retrieving the bookmarks.

The following code performs the check:

deliciousbadge.js *(excerpt)*

```
/* private methods */
// callData - assembles the JSON call and initiates the timeout
function callData(e) {
  if(!document.getElementById(outputid)){
```

 What's this e Parameter, Then?

You might be wondering what the `e` parameter is. It's not defined in our `init` method, so where has it come from? In fact, this is the **event object**, which contains information about what happened when the link was clicked. It's a global object, and can be used in any event listener.

Remember that this function is called when the link is clicked—because we're about to create the `script` element to retrieve the JSON data, we need to begin the timeout that will cancel our attempts at establishing a connection after a certain amount of time has passed. We store this timeout in a property so that we can stop the countdown once the data has been successfully retrieved, as the code below shows:

deliciousbadge.js *(excerpt)*

```
deliciousbadge.to = window.setTimeout('deliciousbadge.failure()',
    timeoutdelay)
```

We'll need to know the username of the del.icio.us account from which we're retrieving bookmarks; we can determine it from the original URL for the user's del.icio.us page. The following regular expression will remove everything (including the trailing slash) from the anchor element's `href` attribute:

deliciousbadge.js *(excerpt)*

```
var user = o.href.replace(/.*\//g,'');
```

If the link is, for example, http://del.icio.us/codepo8/ the variable `user` will be assigned the value `codepo8`.

Now that we know the username, we can begin to indicate to users that we're doing something with the link other than just following it. As I mentioned when we were planning this script, we're going to create a `span` element, add the "loading…" message as a text node to this `span`, and insert the `span` into our document as a new child node to the original link. The following code achieves exactly that:

deliciousbadge.js *(excerpt)*

```
var msg = document.createElement('span');
msg.appendChild(document.createTextNode(loadingMessage));
o.appendChild(msg);
```

Figure 2.6. Showing a "loading…" message to tell visitors what's going on

It's time to initiate contact with the del.icio.us server so that we can retrieve our bookmarks data. We create a new `script` element, assemble the correct URL for calling the del.icio.us JSON API, set the value of our new `script` element's `src` attribute to equal that URL, and add the element as a new child node to the `head` element of the document:

```
                                                    deliciousbadge.js (excerpt)

    var seeder = document.createElement('script');
    var srcurl = 'http://del.icio.us/feeds/json/' +
                 user + '?count=' + amount +
                 '&callback=deliciousbadge.retrieveData';
    seeder.setAttribute('src', srcurl);
    document.getElementsByTagName('head')[0].appendChild(seeder);
```

This code initiates the JSON call which will execute the `retrieveData` method, should it be successful.

As we don't want to follow the link, we'll need to override the browser's default behavior. To do so, we use another helper method, called `cancelClick`, which we'll define later in the script.

```
                                                    deliciousbadge.js (excerpt)

    cancelClick(e);
  }
};
```

Once the JSON call executes successfully, it sends the object containing our bookmarks to the `retrieveData` method, which will call `displayData`, forwarding the object. Since we want to display the bookmarks as a list, we need to create a new unordered list element, and assign it an `id` to allow for styling:

```
                                                    deliciousbadge.js (excerpt)

// displayData - assembles the list of links from the JSON dataset
function displayData(dataset) {
  var output = document.createElement('ul');
  output.id = outputid;
```

We then loop through each of the entries in the data array. For each entry, we create a list item and a link for storing a bookmark:

```
                                                    deliciousbadge.js (excerpt)

  for(var i=0; dataset[i]; i++) {
    var entry = document.createElement('li');
    var entryLink = document.createElement('a');
```

Now, each array item is an object with the properties d (containing the description of the bookmark) and u (containing the URL). We grab both of these properties for each object:

deliciousbadge.js *(excerpt)*

```
entryLink.appendChild(document.createTextNode(dataset[i].d));
entryLink.setAttribute('href',dataset[i].u);
```

We then add the link to the list item, and the list item to the list of bookmarks:

deliciousbadge.js *(excerpt)*

```
    entry.appendChild(entryLink);
    output.appendChild(entry);
}
```

All that's left for us to do now is to add the list to the DOM, right after the original link, so that it displays as shown in Figure 2.7. As there is not a native DOM method that inserts an element *after* another element, we'll insert the list *before the next sibling* of the link node:

deliciousbadge.js *(excerpt)*

```
o.parentNode.insertBefore(output,o.nextSibling);
```

Figure 2.7. Showing the loaded bookmarks as an HTML list

If we've come this far in our script, we've obviously loaded our bookmark data, so we don't need to show the "loading…" message any longer. We added this message to the link as a span element, so to remove it, all we need to do is get rid of the span's last child node:

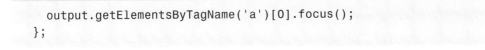

deliciousbadge.js (excerpt)

```
  o.removeChild(o.lastChild);
```

The final line of this method moves the focus from the original link to the first bookmark, using the `focus` method:

deliciousbadge.js (excerpt)

```
  output.getElementsByTagName('a')[0].focus();
};
```

Figure 2.8. Removing the "loading..." message and shifting the focus makes it obvious to the user that something has happened

We're still lacking the `cancelClick` method that will prevent our link from being followed when it's clicked. This is a common helper method that performs some object detection magic in a way that works reliably across several browsers:

deliciousbadge.js (excerpt)

```
// cancelClick - prevents the link from being followed
function cancelClick(e) {
  if (window.event){
    window.event.cancelBubble = true;
    window.event.returnValue = false;
    return;
  }
  if (e) {
    e.stopPropagation();
    e.preventDefault();
```

```
    }
  };
}();
```

Finally, we need to call our `init` method when the document has finished loading. We do this by applying an `onload` handler to the `window` object using `addEvent`:

deliciousbadge.js *(excerpt)*

```
/* initiate when the window has finished loading */
deliciousbadge.addEvent(window, 'load', deliciousbadge.init, false);
```

And that's all there is to it! Because we've used unobtrusive JavaScript techniques, you can add this script to your document simply by including at the top of your page a `script` element that points to it. Just add a link to your own del.icio.us bookmarks that has the correct `id`, and the script will do the rest! You can then make use of the `id`s to style the final result to your liking.

Calling for Server Backup

While the script we've just walked through creates a nifty little badge that will make your personal site the envy of all your friends, there are occasions when you may want to implement a server-side component that acts as a backup, should the client-side script fail. There are several reasons why this can be a good idea:

 Some APIs have **rate limits**, which dictate how many times per day you can call them. With a server-side control you could store a cached copy of the external site's data on your server and only update it every few hours. This type of rate limiting usually only applies to APIs that require a developer key.

 If you're dealing with a flaky API, you could store a copy of the data on your server each time you query the third-party server. This cache can then be used as a backup—the data may not be the most up to date, but at least you can be sure that your badge won't break.

 You can use a server-side component to pare the amount of data you retrieve down to the absolute minimum, or to convert any data that's not in an easily manageable format into something more digestible (like JSON).

Summary

We've come to the end of this chapter, in which we covered:

- why you'd want to use badges on your site
- why so many out-of-the-box badges are unlikely to be right for you
- how badges impact a page's performance
- the limitations of Ajax in a pure client-side environment
- how you can use JavaScript and JSON to retrieve information from some servers without the need for a server-side component
- how to retrieve information using a generated `script` element
- how to make this generated `script` technique more secure by planning for its failure with a timeout
- how to create a badge that incorporates all of these factors

You can now take these techniques and apply them to any API data that you want to include on your site. As more and more API providers realize the benefits of JSON as a lightweight file format, you'll be able to create unobtrusive badges for all kinds of content—whether the person who uploaded it to the Web was you or someone else.

An extensive catalog of APIs exists at Programmable Web;[11] most of the APIs provided by Yahoo and its companies (such as Upcoming and Flickr) provide JSON output.[12]

If you're interested in an easy way to retrieve more del.icio.us data using JavaScript, take a look at a small wrapper library that I've written called Dishy.[13] This library makes obtaining all kinds of information about your bookmarks in JSON format very easy, and is already converted to HTML for immediate use.

---

[11] http://www.programmableweb.com/
[12] http://developer.yahoo.com/
[13] http://icant.co.uk/sandbox/dishy/

Chapter

3

Vector Graphics with **canvas**

Once upon a time, if you wanted to create graphics on the fly on the Web, you had three choices:

- Use server-side generation.
- Use Flash.
- Use Java.

Server-side generation works fairly well when you're producing images for **static data** (stuff that won't change once the page has loaded, like CAPTCHA images). However, the processing time needed to generate a server-side image, and the fact that the image has to be transferred between the server and the client, mean that you can't use the server to create graphics that change in real time. This precludes the use of server-side generation in situations where we want the image to respond dynamically to user input, like mouse movements or keystrokes.

Flash, on the other hand, was built exactly *for* creating graphics that change in real time; when one thinks of Flash, one immediately thinks "animation." But Flash has its downsides, too. First, it requires a plugin—it's not a native browser capability—and while the penetration of the Flash plugin is quite high on desktops, we're beginning to see a resurgence of non-Flash user agents, particularly on mobile and embedded devices. Second, Flash's integration with HTML isn't perfect—it's still very much separated from the web page, which often causes problems with integrated content. And lastly (and to some people, most importantly), Flash is not an open standard: it's developed by Adobe, and Adobe therefore has the first and last word on what Flash can do and how it will work.

Java suffers from many of the same problems as Flash. While it's available in almost every browser, it still runs separately, and its integration with HTML is notoriously clunky. Aside from those real issues, it has had problems escaping its reputation as a 90s-era CPU-hog that will crash your browser; inaccurate as that may now be.

Fortunately, in the past couple of years an alternative technology has emerged that promises to avoid the problems from which Flash and Java have suffered—the **canvas** element.

The canvas element provides a browser-native method for specifying graphics that can be updated with client-side scripting. It's been included as a proposed standard by the WhatWG,[1] an open community of browser vendors and web developers, and is included in the HTML 5 specification. canvas was originally designed by Apple to allow the WebKit component to create vector graphics. WebKit is an open source browser engine that's utilized by a number of applications in Apple's OS X operating system, including Dashboard and Safari. Importantly for us, WebKit can be used to render vector graphics, like the clock shown in Figure 3.1, inside the Safari web browser.[2]

Canvas is now supported by Safari 2+, Opera 9+, and Firefox 1.5+ (and associated Mozilla builds). Internet Explorer does not support canvas, but we'll look at solutions to this later in the chapter.

Figure 3.1. Apple's dashboard clock, which uses canvas to draw and animate the clock's hands

Working with canvas

Canvas is a lot like an img element—it doesn't act as a container for any other elements, it just functions as a space in which you can draw. Think of canvas as an image that you can draw on—it even supports exactly the same attributes as an img (except for src).

Including a canvas element directly into your HTML code is easy:

```
<p>
  <canvas id="graph" width="400" height="400" />
</p>
```

Canvas elements are inline elements by default. If no width or height is specified, a canvas element will automatically be sized to a width of 300 pixels and a height of 150 pixels.

---

[1] http://www.whatwg.org/
[2] http://webkit.org/

canvas is Invalid

Because canvas is an unofficial extension to HTML, it doesn't exist as a valid element in any (X)HTML specification (although it's included in the proposal for HTML 5). So if you include a canvas element in your page, it won't validate according to the W3C validator.

If you don't like having a canvas element in your nicely validating HTML code, it's also possible to create canvas elements dynamically in JavaScript:

```
var graph = document.createElement("canvas");
graph.setAttribute("id", "graph");
graph.setAttribute("width", "320");
graph.setAttribute("height");

document.body.appendChild(graph);
```

However, inserting canvas elements into your HTML in this fashion only follows the letter of the law, not its spirit—the static HTML will validate, but the modified DOM will be invalid.

Which of the two approaches is better is a point of argument among developers … I'll let you make up your own mind. For the purposes of this chapter, we're going to assume that the canvas element we're working with is already included in the HTML code.

Just including a canvas element on your page won't do much, though. You can't specify a source for it, and no markup is available to create graphics via HTML. The only way you'll get a canvas element to make something appear is to use JavaScript.

The canvas API

Alongside the introduction of the canvas element itself, modern browsers now have a new set of JavaScript methods that are specifically designed for creating graphics in canvas elements. All these methods stem from something called a **graphics context**, which is a type of object that gives you access to the drawing capabilities of the canvas.

In order to access the graphics context for a particular canvas, you need to locate the DOM node for the canvas with which you want to work, then call the method getContext, passing an argument that indicates the *type* of context you want to retrieve. At some point in the future, a three-dimensional context will probably be offered in addition to the current two-dimensional one.[3] For the moment, though, we're limited to creating our masterpiece in two planes, so the only value you can pass to getContext is 2d:

---

[3] Work has begun on a three-dimensional canvas context in both Opera and Firefox, but it's not yet available to the public.

```
var graph = document.getElementById("graph");

if (typeof graph.getContext != "undefined") {
  var context = graph.getContext("2d");
}
```

The context variable is now a graphics context that will allow us to draw on the canvas object named graph.

Once you've got a graphics context, you'll have at your fingertips a host of properties and methods that you can use to start pumping pixels onto your canvas. But first, a bit of vector theory.

 Always Provide for Graceful Degradation

You'll notice that the code above includes a conditional check for the existence of the getContext method; this is an excellent way of detecting whether the current browser is capable of working with canvas elements. If that condition isn't met, you can write some code that handles this case, and provide your users with suitable fallback content.

Thinking About Vector Graphics

If you've ever used a vector graphics program like Illustrator or Inkscape, you'll know that creating vector graphics is different from creating an image in Photoshop. Although we might reference points in the canvas as if they were pixels, we're not actually controlling each pixel on the canvas and telling it what color it should be.

What canvas does (as do SVG, and VML, and any other vector graphics languages) is let you specify a series of shapes on a two-dimensional coordinate plane, and have the browser figure out how to represent them in pixels.

Figure 3.2 is a conceptualization of the difference between a vector shape and its rendered pixel form.

Figure 3.2. A conceptualization of the difference between a vector shape and its rendered pixel form

The rendered black circle is magnified by a factor of 20; over the top of the pixels, in red, appears the actual vector shape that defines the final pixel representation. Beneath both circles is the pixel grid to which the browser is typically confined as it renders the circle. However, as the red circle in Figure 3.2 shows, the original vector shape is not constrained by this grid. Vector shapes are clearly much more flexible than bitmap images—while pixels always have to align to the pixel grid, the values for the size and position of a vector are free to take any value, be it 19 or 19.594817205. We can use extreme precision to create whatever shapes we want, and then leave it up to the browser to actually figure out how to represent our shape on the screen.

Most of the time, the coordinate grid of a `canvas` element will correspond to the pixel grid of the HTML page in which it's contained. In fact, this is what happens by default, so you can be sure that 400 units on the coordinate plane equal 400 pixels in the browser. But it *is* possible to transform and distort the coordinate grid of a `canvas` element so that it's totally different from the browser's pixel grid. I won't cover this type of transformation here, but once you've begun to master the basics of `canvas`, you might want to look at these more complex topics as a way of creating more intricate drawings.

For now, remember this: if you want to draw on a `canvas`, you have to use **shapes**.

Creating Shapes

When you think about making bitmap graphics on a computer screen, it's easy to draw a comparison with painting—you pick up a nice digital hog's hair brush, lather it up with some pixel paint, and splash it onto the monitor.

However, when you're creating a shape in `canvas`, what you're really doing is specifying a number of points and connecting them together. The connections can be straight, circular, or curved, but the number of points you need to make a shape, and they way they're connected together, will depend upon the shape you're trying to make.

In other vector graphics languages, we generally have a set of primitive shapes to work with—rectangles, circles, ellipses, polygons—but in `canvas`, there's only one primitive shape: the rectangle. Any other shape has to be constructed from individual lines. A shape that's constructed this way is called a **path**. Because they're easy, we'll take a look at rectangles first.

Creating Rectangles

A graphics context offers three different methods that will let you draw rectangles: `fillRect`, `strokeRect`, and `clearRect`. All of these methods take the same four arguments:

- the *x* coordinate of the rectangle's top-left corner
- the *y* coordinate of the rectangle's top-left corner
- the width of the rectangle
- the height of the rectangle

Each of these arguments represents a dimension on the coordinate plane, as can be seen in Figure 3.3.

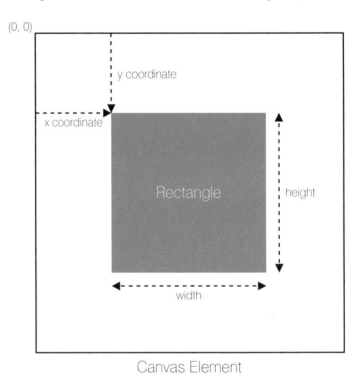

Figure 3.3. The rectangle's dimensions corresponding to locations on a coordinate plane

Let's make our first drawing using a couple of these rectangle functions. First, here's the simple HTML that contains our `canvas` element:

rectangle.html

```html
<!DOCTYPE html PUBLIC "-//W3C//DTD XHTML 1.0 Strict//EN"
    "http://www.w3.org/TR/xhtml1/DTD/xhtml1-strict.dtd">
<html xmlns="http://www.w3.org/1999/xhtml" xml:lang="en" lang="en">

<head>
  <title>Rectangle</title>
  <link rel="stylesheet" type="text/css" href="css/main.css"></link>
  <script type="text/javascript"
      src="scripts/rectangle.js"></script>
</head>

<body>
  <h1>
    Rectangle
  </h1>
  <canvas id="square" width="400" height="400" />
</body>

</html>
```

canvas elements can be styled using CSS, but only as much as img elements can be styled. In other words, position, float, and borders are basically the extent of the functionality. CSS won't affect anything that's drawn inside the canvas.

Stretching with CSS

The dimensions of a canvas element can be controlled via the CSS width and height properties, but this won't change the size of the original coordinate grid specified by the canvas's own width and height attributes. Instead, what will happen is the canvas will stretch to fit the CSS dimensions, and you'll end up with a distorted drawing, just like what happens when you resize the normal dimensions of an img element with CSS.

If width and height attributes aren't specified on the canvas element, the CSS will stretch it from the default width and height of 300×150 pixels.

All of our drawing will be completed through the external JavaScript file **rectangle.js**. Here it is in its first incarnation:

rectangle.js *(excerpt)*

```javascript
window.onload = init;

function init()
{
  var canvas = document.getElementById("square");
```

```
  if (typeof canvas.getContext != "undefined") {
    var context = canvas.getContext("2d");
    context.fillRect(0, 0, 400, 400);
  }
};
```

As we have to wait until the `canvas` element is ready, I've just used a simple `onload` event handler to trigger the initialization function; you can use whatever `onload`/DOM-ready function you normally use in these situations.[4]

When `init` is called, we first have to obtain a reference to the `canvas` element; then, we check whether or not we can retrieve a graphics context for it. If the graphics context is ready and waiting, we know we can start performing some `canvas` operations—the first one we'll do here is called `fillRect`:

```
    context.fillRect(0, 0, 400, 400);
```

This method call tells the browser to create a solid rectangle that's 400 units wide and 400 units high, with its top-left corner at 0, 0 (that's the coordinate for the top-left of the `canvas`, otherwise known as the **origin**). The result looks like Figure 3.4.

Figure 3.4. A rectangle created using `fillRect`

Exciting, huh!?

Our rectangle is black because we haven't specified a fill color, and the default fill color is black (as is the default stroke color). To change the color of the rectangle, we need to modify the `fillStyle` property of the context:

---

[4] If you're new to event handling, the Core library from the SitePoint book *Simply JavaScript* is available as a free download, and is a good place to start: http://www.sitepoint.com/blogs/2007/08/29/simply-javascript-the-core-library/.

rectangle.js *(excerpt)*

```
function init()
{
  var canvas = document.getElementById("square");

  if (typeof canvas.getContext != "undefined") {
    var context = canvas.getContext("2d");
    context.fillStyle = "#0066CC";
    context.fillRect(0, 0, 400, 400);
  }
};
```

This makes the rectangle a nice blue color (nothing's nicer than blue), as shown in Figure 3.5.

Rectangle

Figure 3.5. Changing the color of a rectangle using `fillStyle`

By setting the `fillStyle` property of the context, we're specifying that any fill operations done from now on should use the color #0066CC. If we wanted to change to another color for a different rectangle, we'd have to set `fillStyle` again before drawing it.

`fillStyle` accepts values in a variety of formats (as do all of the other color-oriented properties of the graphics context). It can take:

- a color keyword (e.g. `red`)
- a hex color value (e.g. `#FF0000`)
- an RGB value (`rgb(255, 0, 0)`)
- an RGBA value (`rgba(255, 0, 0, 0.5)`)

This last type of color value may be new to you. It's like an RGB value, except it has an extra number, the **alpha** value, which determines the opacity of the color. This is a number between 0 and 1, so an alpha value of 0.5 means that the color will be 50% opaque.

There are two other rectangle functions: `clearRect` and `strokeRect`. `clearRect` clears the area specified by the rectangle. This doesn't mean it just makes the area white; it removes any drawing that was done in that area and makes the area transparent. With this method we could, for example, clear out a space in the middle of our blue rectangle:

```
rectangle.js (excerpt)

function init()
{
  var canvas = document.getElementById("square");

  if (typeof canvas.getContext != "undefined") {
    var context = canvas.getContext("2d");
    context.fillStyle = "#0066CC";
    context.fillRect(0, 0, 400, 400);
    context.clearRect(75, 75, 250, 250);
  }
};
```

The code above would result in a drawing like the one shown in Figure 3.6.

Figure 3.6. Clearing an area of the `canvas` using `clearRect`

If we have a background color set on our HTML document, the transparency of the new area becomes even more apparent, as Figure 3.7 illustrates.

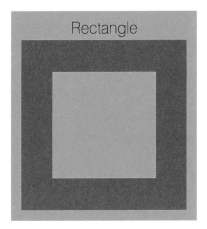

Figure 3.7. Making a cleared area on the canvas transparent

Lastly, strokeRect allows us to create an outline of a rectangle without filling it, as Figure 3.8 shows:

rectangle.js *(excerpt)*

```
function init()
{
  var canvas = document.getElementById("square");

  if (typeof canvas.getContext != "undefined") {
    var context = canvas.getContext("2d");
    context.fillStyle = "#0066CC";
    context.fillRect(0, 0, 400, 400);
    context.clearRect(75, 75, 250, 250);
    context.strokeRect(150, 150, 100, 100);
  }
};
```

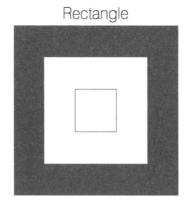

Figure 3.8. Creating an outline of a rectangle with `strokeRect`

The width of a stroke is always centered on the outline of the shape. The stroke above has a default width of one unit, so that means that half of the stroke sits inside the shape, and half of the stroke sits outside, giving the rectangle total dimensions of 101×101, not 100×100. That's why the line might seem a little fuzzy—the browser is trying to figure out how to draw a line along the edge of a pixel column so that half of the line appears in one column, and half in the other. If you wanted the stroke to be crisp (so the whole thing renders exactly on the pixel grid), you'd need to offset the rectangle by 0.5 units. The call to `strokeRect` would therefore become:

```
context.strokeRect(150.5, 150.5, 100, 100);
```

The color of the stroke can be controlled using the `strokeStyle` property, much like we used the `fillStyle` property for the fill. If we wanted a rectangle with a red outline, we'd change the `strokeStyle` to #FF0000 before we applied our stroke:

```
                                                          rectangle.js
window.onload = init;

function init()
{
  var canvas = document.getElementById("square");

  if (typeof canvas.getContext != "undefined") {
    var context = canvas.getContext("2d");
    context.fillStyle = "#0066CC";
    context.fillRect(0, 0, 400, 400);
    context.clearRect(75, 75, 250, 250);
    context.strokeStyle = "#FF0000";
    context.strokeRect(150, 150, 100, 100);
  }
};
```

This would produce the result shown in Figure 3.9.

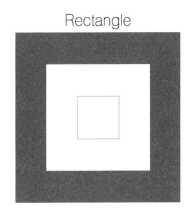

Figure 3.9. Changing the color of a rectangle's outline with the strokeStyle property

Of course, there's only so much you can do with rectangles. If you don't want all of your drawings to look like variations on Tetris, you'll have to start creating your own shapes. And that's where paths come in.

Creating Paths

A path is a series of points that form a shape. You can specify these points in a few different ways, but a path always starts out with a call to the method beginPath.

You can create multiple paths on a canvas, but you can only work on one path at a time. Calling beginPath signifies to the canvas that all the points following that call will belong to the same path, until you either call closePath or start another path with beginPath.

Unlike the rectangle functions that we looked at in the previous section, creating a path does *not* automatically render it to the screen. Once you've mapped out all of the points in a path, you must call stroke or fill in order to instruct the browser to draw the shape.

So, what can you put between beginPath and closePath?

Well, the simplest thing you can do in a path is create a straight line with the lineTo method. This creates a line from the current position of the path to the point defined by the x and y coordinates you specify. Let's start filling out **path.js**:

path.js *(excerpt)*

```
window.onload = init;

function init()
{
  var canvas = document.getElementById("drawing");
```

```
    if (typeof canvas.getContext != "undefined") {
      var context = canvas.getContext("2d");

      context.beginPath();
      context.lineTo(200, 225);
      context.stroke();
    }
  };
```

When you first call `beginPath`, the starting point of the path is set to (0, 0). Any path operations performed straight away will therefore create a line from (0, 0) to your destination point. However, `lineTo` operates a little differently. It only recognizes a starting point once you've made an explicit movement. So the code above would actually create nothing.

If we want to create a straight line as our first operation, we first have to set the starting point:

path.js *(excerpt)*

```
function init()
{
  var canvas = document.getElementById("drawing");

  if (typeof canvas.getContext != "undefined") {
    var context = canvas.getContext("2d");

    context.beginPath();
    context.moveTo(150, 100);
    context.lineTo(200, 225);
    context.stroke();
  }
};
```

Now we're getting somewhere, as Figure 3.10 shows.

Path

Figure 3.10. Creating straight lines using `lineTo`

The `moveTo` method I've used here works a little differently than `lineTo`. If you think of the action of creating a path as being like moving a pencil on paper, the `moveTo` method lets us take the pencil off the paper and place it somewhere else without leaving a mark.

In the code above, we first move our "pencil" to (150, 100)—this gives `lineTo` a starting point to draw from—then, we draw a line from there to (200, 225). Once we've finished creating our path (which consists of two points) we tell the browser to draw it on the screen by stroking it (applying a stroke to the path), with the `stroke` method.

Straight lines and rectangles are a bit boring, though. Let's make something a little more complex:

path.js *(excerpt)*

```
window.onload = init;

function init()
{
  var canvas = document.getElementById("drawing");

  if (typeof canvas.getContext != "undefined") {
    var context = canvas.getContext("2d");

    context.beginPath();
    context.moveTo(150, 100);
    context.lineTo(200, 225);
    context.lineTo(250, 100);
    context.fillStyle = "#D3BEA5";
    context.fill();

    context.beginPath();
    context.moveTo(150, 100);
    context.lineTo(200, 225);
    context.lineTo(250, 100);
```

```
    context.stroke();
  }
};
```

The two paths above actually map out the same shape: three points that form two lines and, ultimately, a triangle. The first path is used to create the fill for the shape, which is done using the `fill` method. Prior to calling that, though, we set the context's `fillStyle` property to a beige-brown color. This means that any fill operations we undertake from now on will use that color.

You should note that we don't call the `closePath` method before we call `fill`. In order to fill a shape, that shape has to be closed, so `fill` takes it upon itself to automatically close the path before rendering anything.

If we wanted the stroke to encompass the entire area that's covered by the fill, we'd have to call `closePath` in order to complete the shape. However, for the moment we want a stroke to be applied to just two of the sides (I'll show you why in a minute!), so in this situation it's okay to call `stroke` without closing the path.

Generally, if you've got a shape that you're going to both fill and stroke, you'll want to fill it before stroking it. As I mentioned before, the stroke is actually centered on the outline of the shape, so if you stroke then fill, the fill will paint over half of the width of the stroke. Also note that if you fill a shape, you don't need to call `closePath`—the fill we be applied without the first and last points being joined. However, if you stroke a path without calling `closePath`, that path will remain open.

The result of all this stroking and filling looks like Figure 3.11.

Path

Figure 3.11. Applying a stroke to our triangular, beige-brown shape

Why Are We Repeating Ourselves?

Ideally, we should be able to use exactly the same path in order to perform a `stroke` operation. However, at the time of writing, Safari has problems applying a fill and a stroke to the same path (it only draws the first operation, ignoring the second). This is why we have the second path replicate the first before applying our stroke.

Ah … what is it? Patience! You'll see.

So what about the times when we want to draw lines that aren't straight (otherwise known as **curves**)? Well, if you want a line that moves in a perfect circle, you can use `arc`.

`arc` lets you specify the center of a circle, the size of that circle, and the section of that circle that you want to draw. The method actually accepts quite a few arguments, which, in order, are:

- the *x* coordinate of the center of the circle
- the *y* coordinate of the center of the circle
- the radius of the circle
- the starting angle of the arc (measured in radians)
- the ending angle of the arc (measured in radians)
- the direction in which the arc is drawn (`true` for counterclockwise, `false` for clockwise)

So, if we wanted to draw a semicircle that capped off the top of our two straight lines, we'd need to determine the point directly between the two end points to get the center of our circle, then halve the distance between them to obtain the radius:

path.js *(excerpt)*

```
window.onload = init;

function init()
{
  var canvas = document.getElementById("drawing");

  if (typeof canvas.getContext != "undefined") {
    var context = canvas.getContext("2d");

    context.beginPath();
    context.moveTo(150, 100);
    context.lineTo(200, 225);
    context.lineTo(250, 100);
    context.fillStyle = "#D3BEA5";
    context.fill();

    context.beginPath();
    context.moveTo(150, 100);
```

```
    context.lineTo(200, 225);
    context.lineTo(250, 100);
    context.stroke();

    context.beginPath();
    context.arc(200, 100, 50, 0, Math.PI, true);
    context.fillStyle = "#FB6CF9";
    context.fill();

    context.beginPath();
    context.arc(200, 100, 50, 0, Math.PI, true);
    context.closePath();
    context.stroke();
  }
};
```

Where have these numbers come from? Well, the halfway point between (150, 100) and (250, 100) is (200, 100), and the distance between them is 100, which gives us a radius of 50 units.

For the angles, you'll need to remember that an angle of zero degrees corresponds to the three o'clock position. Admittedly this is a little unintuitive, but that's how it is so you'll just have to go with it! Now, the values for the angles are measured in **radians**, and 180 degrees actually corresponds to π (3.141592653 …) radians. So, to create a circular curve that travels from the three o'clock position to the nine o'clock position, we need to specify an arc from zero to π. The only question remaining now is in which direction the arc should travel. We want the circle to sit above the straight lines that we've already drawn, so it should move in an counterclockwise direction; the last argument should therefore be `true`.

You'll notice in the code above that, once again, we've redrawn the same path twice in order to achieve both the fill and the stroke. However, this time, when we apply the stroke we *do* call `closePath`. The stroke will therefore be applied around *all* sides of the semicircle, and won't leave it open at the bottom.

Once that's done, we've drawn our first little picture, shown in Figure 3.12.

 Going in Circles

To create a full circle, we need to specify two angles that have a difference of 2π. This is because 2π radians produces one complete rotation.

Any arc angles that are greater than 2π will simply cycle around again. Since the stroke is applied after the angle has been calculated, 3π radians (one and a half rotations) is therefore equivalent to π radians (half a rotation).

Path

Figure 3.12. A combination of straight lines and arcs producing some delicious ice cream

Although there's a shared line between the ice cream and the cone, there's a reason that we didn't just stroke both lines and have them overlapping. If we'd stroked the top of the cone, when the ice cream line overlapped it, we'd have produced a line that was slightly heavier than all the others. The reason why is that most strokes won't fall exactly on the pixel grid, so the browser will try to anti-alias them. And anti-aliasing is achieved by making some areas of the line semitransparent. So when two lines are drawn, one on top of the other, the semitransparent areas combine to produce a darker color, making the line look heavier. If we only draw the line once, we ensure it maintains an evenness of stroke around the entire drawing.

Straight lines and circles are good for creating nice geometric drawings, but if you want more organic forms, you'll need to investigate the complex world of **Bézier curves**.

Bézier Curves

If you've never worked with vector graphics before (for example, in a drawing program like Illustrator), you may not have a clue what a Bézier curve is. A Bézier curve is a smooth, non-circular curve—for example, like those found in ellipses, waves, and bends—that can be specified in a computer program by a number of parameters. Figure 3.13 shows an example of some `canvas` Bézier curves in use in a real application.

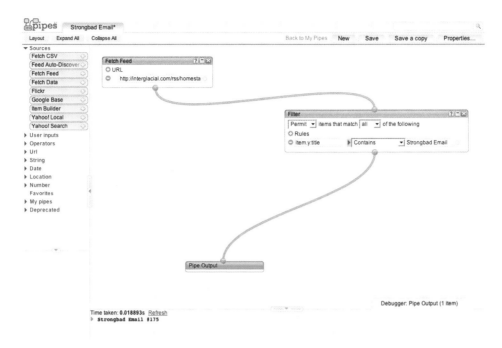

Figure 3.13. The "pipes" that join modules in Yahoo's Pipes application

A Bézier curve consists of two points—the start and the end—but the curve of the line that joins these two points is defined by another point called a **control point**. Control points aren't actually part of the path—you never see them when the path is drawn—but they influence the way the line curves between the start and the end points.

In a **quadratic** Bézier curve, there's one control point that's shared by both the start and end points. In a **cubic** Bézier curve, both the start and end points have their own control points, which are colloquially known as **handlebars**. Cubic Bézier curves therefore have more accuracy than their quadratic counterparts.

Bézier curves are definitely easier to grasp if you visualize them—Figure 3.14 and Figure 3.15 show how they might look.

Figure 3.14. A quadratic Bézier curve with only one control point

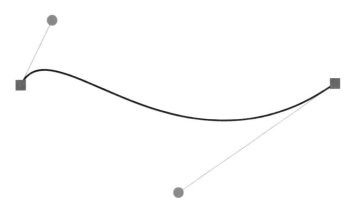

Figure 3.15. A cubic Bézier curve with two control points—one for each end

In those figures, the blue squares mark the start and end points, while the red dots mark the control points. The gray lines connecting the end points to their control points are there to illustrate the effect that a control point has on the direction of the line itself.

A control point indicates the direction in which a curve starts, and how steep the curve is from that point. The shorter the distance between a control point and its path point, the less steep the curve will be. In fact, control points are a little bit like magnets: they exert a force on the line that causes it to bend. The distance to the control point determines how strong that force is.

It can be beneficial to try out a vector drawing program like Illustrator or Inkscape (it's free!) just to get a feel for how these curves work.[5] It's exceptionally hard to create a Bézier curve in JavaScript without first knowing what your final line should look like. If you're creating Bézier curves on a canvas, it's probably a good idea to mock the curve up in Illustrator first, then try to reproduce it with control points in your JavaScript.

canvas allows you to draw both quadratic and cubic curves using the quadraticCurveTo and bezierCurveTo methods, respectively. Any quadratic curve can be reproduced using a cubic curve, but not all cubic curves can be reproduced using quadratic curves. So for the purposes of this chapter, we'll just take a look at bezierCurveTo.

The bezierCurveTo method takes six arguments:

- the x coordinate of the start point's control point
- the y coordinate of the start point's control point
- the x coordinate of the end point's control point
- the y coordinate of the end point's control point
- the x coordinate of the end point
- the y coordinate of the end point

---

[5] http://www.inkscape.org/

Much like the `lineTo` method, `bezierCurveTo` uses the previous point on the path as its starting point, but unlike `lineTo`, it will assume that the starting point is (0, 0) if no points have been laid out yet.

Imagine we left our ice cream out in the sun and it got a bit melty; we could show this using some Bézier curves and a few magic numbers that I've concocted in my top-secret Bézier laboratory:

```
                                                                       path.js
window.onload = init;
function init()
{
  var canvas = document.getElementById("drawing");

  if (typeof canvas.getContext != "undefined") {
    var context = canvas.getContext("2d");

    context.beginPath();
    context.moveTo(150, 100);
    context.lineTo(200, 225);
    context.lineTo(250, 100);
    context.fillStyle = "#D3BEA5";
    context.fill();

    context.beginPath();
    context.moveTo(150, 100);
    context.lineTo(200, 225);
    context.lineTo(250, 100);
    context.stroke();

    context.beginPath();
    context.arc(200, 100, 50, 0, Math.PI, true);
    context.lineTo(160, 100);
    context.bezierCurveTo(170, 100, 180, 110, 180, 120);
    context.bezierCurveTo(180, 125, 172, 140, 185, 140);
    context.bezierCurveTo(198, 140, 190, 125, 190, 120);
    context.bezierCurveTo(190, 110, 200, 100, 210, 100);
    context.fillStyle = "#FB6CF9";
    context.fill();

    context.beginPath();
    context.arc(200, 100, 50, 0, Math.PI, true);
    context.lineTo(160, 100);
    context.bezierCurveTo(170, 100, 180, 110, 180, 120);
    context.bezierCurveTo(180, 125, 172, 140, 185, 140);
    context.bezierCurveTo(198, 140, 190, 125, 190, 120);
    context.bezierCurveTo(190, 110, 200, 100, 210, 100);
    context.closePath();
```

```
    context.stroke();
  }
};
```

When you're creating curves like these, achieving the curve you want really is mostly a matter if trial and error. Again, it does help if you can mock up the layout of the control points in a drawing program. A visualization of the path and its control points would look like Figure 3.16.

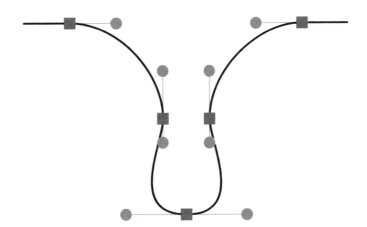

Figure 3.16. A visualization of the control points on the ice cream Bézier curves

If we run `init` now, we get a nice scoop of melty strawberry ice cream, like the one in Figure 3.17.

Path

Figure 3.17. Producing more complex organic forms with Bézier curves

As you can see, Bézier curves *do* give you nice, smooth curves if you have the patience to work with them. They're also the final component we can use in creating paths.

Enough with the cutesy pictures. Let's try to make something useful!

Creating a Pie Chart

The aim of this little project is to produce a pie charting utility that can take a dataset of any size and produce a pie chart of that data. Previously, if you wanted to do this sort of interaction on the client side, you might have used Flash. But now, with `canvas`, we can do it all in our HTML.

Drawing the Chart

Our data will be passed as a simple array of values; it's our job to calculate each data value as a proportion of the sum of all the values, and reflect each graphically as a piece of the pie chart.

To do this, we'll create a new object called `PieChart` that takes two values: the data array to be drawn, and the size of the chart (that is, the radius of the circle):

pie_chart.js (excerpt)

```
function PieChart(data, radius)
{
  this.data = data; ❶
  this.radius = radius;

  this.startColor = [204, 0, 0]; ❷
  this.endColor = [115, 12, 243];

  this.canvas = document.getElementById("chart");

  if (typeof this.canvas.getContext != "undefined") {
    this.context = this.canvas.getContext("2d"); ❸

    this.draw();
  }
}
```

❶ First of all, we store the passed-in data as properties of the object, so that other methods can access them.

❷ Then, we create two arrays for RGB color values (`this.startColor` and `this.endColor`). These will be the start and end colors of the segments in the pie; we'll have to make sure there's a nice gradation between them for the segments that fall in between.

❸ Lastly, there should be the now-familiar code to get the graphics context for our `canvas` element. Once we've got it, we make a call to the object's `draw` method.

The code to draw `canvas` shapes can get fairly lengthy not through complexity of calculation, but because of the number of operations it takes to generate the required shapes. This is the case with `draw`:

```
PieChart.prototype.draw = function()
{
  var cx = this.canvas.width / 2; ❶
  var cy = this.canvas.height / 2;

  var dataTotal = 0;

  for (var i=0; i < this.data.length; i++)
  {
    dataTotal +=  this.data[i]; ❷
  }

  var dataSubTotal = 0; ❸

  for (var i=0; i < this.data.length; i++) ❹
  {
    var red = Math.round(this.startColor[0] - ((this.startColor[0]
        - this.endColor[0]) / (this.data.length - 1) * i));
    var green = Math.round(this.startColor[1] - ((this.startColor[1]
        - this.endColor[1]) / (this.data.length - 1) * i));
    var blue = Math.round(this.startColor[2] - ((this.startColor[2]
        - this.endColor[2]) / (this.data.length - 1) * i));

    this.context.fillStyle = "rgb(" + red + "," + green + ","
        + blue + ")";

    this.context.beginPath();
    this.context.moveTo(cx, cy);
    this.context.arc(cx, cy, this.radius,
        dataSubTotal / dataTotal * Math.PI * 2,
        (dataSubTotal + this.data[i]) / dataTotal * Math.PI * 2,
        false);
    this.context.closePath();
    this.context.fill();

    this.context.beginPath();
    this.context.moveTo(cx, cy);
    this.context.arc(cx, cy, this.radius,
        dataSubTotal / dataTotal * Math.PI * 2,
        (dataSubTotal + this.data[i]) / dataTotal * Math.PI * 2,
        false);

    if (i == this.data.length - 1) {
      this.context.closePath();
    }

    this.context.stroke();
```

```
      dataSubTotal += this.data[i];
  }
};
```

1 The variables `cx` and `cy` are used to determine the exact center of our `canvas` element, because that's where we want the center of our pie chart to be. To calculate these variables, we simply take the `canvas`'s `width` and `height` attributes and divide them by half—easy!

2 The next piece of data we have to calculate is the size of our data set. In order to figure out what proportion of the total pie each data value represents, we first have to know what size the pie is. `dataTotal` uses a `for` loop to add up all of the values in the data array and produce a total value.

3 In order to keep track of the number of data values we've drawn already (and how far around the pie we've come), `dataSubTotal` is initialized now—it can be used as a running counter.

Now we're ready to start drawing each segment.

4 A `for` loop is used to iterate through our data array. We'll calculate two things for each data value: the dimensions of the slice of the pie chart, and the color of the slice.

First up, let's talk about color.

Calculating the Color of a Segment

We can use the two-color arrays that we've specified in our object constructor to create a nice progression of color by programmatically selecting several colors that fall in between the start and end colors. The color wheel in Figure 3.18 is one example of a smooth progression of colors.

To select the colors we'd like to use for our pie chart, we take each of the RGB values and calculate regular intervals by which to move from the start value to the end value.

Let's look at the calculation of the red value:

```
var red = Math.round(this.startColor[0] - ((this.startColor[0]
    - this.endColor[0]) / (this.data.length - 1) * i));
```

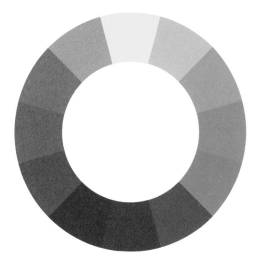

Figure 3.18. A color wheel, showing smooth progression across the color spectrum

The calculation in bold above determines the total difference between the start and end values. By the time we draw the last segment, we want this value to be at its maximum, but for each of the intervening segments we're only interested in a certain fraction of the value. To obtain those fractions, we take the difference between the start and end values and multiply it by the current position, expressed as a percentage, like so:

```
var red = Math.round(this.startColor[0] - ((this.startColor[0]
    - this.endColor[0]) / (this.data.length - 1) * i));
```

The portion of code that's bolded above will tell us how much we're deviating from our initial red value for each segment. If we subtract this difference from the start value, we should get the value we need to assign to the segment itself:

```
var red = Math.round(this.startColor[0] - ((this.startColor[0]
    - this.endColor[0]) / (this.data.length - 1) * i));
```

Just to make sure this number is an integer, we've used `Math.round` to round it to the nearest whole number, and there we have our red value! (Okay, now mightn't be the time to warn you that drawing graphics requires a little bit of mathematics.)

This process is repeated for the green and blue values for the color, producing a complete RGB value to assign to each segment of the chart. We then assign this value to the `fillStyle` of the graphics context, so this color will be used the next time we call a fill operation.

With the color calculation out of the way, we're now ready to start drawing the segment.

Determining the Dimensions of a Segment

If you analyze a slice of pie like the one in Figure 3.19, it's easy to break it down into a couple of the simple path drawing operations that we looked at earlier in the chapter.

Figure 3.19. A nice slice of pie

As you can see, all a segment consists of is two straight lines joined by an arc. In actual fact, we don't even need to worry about creating the two straight lines—this is done for us by the definition of the path:

pie_chart.js *(excerpt)*

```
this.context.beginPath();
this.context.moveTo(cx, cy);
this.context.arc(cx, cy, this.radius,
    dataSubTotal / dataTotal * Math.PI * 2,
    (dataSubTotal + this.data[i]) / dataTotal * Math.PI * 2,
    false);
this.context.closePath();
```

The start of the pie segment is actually the center of the canvas, so we use movePath to place our first point there. From there, we can jump straight into drawing the arc for the outer edge of the segment—the path will automatically connect the first point with the starting arc point.

In order to draw the arc, we give the arc method the coordinates of the center of the circle—(cx, cy)—and the radius that was passed into the object's constructor—this.radius. We're expressing the angle through which we want the arc to be drawn for each segment as a percentage of a complete circle, then multiplying this percentage by 2π (360 degrees expressed as radians). We begin at the point of the circle's circumference that's defined by the first segment (the fraction defined by dataSubTotal over dataTotal). We then draw an arc for the percentage of the circle defining the next segment (the fraction of the current data value over dataTotal).

With the arc complete, closing the path will finish off the shape by drawing a line from the arc back to the center of the canvas. Fill this shape, repeat and stroke the shape, and we've got our first segment of pie.

Don't Re-stroke the Same Line

Note that, right before stroking the path, we perform a check to see if the current segment is the last piece of the pie. Only when it is do we call `closePath`. `closePath` will create the line from the right side of the arc back to the middle of the circle, but this line will coincide with the first line of the next segment, so we don't want to stroke the same line twice (that would generate a heavier stroke).

The last piece of the pie is a special case, because when we fill it with color, that fill will actually overwrite half of the stroke on the first piece of the pie, so we have to close the path of the last piece and make sure that we have a full stroke.

As the `for` loop starts repeating all these calculations, you can see the build-up of segments, and our pie chart taking shape. The iterations of the code affect the `canvas` as shown in Figure 3.20.

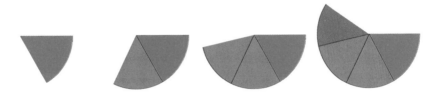

Figure 3.20. Slices of pie being added to the `canvas` as the `for` loop iterates through the data array

You'll notice that the trailing edge of each piece is not stroked, because the next piece of the pie will create that line.

With the `draw` method out the way, our `PieChart` object is complete. All that's required is to initialize the page.

Initializing the Page

Instantiating our `PieChart` object is easy—we just need to pass it some values. For this demo, we'll use a random data array of six values. This means you'll get a new pie chart every time you refresh the page.

Here's the `init` method:

pie_chart.js (excerpt)

```
window.onload = init;

function init()
{
  var data = [Math.random(), Math.random(),  Math.random(),
      Math.random(),  Math.random(),  Math.random()];
```

```
  var radius = 180;

  setTimeout(function()
    {
      new PieChart(data, radius);
    },
    1
  );
};
```

While we've used random values here, it would be particularly easy to link our `PieChart` to an actual data source, as we'll see in a moment. In addition to specifying the data we want to depict through a random data array, we specify the chart's radius via the `radius` variable. Drawing a pie chart thus becomes a simple matter of creating a new `PieChart` object and passing those two variables to it.

Figure 3.21 shows some of the results of the random pie chart generation.

Figure 3.21. Randomly generated data producing different pie charts

 Fixing Firefox

You'll probably be wondering what on earth that `setTimeout` is doing around the object instantiation. That's a fix for a Firefox bug which, when rendering `canvas` files on local documents, sometimes doesn't draw them at all. Putting in a brief delay (in this case, one millisecond) rectifies the problem.

Casting a Shadow

As a final trick in our `canvas`-drawing bag, we'll add a slight shadow to the pie chart—just to make it pop out of the page and hit you in the eye. Kapow!

Now, it would actually be fairly easy to add a drop shadow to the chart: just draw a light gray circle on the `canvas` before you draw the pie chart. However, I'm going to take a slightly longer route that will allow me to show you a very handy feature of the graphics context. What we're going to do is draw the shadow *after* we've drawn the pie. The shadow code is highlighted in bold in the following code listing:

```javascript
PieChart.prototype.draw = function()
{
  var cx = this.canvas.width / 2;
  var cy = this.canvas.height / 2;

  var dataTotal = 0;

  for (var i=0; i < this.data.length; i++)
  {
    dataTotal +=  this.data[i];
  }

  var dataSubTotal = 0;

  for (var i=0; i < this.data.length; i++)
  {
    var red = Math.round(this.startColor[0] - ((this.startColor[0]
        - this.endColor[0]) / (this.data.length - 1) * i));
    var green = Math.round(this.startColor[1] - ((this.startColor[1]
        - this.endColor[1]) / (this.data.length - 1) * i));
    var blue = Math.round(this.startColor[2] - ((this.startColor[2]
        - this.endColor[2]) / (this.data.length - 1) * i));

    this.context.fillStyle = "rgb(" + red + "," + green + ","
        + blue + ")";

    this.context.beginPath();
    this.context.moveTo(cx, cy);
    this.context.arc(cx, cy, this.radius,
        dataSubTotal / dataTotal * Math.PI * 2,
        (dataSubTotal + this.data[i]) / dataTotal * Math.PI * 2,
        false);
    this.context.closePath();
    this.context.fill();

    this.context.beginPath();
    this.context.moveTo(cx, cy);
    this.context.arc(cx, cy, this.radius,
        dataSubTotal / dataTotal * Math.PI * 2,
        (dataSubTotal + this.data[i]) / dataTotal * Math.PI * 2,
        false);

    if (i == this.data.length - 1) {
      this.context.closePath();
    }
```

```
    this.context.stroke();

    dataSubTotal += this.data[i];
  }

  this.context.beginPath();
  this.context.moveTo(cx + this.shadowOffset,
      cy + this.shadowOffset);
  this.context.arc(cx + this.shadowOffset, cy + this.shadowOffset,
      this.radius, 0, Math.PI * 2, false);
  this.context.closePath();
  this.context.globalCompositeOperation = "destination-over";
  this.context.fillStyle = "rgba(0, 0, 0, 0.25)";
  this.context.fill();
};
```

The most important thing to note here is the property that we're modifying on the graphics context, just before we fill the shape: `globalCompositeOperation`.

Typically, when we perform a fill or a stroke operation on a canvas, the item that we've drawn most recently will appear above whatever we've previously drawn on that canvas. What's actually happening here is that the default value of globalCompositeOperation—source-over—is being used with each operation.

In fact, globalCompositeOperation can have any of 12 values, each of which changes the way that the drawing is composited (that is, the way the new shape interacts with what's already on the canvas).

You can see all the values and their effects in Table 3.1. In this table, the green circle is the new shape, and the red circle is the existing content.

Table 3.1. Possible Values of `globalCompositeOperation`

globalCompositeOperation	Description	Effect
source-over (default)	The new shape is drawn over the existing content.	
destination-over	The new shape is drawn behind the existing content.	
source-in	Only the part of the new shape that intersects with the existing content is shown. Everything else on the canvas is made transparent.	
destination-in	Only the part of the existing content that intersects with the new shape is shown. Everything else on the canvas is made transparent.	
source-out	Only the part of the new shape that *doesn't* intersect with the existing content is shown. Everything else on the canvas is made transparent.	
destination-out	Only the part of the existing content that *doesn't* intersect with the new shape is shown. Everything else on the canvas is made transparent.	
source-atop	The part of the new shape that intersects with the existing content is drawn on top of the existing content.	

globalCompositeOperation	Description	Effect
destination-atop	The part of the existing content that intersects with the new shape is kept, while the remainder is made transparent. The new shape is then drawn behind.	
lighter (not supported in all browsers)	Where the new shape and the existing content intersect, their color values are added together.	
darker (not supported in all browsers)	Where the new shape and the existing content intersect, the difference between the color values is displayed.	
xor	The intersection of the new shape and the existing content is made transparent.	
copy (not supported in all browsers)	All existing content is removed before the new shape is drawn.	

In the case of our drop shadow, we've used destination-over as the composite operation, so when we draw the shadow it's positioned behind what's already on the canvas. This makes the shadow appear to be coming from *behind* the pie chart.

The position of the shadow circle is offset by a small amount, so that the pie chart looks like it's casting a shadow onto the page. This offset is stored in this.shadowOffset and is created in the object's constructor, as shown below:

pie_chart.js *(excerpt)*

```
function PieChart(data, radius)
{
  this.data = data;
```

```
  this.radius = radius;

  this.startColor = [204, 0, 0];
  this.endColor = [115, 12, 243];
  this.shadowOffset = 7;

  this.canvas = document.getElementById("chart");

  if (typeof this.canvas.getContext != "undefined") {
    this.context = this.canvas.getContext("2d");

    this.draw();
  }
};
```

As an added bonus, the fill color of the shadow is set using an RGBA value, where the alpha is set to 0.25. So even though the color is solid black, it's actually semitransparent and able to be used regardless of the color of the background upon which it sits. The results of this shadowy transformation can be seen in Figure 3.22.

Figure 3.22. Positioning the shadow of the pie chart behind the chart using a composite operation

Updating the Chart Dynamically

Although the pie chart looks impressive if you understand what's going on under the hood, when it's created using static data, it isn't really that different from an image. In order to take full advantage of client-side drawing capabilities, you need to introduce the facility for interactivity with your site's users.

Luckily, it's really easy to do this with our pie chart! All we have to do is gather some data, feed it into the PieChart object, and the pie chart will be redrawn with the new data.

To take an extremely quick shortcut, I'm going to add a few sliders from Chapter 14 of *The JavaScript Anthology, 101 Essential Tips, Tricks & Hacks*[6] to the page. This requires us to include the **slider_control.js** file, and place some input fields into the HTML:

pie_chart_dynamic.html *(excerpt)*

```
<body>
  <h1>
    Pie Chart
  </h1>
  <div id="chartContainer">
    <form action="">
      <fieldset>
        <input id="data1" name="data1" class="slider" type="text"
            value="100" />
        <input id="data2" name="data2" class="slider" type="text"
            value="56" />
        <input id="data3" name="data3" class="slider" type="text"
            value="23" />
        <input id="data4" name="data4" class="slider" type="text"
            value="75" />
        <input id="data5" name="data5" class="slider" type="text"
            value="115" />
        <input id="data6" name="data5" class="slider" type="text"
            value="30" />
      </fieldset>
    </form>
    <canvas id="chart" width="400" height="400"></canvas>
  </div>
</body>
```

Those input fields are going to be transformed into spiffy slider controls—all we need to do is wire them up and feed their values into our `PieChart` object. In order to do so, we'll need to modify **slider_control.js**. The full code for that file is explained in *The JavaScript Anthology*, or you can take a look at it in the code archive for this chapter.

It's really a very simple change that we're going to be making. Every time that one of the sliders is moved, we'll retrieve the values for all six input fields and create a new `PieChart` object. This means we need to modify the `mousemove` event listener for the sliders:

slider_control.js *(excerpt)*

```
function mousemoveSlider(event)
{
  if (typeof event == "undefined") {
```

---

[6] http://www.sitepoint.com/books/jsant1/

```
    event = window.event;
  }

  var slider = document.currentSlider;
  var sliderLeft = slider.valueX;
  var increment = 1;

  if (isNaN(sliderLeft)) {
    sliderLeft = 0;
  }

  sliderLeft += event.clientX - slider.originX;

  if (sliderLeft < 0) {
    sliderLeft = 0;
  }
  else if (sliderLeft > (slider.parentNode.offsetWidth
      - slider.offsetWidth)) {
    sliderLeft = slider.parentNode.offsetWidth - slider.offsetWidth;
  }
  else
  {
    slider.originX = event.clientX;
  }

  slider.style.left =
      Math.round(sliderLeft / increment) * increment + "px";
  slider.parentNode.input.setAttribute("value",
      Math.round(sliderLeft / increment) * increment);
  slider.valueX = sliderLeft;

  var data1 =
   parseInt(document.getElementById("data1").getAttribute("value"));
  var data2 =
   parseInt(document.getElementById("data2").getAttribute("value"));
  var data3 =
   parseInt(document.getElementById("data3").getAttribute("value"));
  var data4 =
   parseInt(document.getElementById("data4").getAttribute("value"));
  var data5 =
   parseInt(document.getElementById("data5").getAttribute("value"));
  var data6 =
   parseInt(document.getElementById("data6").getAttribute("value"));

  new PieChart([data1, data2, data3, data4, data5, data6], 180);

  stopDefaultAction(event);

  return true;
}
```

As you can see, the value of each input field is retrieved and converted from a string to an integer. All six values are then passed straight into PieChart, with a radius value of 180. That's it.

There are some slight modifications that we need to make to PieChart before we can let the sliders go wild on it, mainly because we're going to be redrawing the chart on the same area over and over.

Firstly, because the edges of the pie chart are anti-aliased, if we start drawing several of the charts on top of one another, we'll see a build up of the transparent edge pixels. This will produce a "heavy" effect, as we've seen in previous line drawings. The way to get around this problem is to clear the canvas every time we want to make an update. The easiest way to do that is to use clearRect on the entire canvas:

pie_chart_dynamic.js (excerpt)

```
PieChart.prototype.draw = function()
{
  var cx = this.canvas.width / 2;
  var cy = this.canvas.height / 2;

  this.context.globalCompositeOperation = "source-over";
  this.context.clearRect(0, 0, this.canvas.getAttribute("width"),
      this.canvas.getAttribute("height"));

  var dataTotal = 0;

  for (var i=0; i < this.data.length; i++)
  {
    dataTotal +=  this.data[i];
  }

  var dataSubTotal = 0;

  for (var i=0; i < this.data.length; i++)
  {
    var red = Math.round(this.startColor[0] - ((this.startColor[0]
        - this.endColor[0]) / (this.data.length - 1) * i));
    var green = Math.round(this.startColor[1] - ((this.startColor[1]
        - this.endColor[1]) / (this.data.length - 1) * i));
    var blue = Math.round(this.startColor[2] - ((this.startColor[2]
        - this.endColor[2]) / (this.data.length - 1) * i));

    this.context.fillStyle = "rgb(" + red + "," + green + ","
        + blue + ")";

    this.context.beginPath();
    this.context.moveTo(cx, cy);
    this.context.arc(cx, cy, this.radius,
        dataSubTotal / dataTotal * Math.PI * 2,
        (dataSubTotal + this.data[i]) / dataTotal * Math.PI * 2,
```

```
        false);
    this.context.closePath();
    this.context.fill();

    this.context.beginPath();
    this.context.moveTo(cx, cy);
    this.context.arc(cx, cy, this.radius,
        dataSubTotal / dataTotal * Math.PI * 2,
        (dataSubTotal + this.data[i]) / dataTotal * Math.PI * 2,
        false);

    if (i == this.data.length - 1) {
      this.context.closePath();
    }

    this.context.stroke();

    dataSubTotal += this.data[i];
  }

  this.context.beginPath();
  this.context.moveTo(cx + this.shadowOffset,
      cy + this.shadowOffset);
  this.context.arc(cx + this.shadowOffset, cy + this.shadowOffset,
      this.radius, 0, Math.PI * 2, false);
  this.context.closePath();
  this.context.globalCompositeOperation = "destination-over";
  this.context.fillStyle = "rgba(0, 0, 0, 0.25)";
  this.context.fill();
};
```

 ### Opera Handles `clearRect` and `globalCompositeOperation` Differently

I had originally placed the default `globalCompositeOperation` setting right before the first `fill`, but then I noticed that Opera wasn't clearing the `canvas`. This is because Opera, unlike other browsers, actually applies the `globalCompositeOperation` to `clearRect`. So on successive calls to `PieChart.draw`, Opera was only clearing the content beneath what already existed. By resetting `globalCompositeOperation` *before* calling `clearRect`, we can be sure that everything is removed from the `canvas`.

You may remember from our little rectangle drawing exercise that `clearRect` clears the specified area of the `canvas`, making it entirely transparent. If we position the top-left of the rectangle at (0, 0) and specify the width and height of the rectangle as the `width` and `height` of the `canvas` element, we'll clear the entire `canvas` view. This gives us an empty space upon which we can draw our updated pie chart.

The second change in the code above is the addition of another `globalCompositeOperation` setting—just before we call `clearRect` and, most importantly, before we perform the first `fill` of the pie chart. The reason for this is that the last fill of the pie chart (the shadow) uses a `globalCompositeOperation` that's different from the default. The graphic context remembers this last setting, so when we draw a new pie chart, it uses the non-default method. We'll want to revert to the default before we perform any operations, so every time that `draw` is called, we make sure the `globalCompositeOperation` property is set to `source-over`.

The last thing for us to do is to use the initial position of the sliders as the first set of data for the pie chart. Let's edit `init` as follows:

```
                                                    pie_chart_dynamic.js (excerpt)
function init()
{
  var data1 =
   parseInt(document.getElementById("data1").getAttribute("value"));
  var data2 =
   parseInt(document.getElementById("data2").getAttribute("value"));
  var data3 =
   parseInt(document.getElementById("data3").getAttribute("value"));
  var data4 =
   parseInt(document.getElementById("data4").getAttribute("value"));
  var data5 =
   parseInt(document.getElementById("data5").getAttribute("value"));
  var data6 =
   parseInt(document.getElementById("data6").getAttribute("value"));

  var data = [data1, data2, data3, data4, data5, data6];
  var radius = 180;

  setTimeout(function()
    {
      new PieChart(data, radius);
    },
    1
  );
};
```

This code is almost identical to the changes we made to the slider event listener: we're taking the values of each of the input fields and passing them into a new `PieChart` object.

And with those few small changes, we're done. Now when the sliders are moved, they'll force a redraw of the pie chart that reflects the new data. The redraw is so quick that the users won't even see it—they'll just get smoothly moving pieces of pie.

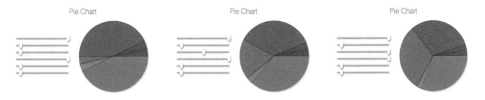

Figure 3.23. The completed implementation, which enables user interaction with the graphs

You can sort of get the effect if you wobble this book in front of your face, but for the full experience, load up the example from the code archive and start sliding those sliders!

canvas in Internet Explorer

Earlier in the chapter I mentioned that canvas was supported in most modern browsers—all, in fact, except Internet Explorer. Given IE's dominant share of the browser market, this poses a problem for the adoption of canvas. Luckily, however, there's a solution.

Although it doesn't support canvas, Internet Explorer *does* support something similar, called VML (Vector Markup Language). At the end of 2005, Emil Eklund had the brilliant idea—and technical nous—to write a JavaScript module that automatically translates canvas to VML, thereby allowing canvas to "work" in Internet Explorer. Google has since taken up the responsibility of developing this technology and now provides it as a module called ExplorerCanvas.[7]

It's a marvel how simple ExplorerCanvas is to use. All you need to do is include the **excanvas.js** file on your page. Let's get it working for our static pie chart:

pie_chart_excanvas.html *(excerpt)*

```
<!DOCTYPE html PUBLIC "-//W3C//DTD XHTML 1.0 Strict//EN"
"http://www.w3.org/TR/xhtml1/DTD/xhtml1-strict.dtd">
<html xmlns="http://www.w3.org/1999/xhtml" xml:lang="en" lang="en">

<head>
  <title>Pie Chart</title>
  <link rel="stylesheet" type="text/css" href="css/main.css"></link>
  <script type="text/javascript" src="scripts/pie_chart.js"></script>
<!--[if IE]>
  <script type="text/javascript" src="scripts/excanvas.js"></script>
<![endif]-->
</head>
```

<hr>

[7] http://excanvas.sourceforge.net/

Once the **excanvas.js** file has been included in the page, the graphics context and its associated methods and properties are exposed to Internet Explorer. We don't have to change any of our original `canvas` code in order to get it to display.

As you can see in the code above, the best way to include the ExplorerCanvas script is inside some Internet Explorer conditional comments. That way, no other browsers will try to run the code. The file itself is reasonably small (12KB when compressed), so you don't introduce much overhead by using it.

Although it works fairly well with normal shapes and lines, ExplorerCanvas does lack some of the finer features of `canvas`. For example, if we take our pie chart with a shadow and draw it into Internet Explorer as is, we experience a bit of a layering issue, as Figure 3.24 illustrates.

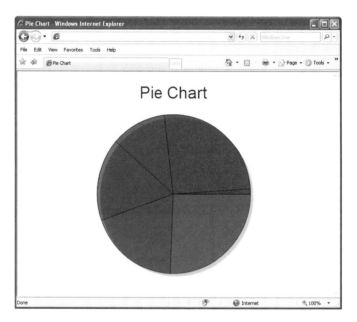

Figure 3.24. ExplorerCanvas's imperfect translation of `canvas` into VML

The error occurs as a result of the fact that VML doesn't have anything that can reproduce the different types of compositing available via `globalCompositeOperation`. Therefore, we can't draw the shadow of the pie chart *behind* the slices.

Because of this lack of `globalCompositeOperation` support, we have to approach the drawing of our pie chart in a more straightforward manner. So, instead of drawing the shadow *after* the pie slices have been drawn, we should draw it *before* the slices, then let the slices automatically be drawn on top of the shadow:

```javascript
PieChart.prototype.draw = function()
{
  var cx = this.canvas.width / 2;
  var cy = this.canvas.height / 2;

  this.context.beginPath();
  this.context.moveTo(cx + this.shadowOffset,
      cy + this.shadowOffset);
  this.context.arc(cx + this.shadowOffset, cy + this.shadowOffset,
      this.radius, 0, Math.PI * 2, false);
  this.context.closePath();
  this.context.fillStyle = "rgba(0, 0, 0, 0.25)";
  this.context.fill();

  var dataTotal = 0;

  for (var i=0; i < this.data.length; i++)
  {
    dataTotal +=  this.data[i];
  }

  var dataSubTotal = 0;

  for (var i=0; i < this.data.length; i++)
  {
    var red = Math.round(this.startColor[0] - ((this.startColor[0]
        - this.endColor[0]) / (this.data.length - 1) * i));
    var green = Math.round(this.startColor[1] - ((this.startColor[1]
        - this.endColor[1]) / (this.data.length - 1) * i));
    var blue = Math.round(this.startColor[2] - ((this.startColor[2]
        - this.endColor[2]) / (this.data.length - 1) * i));

    this.context.fillStyle =
        "rgb(" + red + "," + green + "," + blue + ")";

    this.context.beginPath();
    this.context.moveTo(cx, cy);
    this.context.arc(cx, cy, this.radius,
        dataSubTotal / dataTotal * Math.PI * 2,
        (dataSubTotal + this.data[i]) / dataTotal * Math.PI * 2,
        false);
    this.context.closePath();
    this.context.fill();

    this.context.beginPath();
    this.context.moveTo(cx, cy);
    this.context.arc(cx, cy, this.radius,
        dataSubTotal / dataTotal * Math.PI * 2,
```

```
        (dataSubTotal + this.data[i]) / dataTotal * Math.PI * 2,
        false);

    if (i == this.data.length - 1) {
      this.context.closePath();
    }

    this.context.stroke();

    dataSubTotal += this.data[i];
  }
};
```

With this slight reorganization, we get a picture-perfect rendition of the pie chart in Internet Explorer, as Figure 3.25 shows.

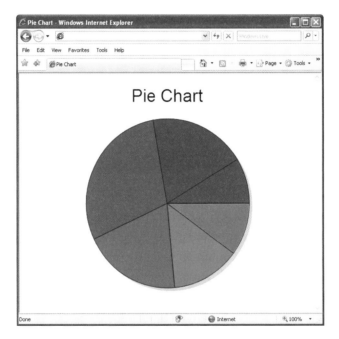

Figure 3.25. Producing a consistent cross-browser drawing with ExplorerCanvas

Similar layering operations, such as clearRect, will also cause problems in ExplorerCanvas, but for most other simple drawings like those we've dealt with in this chapter, ExplorerCanvas should produce a stable and reliable cross-browser canvas drawing.

Summary

We've only touched on the very basics of canvas drawing in this chapter. There's so much more you can learn about and experiment with, but I hope this grasp of the fundamentals will lead you to produce more complex and interesting examples out there in the real world. See you in vector land!

Debugging and Profiling with Firebug

Two things are inevitable in software development: bugs, and more bugs. Unfortunately, JavaScript development is no exception to this rule!

Front-end developers need tools to help them squash those bugs, and one such tool, Firebug,[1] has in a very short time become almost ubiquitous within the JavaScript development community—it's now quite possibly the most popular JavaScript development tool out there. Firebug is a free, open source project that works as a plugin for the Firefox browser. Its creator, Joe Hewitt, was one of the co-founders of the Firefox project.

Firebug, as its name implies, is a debugger in the traditional sense—it lets you pause program execution, step through your code line by line, and access the state of variables at any time.

But Firebug is much more than that. With Firebug, you can examine the entire DOM (HTML and CSS), view built-in browser details, and easily inspect anything on the page simply by clicking on it. The program also includes powerful tools for monitoring network traffic and profiling your Ajax applications. All this takes place inside a compact interface that's integrated into the browser.

The most compelling reason to use Firebug is to find and fix problems in your code, but as you might expect, it offers a range of other benefits. One is that you can use Firebug for rapid development, since Firebug makes most aspects of your application editable, and lets you author and execute

---

[1] http://getfirebug.com/

JavaScript on the fly. With its ability to analyze HTTP traffic, Firebug is also a suitable tool for the "quick and dirty" exploration of web services—an alternative to using client applications such as telnet and curl.

Firebug can also help you discover how other people's JavaScript applications work. Exploring other apps can be a powerful educational experience and, after all, one of the reasons why a technique such as Ajax flourished so quickly was the ease with which the innards of an Ajax application could be examined. If I was going to write a Google Maps mashup like the one in Chapter 7, for instance, the first thing I'd do would be to find one or two sites that already use Google Maps, and spend a few minutes dissecting them with Firebug. The ability to dissect an existing site offers more direct benefits, too—it can speed up the development process for applications that don't run in a browser. So, for example, it can hasten the development of a desktop application that interacts with another site's API, such as a command line scraper or a site-specific browser plugin.

Installing and Running Firebug

Okay, so I've convinced you that you need Firebug (and the Firefox browser in which it runs). Go ahead and install it if you haven't already—the process is fairly straightforward.

Installing Firefox and Firebug

On the remote chance that you don't have Firefox installed, now's the time to download the latest version from http://getfirefox.com/. Like Firebug, Firefox is an open source product that can be downloaded free of charge.

Once you've installed Firefox, you can install Firebug. If you've never installed a plugin before, fear not—the process is quick, if somewhat convoluted. Here are the steps that work for Firefox 2.0; other versions may vary slightly.

1. Launch Firefox if it's not already running.

2. Type http://getfirebug.com/ in the address bar, and press **Enter**.

3. When the Firebug homepage has finished loading, click the **Install Firebug** link. At the time of writing, the latest release was version 1.0, and the Firebug download link was a big orange button. You should see a yellow warning bar appear at the top of the browser, like the one shown in Figure 4.1. Click on the **Edit Options...** button, and click **Allow** to add the getfirebug.com domain to your list of approved sites.

4. Click the **Install Firebug** button again.

5. A popup window will appear to ask you to confirm the installation; accept the installation request. Hooray! Firebug is now installed. Unfortunately, you can't use it … yet.

Figure 4.1. The Firebug installation page

6. Quit Firefox and relaunch it—you can do this by clicking the **Restart Firefox** window at the bottom of the Firebug installation dialog window.

7. Firebug should now be running—if it is, a **Firebug** submenu will be available within the **Tools** menu. If you don't see this menu item, Firebug hasn't installed successfully—repeat the steps above to install it again.

8. Open the **Firebug** submenu from the **Tools** menu, and click **Disable Firebug** to remove the tick next to the menu item. Firebug is disabled by default; you've now enabled it.

First Steps with Firebug

Now that Firebug is installed and running, let's see how we can open up Firebug and start inspecting and debugging a web site. To begin with, point Firefox at http://digg.com/spy/. You'll see a display like the one shown in Figure 4.2.

We'll launch Firebug from the **Tools** menu. Open the **Tools** menu, navigate to the **Firebug** submenu, and choose **Open Firebug**.

Squinting at the Bug?

You can change the text size easily in Firebug. Open Firebug's main menu by clicking the Firebug icon located at the top-left of the Firebug window, and select the **Text Size** submenu. A small font size, if you can bear it, packs a lot of debugging content into a small space, which means you won't have to resize the window as often. Unfortunately, there's currently no keyboard shortcut for this feature.

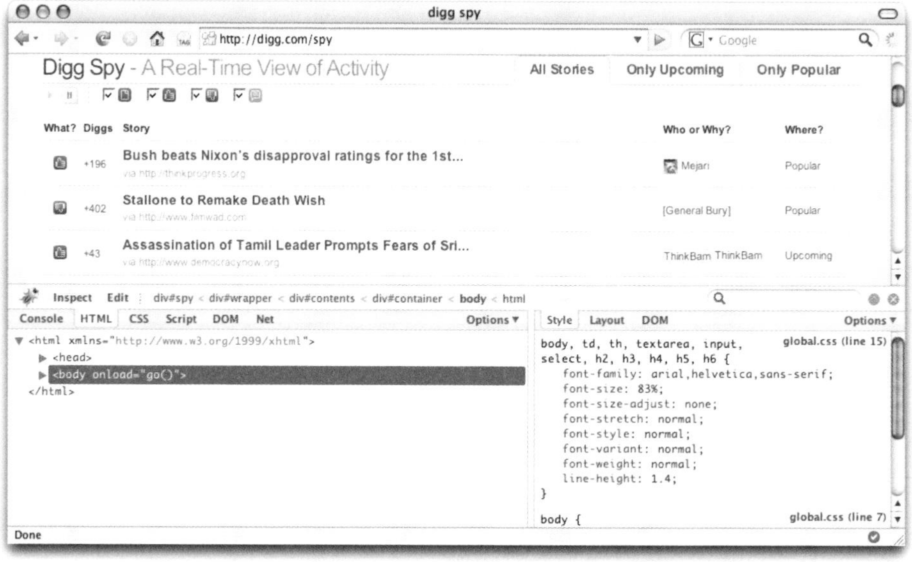

Figure 4.2. Looking under the hood of the Digg Spy

Next, select the **HTML** tab, and click on the arrows to expand some of the HTML elements on the page. You'll notice that, by default, the window is docked (fixed to the bottom of the browser). It's possible to run Firebug in a separate window, but let's not get ahead of ourselves just yet!

Before we get our hands dirty with Firebug, there's one important point that you should understand: each time you launch Firebug, you create a new instance of Firebug that's tied to the current page. So if you open a second tab (or window) in Firefox, and open Firebug for that tab, the page in that tab will receive its own instance of Firebug—and the information that's visible will be completely independent of the other instances of Firebug.

To see this facility in action, open up a new browser tab (**File** > **New Tab**) and enter the URL http://twittervision.com/.

The first thing you'll notice is that the Firebug window is not open on this tab, though it's still open on the original one. Open Firebug again from the **Tools** menu, and verify that the HTML displayed in this instance of Firebug is different from that of the previous tab. Select the **Console** view for both the Digg Spy and Twitter Vision sites open in your tabs, and you'll see that they're also different from one another. This should be enough to convince you that multiple instances of Firebug running in different Firefox tabs (or windows) are completely independent of one another—the only aspects they have in common are Firebug's global options, which we'll look at later on.

Opening, Closing, and Resizing Firebug

So far, we've used the **Tools** menu to reveal the Firebug window, but you can actually use quite a few techniques to show (and hide) Firebug. Here's a complete list:

the Firefox menu

As we saw earlier, selecting **Tools** > **Firebug** > **Open Firebug** will also launch Firebug, but, as you'll see, it's a little laborious when compared with some of the alternatives.

the Firebug status icon

Clicking the Firebug status icon (which appears in the bottom-right of your browser's status bar) is probably the most popular technique. However, the icon's appearance can vary, as Figure 4.3 shows. If the current page has no errors, the icon will be a small, green circle with a check mark in it; if errors occur in the page, the icon will display as a red cross next to a number—that's the number of errors on the page; if Firebug has been disabled, the icon will be a gray circle with a slash (/) through it. Whatever the icon's appearance, if you click on it, you'll see Firebug; clicking the icon again will hide it.

keyboard shortcuts

On a Windows system, pressing **F12** will launch and hide Firebug. By default, **F12** is used by OS X to show the Dashboard, so if you want to use **F12** to launch Firebug, you'll need to remove the **F12** keyboard Dashboard mapping manually (you can do so through your Mac's **System Preferences** panel).

However, this is probably unnecessary given the huge array of other keyboard shortcuts available. For example, **Ctrl-Shift-L** (**Command-Shift-L** on a Mac) opens Firebug and places focus on the **Console** tab. Another useful shortcut is **Ctrl-Shift-K** (**Command-Shift-K**), which opens Firebug and places focus on the Search box, ready for you to type the ID of that elusive element that's nested several layers deep on your page. Additionally, **Ctrl-F12** (**Command-F12**) will launch Firebug as a standalone window (I'll talk more about standalone window mode in a moment).

the context menu

Right-click on any element in a web page to reveal the context menu, then choose **Inspect Element**. This action not only displays the window, but takes you straight to the element's representation in the Firebug HTML view. This menu is useful for navigation even if the Firebug window's already open.

the toolbar

You can add a Firebug icon to your Firefox toolbar. Right-click on the toolbar (near the top of the window) and select **Customize**. A dialog will appear showing a number of icons, Firebug among them. Drag the Firebug icon from the dialog to your toolbar—adding this icon will cause Firebug to be opened as a standalone, rather than docked, window. This approach can be useful if you prefer to operate Firebug in standalone mode.

No errors icon

11 Errors   Errors icon

Disabled icon

Figure 4.3. One of these icons will appear in the bottom-right of the Firefox window

You can use one of the relevant keyboard shortcuts mentioned above or click on the Firebug status icon to show and hide Firebug. There's also a button to close Firebug (a gray circle containing an **X**) located in the top-right corner of the Firebug window. However, it's important to note that this doesn't actually close Firebug, as I'll explain in a moment—it just hides it.

As you can see, there are many different ways to perform the simple task of opening and closing the Firebug window! This is true of many tasks in Firebug—instead of having to perform actions in a certain way, you can usually choose a technique that suits your style and the task you're working on.

If you hadn't noticed yet, it's also possible to resize the Firebug window (and the columns within the Firebug window). Changing the height of the window is as simple as dragging its upper edge up and down—the standard technique for docked windows. The default size is usually fine, but a little extra height can sometimes be useful, particularly when you're examining complex stack traces.

 Docked or Standalone?

The Firebug window is docked by default—in other words, it's permanently attached to the bottom of the browser window, and this is how most people like it. In docked mode, you can resize the window vertically, and you can toggle between hiding and showing the window. When visible, it's always fixed to the bottom of the page, and always occupies the entire browser width.

The alternative to using Firebug in docked mode is to "tear it off" and use it in a standalone, floating window. To do so, click on the New Window button, which is labeled with a caret (^), in the top-right corner. Alternatively, use the **Ctrl-F12** keyboard shortcut (**Command-F12** on a Mac). You can then drag the window anywhere on your desktop—even to another monitor, if you have that luxury—and resize the window's height or width. To return to docked mode, just close the window.

A standalone window can be useful if you have a widescreen monitor and would prefer to run Firebug side by side with Firefox. If you have several tabs open, it's possible to open a separate standalone window for each tab. This can be useful in certain circumstances—for example, when comparing one Firebug instance with another, or when cutting and pasting between them. It can also be less resource intensive to run Firebug this way, for reasons that I'll explain in the next section. Most of the time, though, you'll probably want to stick with docked mode.

Enabling and Disabling Firebug

Firebug isn't a massive memory hog, but it can have a noticeable effect on your computer's performance—especially when you have 50-odd browser tabs open, as any red-blooded developer is prone to do. Even when Firebug is hidden in docked mode, it's still ticking away in the background, capturing every HTTP connection and updating itself each time the page changes. Given that each of your browser's tabs has its own instance of Firebug, you can see how these multiple instances of Firebug might eventually slow things down.

To ease the pain, you can disable Firebug when you're not using it. The **Disable Firebug** option appears in multiple menus: the Firebug submenu (**Tools** > **Firebug**); the main Firebug menu (click the Firebug icon at the top-left of the Firebug window); and the smaller context menu (right-click the Firebug status icon in the bottom-right of your browser). You can also disable Firebug for the site you're currently viewing by choosing the **Disable Firebug for** *example.com* menu option.

Blacklisting and Whitelisting

Choosing the **Allowed Sites...** option in the Firebug menu launches a dialog through which you can control where Firebug runs: you can have it run on some sites and not others.

The list of sites to which you assign a status of **Allow** constitutes a whitelist of sites that will always run Firebug—even when you've disabled Firebug. Those with a status of **Block** constitute your blacklist, and Firebug will always be disabled on these sites.

This feature can be useful if, for example, you wish to enable Firebug only for local testing purposes—set http://localhost/ to **Allow** and disable Firebug. On the other hand, you may find that running Firebug on http://example.com/ makes your browser too slow. In that case, set http://example.com/ to **Block**, but keep Firebug enabled.

The Many Faces of Firebug

Now that you're comfortable opening Firebug in your browser, let's take a whirlwind tour of its various components. This section will provide an overview of the parts of Firebug; in subsequent sections, we'll explore them in more depth as we examine how to use Firebug's components for specific tasks.

Common Components

If you've jumped ahead and clicked on any of the tabs in Firebug (you devil, you!), the first thing you'll have noticed is that some parts of the Firebug window change with each tab, while others remain the same. The following components are always present, regardless of which tab you're viewing:

the header bar

The header bar runs across the top of the Firebug window. There are always at least two buttons present in the left of the header bar: the Firebug icon, which, when clicked, displays the main menu, and the **Inspect** button, which lets you inspect specific pieces of page content by hovering the cursor across the elements you're interested in. In the right-hand side of the header bar appear three controls: a search field, a button to open Firebug in a new window, and a button to close Firebug.

the tabs

The six Firebug tabs sit just below the header bar, and are the means by which you can switch between the six views offered by Firebug.

Options menu

To the right of the tabs bar is the **Options** drop-down menu. From this menu, you can set options that are specific to the current view.

The content of the following components changes depending on the current view:

the top controls

These controls appear in the header bar, between the permanent controls on the left and the search box on the right. For instance, the **Console** view has **Clear** and **Profile** buttons at its top left, while the **Script** view has a drop-down menu on the left-hand side, and a set of debugging buttons on the right.

the main content window

The main content window takes up most of the Firebug window, and displays information that's specific to the current view.

Let's look at each of the views now.

The Firebug Views

As we step through the different Firebug views, I encourage you to experiment with each; explore the options, and don't be afraid to click on different items inside the view.

We're going to treat these as read-only views for now, but as we'll see in the next section, there's more than meets the eye here; many aspects of the views can be edited, allowing you to tweak your web application in real time.

The Console View

Let's begin by clicking on the **Console** tab. The Firebug console displays JavaScript errors as they occur, as well as any log messages that you might have included in your script. Figure 4.4 shows the result of a few log messages in our script. These have been added using the syntax `console.log` (*variable*). As we'll see later, the Console view also serves as a real-time editing environment in which you can type new JavaScript code, and have it executed there and then.

Figure 4.4. Viewing log messages in Firebug's Console view

What About the Firefox Error Console?

Firefox has its own error console, and before Firebug was launched, it was one of the main advantages of using Firefox as a development tool. You can still reach the error console from the **Tools** menu, but it's not much use in the age of the Firebug console, which has the advantage that it can be docked in the browser or launched as a standalone window. It also comes enhanced with the goodies we talked about above, like hyperlinks to other Firebug content, and is specific to a single browser tab (unlike the less capable Firefox console).

The HTML View

Let's move to the HTML view. Click on the HTML tab and you'll see—as you'd expect—a slab of HTML in the main content window. You can click on the gray arrows to expand and collapse the markup tree, which you'll notice has been nicely indented for you. It's important to note that what we're viewing here is the browser's model of the DOM after the page has been rendered, which is not necessarily the page's original HTML—that is, the HTML you'd see if you were to click **View Source**). If, for example, the page used JavaScript to remove an element, that element would not be present in the HTML view.

On the right of the main content window is a pane containing three tabs: **Style**, **Layout**, and **DOM**. Each of these tabs displays distinct information about the currently selected HTML element. As with the content window, this information is based on the page *after* it has been rendered, so the details may differ from the raw source. For instance, layout errors in the original source may have been corrected by the browser as part of the rendering process.

In Figure 4.5, the cursor is hovering over the averageDuration element in the HTML, causing the corresponding element to be highlighted on the page (the value 3.36s).

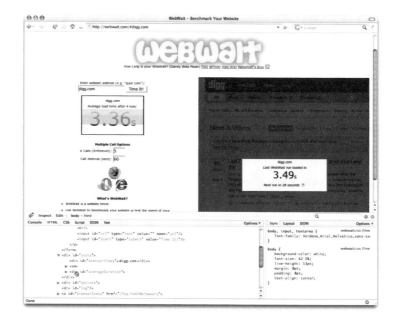

Figure 4.5. Highlighting elements in Firebug's HTML view

The CSS View

The CSS view, shown in Figure 4.6, shows the style rules that are defined in each CSS file; a drop-down menu in the header bar allows you to switch between multiple CSS files (if they're linked using the `<link>` tag). This is a great improvement over the bad old days when you had to **View Source** just to find out which CSS files were being invoked, then open each of them manually.

Figure 4.6. Exploring style rules in Firebug's CSS view

The CSS view will also display any CSS that's embedded in the HTML source. As with the HTML view, the information that's displayed in the CSS view is the browser's interpretation of the CSS after it has been parsed—it's not the raw CSS source.

Visual CSS

One of the neat features of the CSS view is that you can hover over certain properties in the CSS to view a visual representation of those properties. For example, if you hover the cursor over code that represents a color (whether it's a hexadecimal code, an RGB value, or a color name) a small box of that color will appear alongside your cursor. Similarly, hovering over an image's URL will display a thumbnail of that image.

The Script View

Similar to the CSS view, the Script view contains a menu that lists all files that contain JavaScript either as external and embedded code. As with the CSS, this means we no longer need to trawl through the HTML source in order to work out which scripts are being executed. Unlike the HTML and CSS views, though, you *do* see the raw JavaScript source in Script view.

To the right of the JavaScript code are a collection of user interface components in which Firebug's more sophisticated debugging happens—monitoring variable states, setting breakpoints, and stepping through code. We'll give these tools a workout later. Figure 4.7 shows what the Script view looks like.

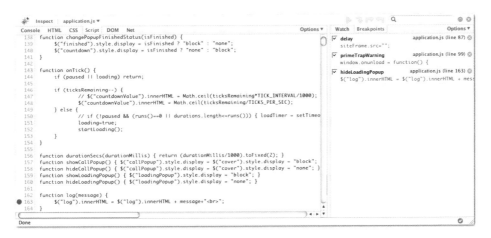

Figure 4.7. Perusing JavaScript code in Firebug's Script view

The DOM View

The DOM view is an exhaustive, no-frills listing of all elements in the current page's DOM tree. This list includes many things you wouldn't normally consider to be part of your application, like Firefox's model of the page and native JavaScript functions. Your page's application objects are listed at the top of the list, although you'll probably find yourself relying on the search function heavily whenever you're wading through the DOM view.

The left-hand column lists the objects in the DOM tree, the right-hand column lists the values of these objects, and the breadcrumb trail in the header bar indicates your current position in the DOM tree. You can expand and collapse branches in the tree by clicking on the gray triangles alongside them. You can also click on object values in the right-hand column to drill down into the hierarchy, and climb back up the tree by clicking on one of the parent nodes in the breadcrumb trail. Figure 4.8 shows the DOM view in action.

Figure 4.8. Navigating the DOM tree in Firebug's DOM view

The Net View

Finally, the Net view helps you to understand the HTTP traffic and loading times for the various components that make up your application. The list of entities that are measured includes any item that comprises an individual HTTP request—HTML markup, CSS rules, images, JavaScript code (including any remote Ajax calls that take place), and embedded media such as Flash.

The Net view displays packet sizes and loading sequence details, as you can see in Figure 4.9. Clicking on a row expands the details for that row, revealing the nitty-gritty HTTP packet content.

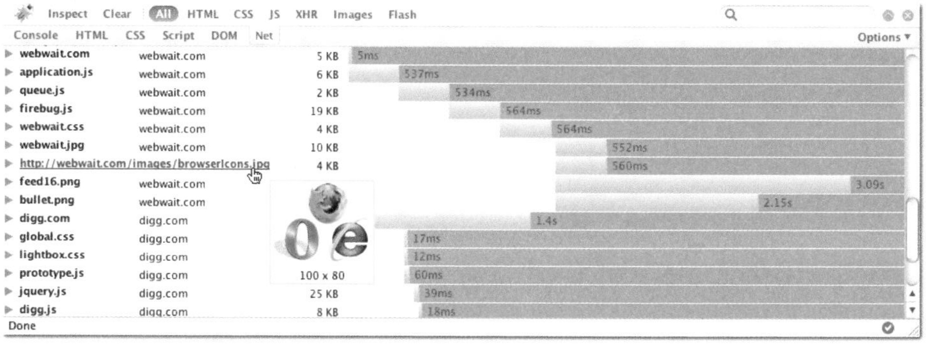

Figure 4.9. Analyzing load times in Firebug's Net view

Switching Views

You probably won't be surprised to learn that Firebug provides more than one way to switch between its different views. The following mechanisms are available:

tab selection

The obvious, direct, route to change views is simply to click the Firebug tab you're interested in.

cross-linking within Firebug

A very nice feature of Firebug is cross-linking between views. For example, if a page element is displayed in the Console view, clicking on it will switch to the HTML view, with the view centered on that element. Experiment with clicking on items in the content window and you'll find many more examples like this.

inspecting elements

When you inspect an element on your page (which we'll explore further in a moment), Firebug always switches to the HTML view. Inspecting an element can be performed via the browser's contextual menu (which you can access by right-clicking any element on the page), the Firebug submenu of Firefox's **Tools** menu, or the Firebug **Inspect** button.

inspect command

In the console, enter `inspect($('score'))` to jump to the HTML view, focused on the `score` element.

console entry

In the console, enter the name of a DOM element you'd like to view. Instead of hitting **Enter** to view the element, hit **Shift-Enter** and you'll be transported to whichever view is appropriate, centered on the element.

Using Firebug

So far, we've talked mostly about Firebug as a read-only tool—we've seen how the HTML tab lets us view the HTML, and so on. But there's one particularly cool feature of Firebug that we haven't discussed yet: it lets us make changes to our code on the fly.

Being able to change a live application is useful in a number of ways. It can assist the development process, it can aid with debugging errors in your code, and it can support the performance-tuning effort. Let's see how.

Performing Rapid Application Development

Firebug exploits the fact that HTML, CSS, and JavaScript are interpreted languages by allowing you to alter your web application's state in real time. Here are some examples:

- The Firebug console includes a text entry area into which you can type arbitrary JavaScript commands: console log messages, queries, variable assignments—even the creation and execution of entire functions! The text entry area is displayed either as a multiline pane to the right of the main content window, or as a command line along the bottom of the window, and you can switch between the two easily by clicking the small arrow icon in the bottom-right corner.

■ You can double-click *any* object, element, or property in the HTML and CSS views to modify its value. You'll see the page update with your changes incorporated immediately.

■ You can also edit the value of objects in the DOM model. Either double-click the object you wish to edit, or select **Edit Property...** from the context menu, which can be accessed by right-clicking on the object name or value.

This last feature is especially appealing to developers who are burdened with a tedious build (or deployment) process and want to try out a few quick tweaks or diagnose a problem. For example, you might run a function manually to see if it updates the page correctly, or you might experiment with a library function to confirm that you're using it the right way.

Searching in Firebug

A search field that's modeled closely on Firefox's own search appears at the top-right of the Firebug window. Type some text into it and hit **Enter** in order to search; you can keep hitting **Enter** to repeat the search. There's also a keyboard shortcut: **Ctrl-Shift-K** (**Command-Shift-K** on a Mac).

Note that you'll only be able to search content in the current Firebug view—if you were to search for "table" with the HTML view open, you'd find all of the `<table>` tags in the document's HTML, but your search wouldn't return any information about how they were styled in the page's style sheet. To get those details, you'd have to open the CSS view and repeat the search. Firebug only searches the left-hand pane in those tabs with two panes.

Lead developer Joe Hewitt has stated that Firebug users sometimes have trouble with the search function.[2] He realizes that many don't even know that it exists, let alone how to use it. Watch out for a user interface redesign of this feature at some stage.

Monitoring, Logging, and Executing with the Console

Perhaps the most useful feature of the Console is simply that it shows warnings and error messages in an unobtrusive manner (as compared to the "alert window" method that was popular in the early days of JavaScript development). There's an example on my own Firebug demo page;[3] the script on this page references an invalid variable name that leads to the error message "undefinedVar is not defined." While this is already reasonably useful, what's even better is that you can obtain a stack trace simply by clicking on the error, and that the methods within the stack trace are all clickable. Clicking one of the methods will open the Script view, where the line of JavaScript code that caused the error will be highlighted for you.

---

[2] http://ajaxian.com/archives/audible-ajax-episode-22-joe-hewitt-on-firebug-firefox-and-iui/
[3] http://ajaxify.com/run/firebug/

Retaining Type in Log Messages

Suppose we wanted to write the value of an object in the DOM tree that had an ID of `message`. We could try the following:

```
console.log("Message element is "+document.getElementById("message"));
```

However, all we're doing here is logging a single string. When working with Firebug, a better strategy is to pass our preamble text and our DOM element as separate arguments, like this:

```
console.log("Message element is ",document.getElementById("message"));
```

This way, the preamble string will be explicitly separated from the variable. The Console will then render two separate items, and the second item will be displayed as a proper DOM element.

The advantage of this approach is that the element that's displayed in the Console will be hyperlinked to its corresponding location in the HTML view. You can pass in any number of arguments to the logging functions, like so:

```
console.log("Message elements are", x, y, z);
```

The console also offers a helpful logging API, as Figure 4.10 illustrates. You can log messages at different levels; those levels will then be rendered in different colors and with cute little icons that reflect the messages' differing levels of urgency:

```
console.log("A normal log message.");
console.debug("Just some debugging.");
console.info("Here's some info for you.");
console.warn("I'm warning you!");
console.error("Error. That's just great.");
```

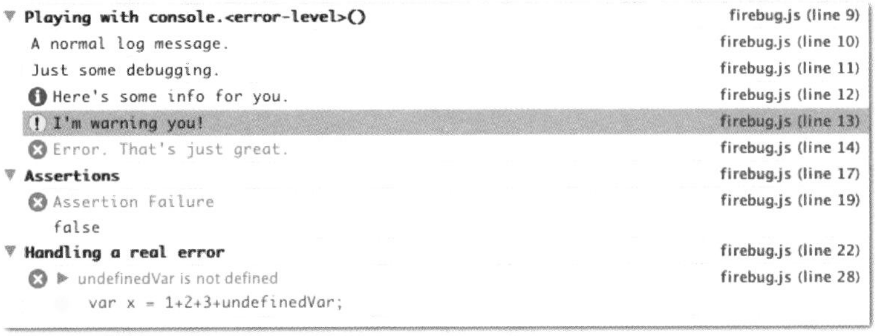

Figure 4.10. Showing log messages and errors on the console

Assertions in JavaScript

If we were to be honest, we JavaScript developers probably don't test our code as thoroughly as do software developers who program in other languages.

For this reason, it's important to apply other defensive programming techniques, and one of the best is the use of **assertions**—small test cases that confirm whether a unit of code produces the expected output.

Firebug lets you run assertions; if the assertion fails, an error will occur—complete with stack trace. Here's an example:

```
assert(count>0);
```

You can even display a message when an assertion fails. For the above assertion, you might try this:

```
assert(count>0, "counting hasn't started")
```

The console also shows you XMLHttpRequest calls as they happen. Point your browser once more at Digg Spy,[4] and watch the console fill up as the remote calls take place! You'll see a summary line showing the URL that was the target of the remote request. Click to expand it, and you'll see no fewer than three tabs full of call details: **Params**, **Headers**, and **Response**. There's also a **Post** tab that appears if the request is a POST request.

Params displays the CGI parameters going into the remote call. This information isn't particularly useful for GET calls, as the same information is already available as part of the URL, but it's very handy for working with POST and PUT requests.

The **Headers** tab shows all of the request and response headers. This view is incredibly useful, since a large number of remote scripting bugs arise from issues with headers (including incorrect mime types, cookies not being set, caching directives being too strong or weak, etc.).

The next two tabs—**Post** and **Response**—display the request and response bodies. This is also incredibly useful information, as it helps you understanding what data you're uploading and what the server's sending back to your browser. Unfortunately, the **Post** tab is strictly available for POST requests, even though other HTTP requests (such as PUT) also include a request body.

You can also run arbitrary JavaScript commands with the console. Where you do this depends on the "larger command line" setting in the Console view. If this option is turned on, you'll see a single pane at the bottom of which is a command line. If the command line is disabled, you'll see a scratchpad area in the right-hand pane. The command line option has a few advantages—you can

---

[4] http://digg.com/spy/

press the up arrow key to scroll through a history of your previous commands, and you can take advantage of auto-completion functionality by hitting the Tab key.

Making the Most of Auto-completion

With method names like `getElementsByTagName` being so common in JavaScript programming, you'll be relieved to discover Firebug's auto-complete functionality in the Console command line.

It works much like the same functionality at a DOS or UNIX prompt: start typing a word, press Tab, and the entire word will appear; keep hitting Tab to cycle through all the possible completions Firebug has to offer. Not only can using auto-completion save you keystrokes, it can prevent you from entering typos as well!

Auto-completion has been implemented in Firebug in an intelligent way; if you press Tab after typing `person.` (a variable name followed by a period), Firebug will show you all the properties of the `person` variable.

Firebug offers some other conveniences at the command line. For example, when you include $1 in a console command, Firebug will interpret this as the most recent variable that you inspected in the HTML view.

So you could, for instance, enter this command:

```
$1.style.background = 'red'
```

This command will change that element's background style. This is a useful way to get a handle on elements that don't have an ID. Entering $$1 will get you the most recent DOM element. There's also a history feature here; $2 gives you the second-most recent element, $3 the third-most recent, and so on.

Creating Bookmarklets

Bookmarklets are snippets of JavaScript that you can attach to an element on the page. Bookmarklets are useful because they make a small amount of functionality available to be executed on any site. Users store the script their browser's bookmarks; the script is then available to be executed on any page—the user simply needs to click on the bookmark that was stored. A bookmarklet consists of only a single line of code, and is prefixed with the `javascript:` protocol.

Firebug (in particular, the right-hand "scratchpad" pane of Firebug's Console view) is ideal for making and testing quick bookmarklets. Type your code into the scratchpad, and hit **Run** to test it out. When you're satisfied that your bookmarklet code is complete, click **Copy** to have Firebug copy to the clipboard the entire code in bookmarklet form (that is, it will be reformatted so that it occupies a single line and is prefixed with `javascript:`).

Beware of Phantom Errors

Sometimes you'll notice in the Console an error or warning that seems to have nothing to do with the page you're viewing. At first, you might wonder whether the error is coming from another browser tab, but as we learned earlier in this chapter, this would be impossible because each browser tab (and window) has its own Firebug instance.

In fact, the source of these phantom errors will usually be a browser **add-on** that you've installed—add-ons (or plugins) often perform their magic by interfering with the page content and script, and if this occurs, Firebug has no way to determine the source of the error. A telltale sign that an add-on might be the culprit is that the error appears every time you load a page, regardless of which web site you're visiting.

In most cases, your phantom error will be harmless, but the continual appearance of messages like this can make our lives more complicated. (It's always nice to know you have a clean slate when everything's working fine.) To remove the error, your best option is to disable the offending plugin (assuming you're willing to live without it). In order to determine *which* plugin you should disable, you'll need to progressively remove or disable add-ons until you've narrowed the range down to just one. If you're feeling lucky—or particularly talented!—you could try using some guesswork to identify the offending plugin. This could save you a lot of effort, as you'll need to restart Firefox each time you disable or enable a plugin.

Viewing and Editing On the Fly

As we've already seen, the HTML view displays a version of the page's markup in its *current state*, rather than the original HTML source. In HTML view, you can expand and collapse nodes, and jump to particular locations in the markup by selecting the **Inspect Element** menu item from the browser's context menu. You can also do the reverse: pick an element in the HTML and force the web page to scroll to that element. Right-click the element in the markup, and select **Scroll Into View** from the Firebug context menu.

You should also experiment with the Firebug **Inspect** button. Clicking **Inspect** puts Firebug into a special mode in which the Firebug HTML view is synchronized with the browser's page view. As you scroll through the elements on the web page, the Firebug HTML view will scroll to center on those elements in the page's markup. The reverse is also true ... sort of. Hovering over the tags in the HTML view will highlight the corresponding elements on the page, although the browser page won't scroll to keep up.

As we saw in the previous section, the HTML view has on its right-hand side a supporting pane that provides additional information about the currently selected element.

There are three subviews here, each represented by a tab:

Style   Clicking on the **Style** tab, you can see all of the style rules that apply to this element. If you've ever wondered why on earth an element displays the way it does, you'll understand how powerful this view is. The cascading nature of CSS rules often takes developers by surprise—sometimes you might use the wrong rule (for instance, `display: hidden` instead of `display: none`); other times you might forget that another rule takes precedence. There may even be occasions when you forget about a dynamic change that you've instigated from your JavaScript, or you fail to anticipate its effect on your page.

The Style subview shows you exactly which rules apply, and which rules don't. Overridden rules are also shown, but they're struck out. The most general rules appear at the bottom of the window; the most specific rules are at the top. So if the same style is defined in two places, the rule that appears lower in the list will be struck out, and the one that's higher (that is, the one that's actually used) will be displayed as normal.

Suppose you were looking at some CSS in your raw CSS file that was similar to this:

```
h1 { font-color: red; }
```

If you were wondering why a particular heading was blue rather than red, you could easily check whether the rule was parsed correctly by the browser, whether it was applied to the heading in question, and whether it had been overridden by a more specific selector. As with the Firebug CSS view, you can edit style values in this view with immediate effect, which can be a fast way to tweak your user interface.

Layout Next is the Layout subview, which displays a handy outline of the current element within the CSS box model framework. As Figure 4.11 demonstrates, this subview shows you the element's dimensions, padding, border, margin, and offset; you can hover over each of these properties in this view to see where they're on the rendered page.

The important thing to note here is that these values reflect the actual dimensions of these elements in the browser—not the dimensions that were specified in the style sheet. Indeed, even if your web application contained no CSS at all, you'd still be able to view the default styles that the browser applies to each element in the Layout subview.

Because of the way the CSS box model works, the dimensions you specify in your CSS won't always correspond to the dimensions your elements ultimately take on, and this subview will help you identify occasions when you might have misinterpreted the box model. For instance, you might set a rule like this:

```
div {width: 100px;}
```

If you then discovered that your `div` was expanding to fill the full browser width, you could use the Layout subview to determine the exact size of the element and its boundaries, and correct your style rules accordingly.

Figure 4.11. The HTML view, with the Layout subview on the right

DOM   The DOM subview shows all of the attributes and functions that are available for the
current element. This view is basically a subset of the larger DOM tree that's visible in
the main DOM view. Like its big brother, the DOM subview is also editable, and contains
cross-links to other DOM elements on the page.

Debugging Your Application

At first glance, the Script view appears to be a very basic listing of all of the source files used in
your application. But take a closer look and you'll notice some extra controls on the right-hand side
of the header bar—controls that give you the ability to perform tasks you'd expect to complete using
a debugger for any language: stepping through code line by line, stepping in and out of functions,
and monitoring variable state. Most of the time these controls are grayed out, and aren't clickable.

Let's look at a simple example that I've hosted at http://ajaxify.com/run/firebug/debug/. When you
click the button on this page, a counter variable is incremented by one, and a message that contains
the new value of the counter is displayed.

To begin debugging, ensure the Script view shows **firebug.js** (use the drop-down menu an the top
to switch between JavaScript files). We'll then set a couple of breakpoints—do this by clicking in
the left margin of the Script view, where the line numbers appear. You should see a red spot toggle
on and off each time you click in that zone. The red spot is a **breakpoint**, which is an indicator that
program execution will pause when it reaches that line.

Set a breakpoint at line 10. Incidentally, notice how the **Breakpoint** subview on the right contains a
list of all breakpoints that you've set. This view is especially useful when you've placed breakpoints
in multiple script files.

Now reload the page and hit the **Change the Message!** button. Your Script view should look something
like that shown in Figure 4.12.

Figure 4.12. Debugging with Firebug: a breakpoint at line 10 and execution paused at line 11

The script has made its way to our breakpoint, and a yellow arrow in the margin indicates which line we're on. Also, notice the debugging controls at top-right (next to the search field) are no longer grayed out; now that the script is paused, the debugging controls are active. If you've used a debugger before, the meaning of these controls will be familiar to you:

Continue   This button resumes execution. The script will only pause again if and when the script reaches a breakpoint.

Step Over   This button executes the current line, including any functions that are invoked along the way, and moves to the next line.

Step Into   This button ordinarily moves to the next line, as with **Step Over**. However, if the debugger happens to be paused at a line that invokes a function, the script will instead jump to the first line of that function.

Step Out   This button causes the script to jump out of the current function, returning to the method from which it was called.

Got all that? Great!

Conditional Breakpoints

Sometimes you may want a set a breakpoint, but make it apply only in certain conditions. You need **conditional breakpoints**.

Right-click on a breakpoint and you'll see a balloon-styled dialog asking you to enter a condition. This is simply a JavaScript expression; each time the breakpoint is reached, Firebug will evaluate the expression. If—and only if—the expression is true, the breakpoint will be applied and execution will pause.

In our demonstration which updates a message with an incrementing variable, for instance, we could make our conditional breakpoint's expression read `finished==true`. This would cause the breakpoint to pause only when the `finished` variable is `true`, instead of every time the breakpoint is passed.

Next we're going to step *into* a few functions, so we can see every line of JavaScript that's executed. Keep your cursor pointed firmly at the **Step Into** button and get ready to click. The first time you click, the pointer moves down to line 11. `counter` has been incremented, but the message has not yet changed.

If you like, switch to the Console view and verify that `counter` now has a value of 1 (try typing `console.log (counter)`). From line 11, click **Step Into** again—suddenly we're transported into the $ function, over in **util.js**. Keep clicking through to complete the entire thread of execution you triggered by hitting the button. I suggest you experiment with this a few times. For instance, you might click the button, step into $, and then immediately **Step Out**. Or perhaps you might click the button, then immediately click **Continue** to resume execution.

Step Into and Step Over

Over time, you'll get a feel for when to use **Step Into** and when to use **Step Out**. Until you do, here are a few rules of thumb:

- If you're working with a third-party JavaScript library like Prototype or YUI, you can (hopefully!) trust that the library works correctly, so most of the time you'll step over calls to the library.

- On the other hand, if you're not sure what a library is doing, you can step into it to have a dynamic code walk through applied specifically to your code—this is probably more useful than poring over the library source code.

- It's sometimes easier to diagnose a problem in several passes. If your code is well layered, each function should be self-contained and work at the same level of abstraction. Thus, you'll often want to start with a high-level function and exclusively click **Step Over** to see only what happens inside it, treating any functions that may be invoked as black boxes that you don't enter.

  Then, if you're satisfied that the high-level function works, you can instigate further passes where you step into each invoked function and do the same thing inside them: step over each line without diving any deeper. Keep following this approach until you find the bug. This strategy can be quite efficient, provided you don't stick to it rigidly and you're willing to employ some guesswork alongside it.

Another useful feature of the debugger is the **Watch** subview in the right-hand pane.

A **watch** is a JavaScript expression that you can request the debugger to continuously evaluate, so you don't have to keep querying it manually in the Console. Just click the yellow **New watch expression...** line to create a new watch. The expression could be as simple as a variable, or as complex as a formula involving calls to other functions.

In our current example, try entering `counter` to monitor the `counter` variable, and `$("message").innerHTML` to monitor the message contents. As you click the page's **Change the message!** button, you'll see how the variables change. This kind of data can be incredibly useful when you know your script is causing an incorrect value for a variable or DOM element. By adding a watch for the variable, you can step through the script and pinpoint the exact moment when it goes wrong.

Performance Tuning Your Application

One of the key challenges of JavaScript development—in particular, Ajax development—is performance optimization. Not only do you have the network to consider, but processing speeds in the browser are significantly slower than those for equivalent native applications.

Firebug provides you with the tools to measure your application's performance. As any engineer will tell you, measurement goes hand in hand with optimization; if you can't measure performance objectively, how can you be sure you've really improved it, and how will you know when it's no longer worth optimizing?

We've already seen how the **Net** view helps you measure times for each component and each remote call, providing you with a kind of Gantt chart that illustrates exactly when the components of a page were loaded. You need to be pragmatic in applying this information and, above all, consider what it really means for the user experience.

For example, an image might take a long time to load, but that's probably okay as long as users were already in a position to read page content and navigate elsewhere if they wanted to. On the other hand, you should probably be more concerned if users are waiting a long time for XMLHttpRequest requests to complete.

Below are a few items you might see in the **Net** view graph, and some potential fixes that might help in each situation.[5]

Table 4.1. Common Performance Problems and Recommended Solutions

Problem	Solution
Critical page content loads too late.	Load critical content first, in the initial HTML, and issue remote calls to retrieve less important information afterwards.
JavaScript takes too long to load.	Combine all JavaScript into a single, compressed, file. Consider using the gzip protocol to ensure all of your HTTP traffic is compressed at a low level, but be aware that in some cases, the decompression process will noticeably slow down your client.
Many images are loading.	Combine the images into one big image and render them separately using the CSS `background-offset` property.

---

[5] For more information, see http://ajaxpatterns.org/.

The other type of performance optimization that you can apply is **profiling** execution, which is handled in the Console view. Profiling is straightforward—it's a process that has a very definite start and finish, and the end result is a report on what happened and how long it all took.

Here's how you can see Firebug's profiling capabilities in action:

1. Visit http://ajaxify.com/run/firebug/profile/, where you'll find a Fibonacci sequence calculator.
2. In the Console view, click **Profile**. This turns on profiling.
3. In the application, hit the **Calculate it!** button.
4. In the Console view, click **Profile** again to complete profiling.

What you'll receive is a report listing all of the functions that were called, and how much time was spent in each. The report also includes average, minimum, and maximum times. Most importantly, the **Percent** column shows the proportion of time spent in each function.

Can you guess the difference between **Own Time** and **Time**? **Own Time** is time spent purely inside the function you're looking at, ignoring any functions it calls. **Time** adds on the time spent in those called functions. Notice in Figure 4.13 that the `onclick` function doesn't do very much itself—it delegates everything to two other functions. That's why it has a big **Time**, but a small **Own Time**.

 Using Profile Data

Here are a few tips for using profile data.

- Go for low-hanging fruit—attack the easy stuff first, and then you many not need to bother going any further. If the **Percent** column informs you that a particular function is taking up 80% of the overall time it takes your page to load, this should be the function that you investigate first.

- Look for functions that are called many times. You might be able to reduce the number of calls just by caching the results or restructuring the code that calls this function.

- Look for any function that has a maximum time far exceeding its average time, then see if you can eliminate the conditions that cause such disproportionately long calls.

- All the columns are sortable (just click on their headings), so take advantage of this fact to explore the data in different ways.

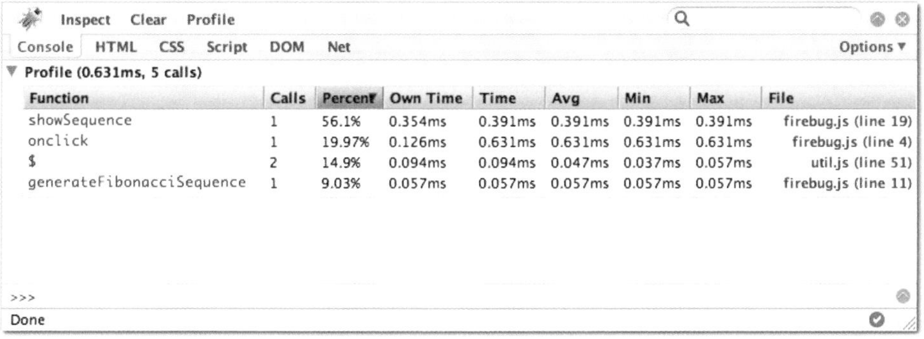

Figure 4.13. Profiling report inside the Console

In the example above, we used the **Profile** button to start and stop profiling. An alternative approach is to embed profiling instructions in your code—type `console.profile()` to start profiling, and `console.profileEnd()` to end it. An example can be found at http://ajaxify.com/run/firebug/profile/console/.

Related Tools

A few other tools that are either affiliated with Firebug, or complement it nicely, should appear in the arsenal of every good web developer.

Firebug Lite

Firebug Lite is part of the Firebug project, although it's not actually a plugin.[6] Rather, it's a small library included for non-Firefox browsers.

You'll need Firebug Lite if you're attempting to run code with Firebug-specific commands (`console.log()`, `console.debug()`, etc.) on other browsers. There are two versions available—one actually provides you with this console functionality on other browsers, which at least makes those browsers slightly easier to debug and test on. This is effectively a light form of Firebug, hence the name of the library.

The other version might be called "ultra-lite"—it doesn't actually add any debugging capability to other browsers, but instead provides some trivial stubs for the Firebug commands so they won't cause errors. This can be very useful if you want to ship your app without bothering to strip all the console commands.

Many developers would be well advised to routinely ship with the ultra-lite edition; it's too easy to forget to remove a console line at the last minute—and the omission makes the live application inaccessible for non-Firefox users. The argument for this approach is especially strong if you're compressing your JavaScript, in which case the difference in the footprint will be negligible, or if

[6] http://www.getfirebug.com/lite.html

you don't have critical footprint requirements in the first place (as is the case for the vast majority of applications out there).

The fact that logging works on multiple browsers once Firebug Lite has been included means that Firebug's logging features may well emerge as the de facto standard for JavaScript logging. The Dojo Toolkit is one library that has adopted Firebug as its standard logging mechanism; the standard distribution ships with Firebug.[7]

YSlow

YSlow is a plugin from Yahoo that augments Firebug to provide advice about optimizing your page's performance.[8] It analyzes your application and grades it on various performance criteria, as well as providing some enhanced statistics. YSlow installs as a regular Firefox plugin.

Microsoft Tools

Unfortunately (from an ease-of-development perspective), Internet Explorer remains a browser in which almost all JavaScript applications must run. Firebug can help you to create an immaculate JavaScript application, but what happens when it falls over in IE? Firebug Lite (mentioned above) will help a bit, but there's still a lot of missing functionality.

Here are a few *free* tools that may help:

- Microsoft Script Editor and its predecessor, Microsoft Script Debugger, are two tools that perform some basic debugging. (I recommend you search for the download page using Google, as the page is different depending on the platform you require, and page locations may change in the future.) At the very least, these tools should point you to the line of JavaScript which is breaking, which is already a step above what IE itself provides.

- The IE Developer Toolbar, available from the Microsoft Download Center,[9] can be useful in understanding the state of your page's DOM tree in IE.

- Fiddler is a popular Windows tool for HTTP proxying,[10] and is useful for analyzing traffic and tracking XMLHttpRequest calls.

---

[7] http://www.sitepen.com/blog/2007/07/05/hacking-firebug/

[8] http://developer.yahoo.com/yslow/

[9] http://www.microsoft.com/downloads/

[10] http://www.fiddlertool.com/fiddler/

Other Firefox Extensions

Firebug is arguably the champion of developer-focused Firefox add-ons right now,[11] but don't ignore all the others out there. Many other add-ons, such as the Web Developer Toolbar,[12] Fasterfox,[13] and Measure-It,[14] offer features that complement Firebug nicely.

Summary

In this chapter, we've looked at the many ways that Firebug can help you develop and debug you scripts, and explore the internals of other people's applications. Firebug doesn't take up much space in the browser, but as we've seen, it manages to pack in a rich set of features. Most of these features can be activated in many different ways—as an example, we saw five techniques for showing and hiding the Firebug window. You'll find it useful to learn more than one way to achieve any given goal, as some are more suited to particular situations than others.

I'd encourage you to explore Firebug and familiarize yourself with all the features we've covered here. Choose an application that you've developed, and devote an hour or two to viewing and tweaking it, trying out as many Firebug features as possible. The effort will be rewarded handsomely, starting from that next, inevitable bug.

---

[11] https://addons.mozilla.org/

[12] https://addons.mozilla.org/en-US/firefox/addon/60/

[13] https://addons.mozilla.org/en-US/firefox/addon/1269/

[14] http://addons.mozilla.org/firefox/539/

Metaprogramming with JavaScript

Metaprogramming is defined on Wikipedia as:

"the writing of computer programs that write or manipulate other programs (or themselves) as their data, or that do part of the work during compile time that is otherwise done at run time."[1]

In modern scripting languages, however, metaprogramming normally involves the manipulation of the very mechanics of the language. Essentially, we're talking about working with classes, functions, method calls, and concepts like inheritance, all from within the program itself.

Although at first this may seem like a rather academic pursuit, there's actually a lot of utility to be gained from these techniques. The Ruby on Rails framework,[2] for instance, owes a lot of its usability and "programmer friendliness" to metaprogramming techniques. One of the best examples is its implementation of the ActiveRecord pattern, which builds class definitions (including methods and properties) automatically by examining the tables within a database. So if your `people` table has a field called `name`, ActiveRecord ensures that your `Person` class has a method called `name`—it essentially writes the code for you. Of course, this chapter isn't about metaprogramming Ruby—that topic has already been covered extensively in the Ruby world. Instead, this chapter will address the use of metaprogramming techniques within the realm of JavaScript.

JavaScript has never had a reputation as a particularly powerful or clever language. In fact, until recently, it's been viewed by most programmers as a rather "dumb" language for programming web

---

[1] http://en.wikipedia.org/wiki/Metaprogramming/
[2] http://www.rubyonrails.com/

browsers. However, as you'll see, JavaScript actually contains some powerful features that make it a perfectly suitable language for implementing several metaprogramming techniques. Although you'll read about or find code that implements many of these techniques across the Web, my intention with this chapter is to collect all of these techniques and examine them together. I hope to show how metaprogramming can be used to make your code more usable (from a development point of view), flexible, and optimized. We'll also take a whirlwind tour of JavaScript's inner workings, and some of its lesser-known but very important features.

We'll start by exploring the basic language features that facilitate metaprogramming in JavaScript. I'll then show you how these building blocks can be assembled into a selection of useful techniques, providing a number of examples from real-world projects along the way. Finally, we'll look at how some of these techniques have been used in existing projects and libraries.

Tinkering with the Examples

As you read through the examples presented here, it's a good idea to have Firefox open, with a copy of Firebug installed so that you can try the techniques out. Just open Firebug on any web page, click **Console**, then type the example in line by line and see what happens. Tinkering with code like this is the best way to understand some of the trickier points of the techniques we'll discuss.

The Building Blocks

Although JavaScript is a relatively basic language with a fairly small number of built-in objects and methods, its clever construction makes it very flexible. As such, the task of metaprogramming JavaScript is a matter of understanding a few basic facts about the language. Some of these facts are well known to most capable JavaScript programmers, others less so. However, most of the concepts, when taken in isolation, are easy to understand. Let's start at the beginning, and break down JavaScript's metaprogramming building blocks.

(Nearly) Everything Is a Hash

In JavaScript, *all* objects (aside from the primitive types of string, number, and boolean) descend from `Object`. `Object` is effectively a **hash**—a set of properties that can have a key of any type, and can contain any type of data. You can add properties to any JavaScript object whenever you like.

Start up Firefox, load up any web page, and using the Firebug console, try some of these examples:

```
var myObj = new Object;
myObj['myProperty'] = 454;
myObj[45435] = true;
myObj[true] = 'hello';
console.log(myObj['myProperty']); //=> 454
console.log(myObj[true]); //=> 'hello'
var myDate = new Date;
```

```
myDate['a'] = 'You can use any type of object as a hash';
location['bingo'] = 'Yes, I mean _any_ object';
console.log(location['bingo']); //=> 'Yes, I mean _any_ object'
```

Note that a special-case syntax exists for properties with string keys—these properties can be accessed and set using the dot notation as well as the square brackets. Because of this capability, these properties are known as **expando properties**.

Following on from the examples above, try these:

```
console.log(myObj.myProperty); //=> 454
console.log(myDate.a);
  //=> 'You can use any type of object as a hash'
myDate.fluffyMonster = 'Expando!';
```

The only restriction is that the key/property name must be a valid variable name and not a reserved word. For instance, setting myObj.bad-var-name or myObj.class won't work, because - characters aren't allowed in variable names, and class is a reserved word (although it's not used by the language at this time).

Now that we know that we can write to and read from properties using a string key or the dot syntax, we can deduce that it's possible to construct objects with dynamic property names:

```
var myObj = {};
for (var i = 0; i < 5; i++) {
  myObj['prop_' + i] = i;
}
myObj.prop_2 //=> 2
```

This facility is a powerful weapon in our metaprogramming arsenal.

Finding and Iterating through Properties in an Object

Now we know that nearly everything in JavaScript is a hash with properties that have keys and values. But, if we're given an object, how do we find out which properties it contains? For this task, we need one of JavaScript's internal constructs—the for-in loop:

```
var person = {
  name: 'Bob',
  email: 'bob@bob.com',
  tel: '0258305964'
};
```

```
for (var key in person) {
  console.log(key);
} //=> 'name', 'email', 'tel'
```

Here we can see how using a for-in loop allows us to loop through all the keys in an object. We can use this technique to **introspect**, or find out information about, the contents of an object. However, the in keyword also has another purpose: it can be used within a condition statement to ask an object if it possesses a specific property:

```
// using the person object from the above example…
if ("tel" in person) alert(person.tel);
```

We'll use the in keyword for both of these purposes later in the chapter.

Detecting Types

JavaScript is a **dynamically typed language**, which means that you can stuff any type of value that you want into a property or variable. As such, you'd expect it to have some solid means for detecting the types of data that are contained in these variables, but in fact JavaScript is quite lacking in this area—all we have available are the typeof and instanceof operators.

Our first port of call is typeof, which can tell you the primitive type of an object:

```
var a = 5;
console.log(typeof a); //=> 'number'
var name = 'Sam';
console.log(typeof name); //=> 'string'
console.log(typeof aVariableThatDoesntExist); //=> 'undefined'

function doSomething() {
  console.log('yay!');
}

console.log(typeof doSomething); //=> 'function'

var anObject = {};
console.log(typeof anObject); //=> 'object'

var anArray = [1,2,3,4,5,6];
console.log(typeof anArray); //=> 'object' (not 'array', unfortunately)
```

As you can see, the typeof operator can tell us the types of strings, numbers, functions, booleans, and even undefined variables. However, typeof will describe all other variables simply as being objects. Not very useful, is it?

Of course, typeof isn't lying to us—all variables that aren't one of the aforementioned primitive types *are* objects—but that information's no help to us! We need to find out what types of objects they are. That's where instanceof comes in handy:

```
console.log(anArray instanceof Array) //=> true
console.log(anObject instanceof Array) //=> false
```

Between these two operators, you can usually work out the type of a property or variable.

We're now armed with all the techniques we need to examine all of the properties and types of an object. And seeing as almost everything in JavaScript is an object, we already have most of the knowledge we need to metaprogram JavaScript!

Before we take that step, however, there's one more fundamental aspect of the JavaScript language that you need to understand …

There Are No Classes in JavaScript

That's right: there are no classes in JavaScript! Although many people refer to JavaScript's constructor functions as classes, JavaScript is actually a classless language. Constructor functions are *similar* to the constructors of a class-based language like Java, but they're not identical. As such, I find it best to just forget this comparison completely.

Instead, I think of constructors as being like "cookie cutters" for objects. When a function is used with the new operator, it's called in a special way: instead of executing the function normally and returning a result, a new blank object is created. Then, when the function is called, its this operator points to that new blank object. Additionally, the constructor property of the blank object is set to point to the constructor function itself.

Try these simple examples to get your head around these concepts:

```
function Coord(x, y) {
  this.x = x;
  this.y = y;
}
var home = new Coord(132,223);
console.log(home.x); //=> 132
console.log(home.y); //=> 223
console.log(home.constructor); //=> Coord
var myArray = [];
console.log(myArray.constructor); //=> Array
```

The Coord function above is no different from any other function—it's just that the new operator changes the way the function's called. Also note that, if a function is intended as a constructor, JavaScript convention dictates that its first letter be uppercased.

If the constructor function has a `prototype` property, all objects created from this constructor will inherit the properties of that prototype object. When it's looking for a property, the interpreter will look first at the object's properties. If the property isn't found, the interpreter will look in the constructor's prototype object to find the property. If the property in question isn't there, and the prototype object has a constructor with a `prototype` property, the interpreter will look at *that* prototype object, and so on. The interpreter will continue to travel up the chain of `constructor` and `prototype` properties until it can look no further, at which point it will report definitively that the property does not exist.

This **prototype chain**, as it's called, provides a very primitive form of inheritance, and you shouldn't expect too much of it in its basic form. However, as we'll see later on, it's a good foundation upon which we can build all kinds of inheritance models. You can see the `prototype` property in action by trying out the following code (which continues from the previous example):

```
Coord.prototype.units = 'cm';
var a = new Coord, b = new Coord;
console.log(a.units); //=> 'cm'
console.log(b.units); //=> 'cm'
// To prove that each instance points to the prototype rather
// than a copy, consider the following:
Coord.prototype.units = 'mm';
console.log(a.units); //=> 'mm'
console.log(b.units); //=> 'mm'
// To demonstrate the prototype chain...
function Coord3D(x, y, z) {
   this.x = x;
   this.y = y;
   this.z = z;
}
Coord3D.prototype = new Coord;
var home3D = new Coord3D(323, 2323, 4435);
console.log(home3D.units); //=> 'mm' inherited from Coord
```

The `prototype` property is so crucial to object orientation in JavaScript that it lends its name to an entire library—the Prototype JavaScript library.[3] We'll dissect the Prototype library in detail later in the chapter.

Detecting whether a Function Was Called with new

As I noted previously, constructor functions are just standard, regular functions—there's nothing special about them at all. What is special is that when a function is called with the `new` operator, its behavior changes to reflect the cookie cutter I mentioned previously. However, there are some

---

[3] http://prototypejs.org/

circumstances in which we might want a function to be used as both a constructor and a normal function.

JavaScript itself contains a number of functions that act in this way—Boolean, String, and Number, for example. Let's see some of them in action:

```
// When called as functions, the following perform type conversions:
String(46546); //=> "46546"
Number('46546'); //=> 46546

// However, when called with new they construct objects:
a = new String;
b = new Number;
```

It's sometimes useful to be able to mirror this behavior, but how can we tell from *inside* a function that's in the middle of executing whether that function was called normally or via new?

The trick is to inspect the value of this. When a function is called with new, this points to a blank object; if it's not called with new, this either points to the window object (which is always the default value of this), or to the object of which it is a property.

Here's some sample code that performs this check:

```
function Element() {
  if (this == window || 'Element' in this) {
   // the function is being called normally
  } else {
   // the function is being called via new
  }
}
```

Using such a check allows us to create our own constructor methods, and is an important step in extending and customizing the JavaScript language to our own needs.

Functions Are Objects

We've seen how functions can create objects, but did you know that functions are *themselves* objects? This fact has a few implications. First of all, it means that functions can be assigned to variables and properties of an object, and can be passed as arguments to other functions—something you've almost certainly come across if you've used a library like Prototype or jQuery.[4]

There are three ways to create a function in JavaScript:

---

[4] http://jquery.com/

```
// the basic form
function myFunc(my, args) {
  // some code here
}
// the 'anonymous' form
var myFunc = function(my, args) {
  // some code here
}
// via the new keyword; don't try this at home, kids!
var myFunc = new Function("my, args", "// code as a string here");
```

Each of these types of function creation is useful in different situations, and each has slightly different characteristics:

- The basic form simply creates a named function in the current scope, similarly to the way that var creates a variable.

- The second form, where we've created an anonymous function, and used var to store it in a variable, produces a function that's equivalent to that created by the basic form. What gives the anonymous form an edge is that you can use it to assign a *function* as a property of an object (a technique we'll use later). It's worth noting that this form simply assigns an object of the type Function to the property of another object, much like we would assign any other type of object to the property.

- The third form is potentially the most powerful, but it's essentially a glorified eval—with similar potential security pitfalls—so be extra careful when using this form.

For now, we'll focus on the anonymous form of function creation. This form gives us the flexibility to extend JavaScript in a couple of interesting ways.

First, it allows us to assign a function to the property of an object, thereby simulating the object oriented concept of an object having a method. However, this implementation entails one important difference that often confuses even fairly experienced JavaScript programmers: no binding exists between the function and the object to which it is assigned. Rather, the this keyword, when referenced from within the body of the function, will point to the object upon which the function is called.

The following code demonstrates this behavior:

```
var a = {
  counter : 5
};
var b = {
  counter : 10
};
```

```
a.increment = function(amount) {
  this.counter += amount;
};
a.increment(3);
console.log(a.counter); //=> 8
b.increment = a.increment;
b.increment(15);
console.log(b.counter); //=> 25  When called on b, the 'this'
                        //       property points to b instead of a.
```

The second way in which we can utilize anonymous functions is to take advantage of two very useful built-in methods: `call` and `apply`. These methods allow you to change the context in which a function is called by modifying the value of `this`. Both of these methods produce the same result; the only difference between them lies in the ways in which we pass arguments to them.

Try the following variation of the previous code sample to get a feel for how we can change the scope using `call` and `apply`:

```
var a = {
  counter : 5
};
var b = {
  counter : 10
};
a.increment = function(amount) {
  this.counter += amount;
}
a.increment(3);
console.log(a.counter); //=> 8
// Execute a.increment in the context of b:
a.increment.call(b, 15);
a.increment.apply(b, [15]); // Alternatively, pass the arguments
                            // as an array, rather than as a list.
```

It's worth noting that you can check the `length` property of any function to ascertain the number of arguments it expects. Additionally, while it's not part of the ECMAScript standard, many browsers implement the `caller` property, which gives a reference to the function that invoked it.

Understanding the `arguments` Array

When a function is called, two built-in variables are made available within the local scope of the function. The first is `this`, which we've already encountered; the second is the `arguments` array, which contains information about the arguments passed. The `arguments` array, coupled with JavaScript's ability to pass any number of arguments, gives us a mechanism by which we can simulate a method that accepts optional arguments, or takes a variable number of arguments:

```
// add up all the arguments sent to the function
// no matter how many there are
function sum() {
  var total = 0;
  for (var i = 0, l = arguments.length; i < l; i++)
    total += arguments[i];
  return total;
}
console.log(sum(2,5,90)); //=> 97
console.log(sum(100,200,50,18)); //=> 368
```

There are circumstances in which you might be tempted to manipulate the `arguments` array, but this isn't as easy as you might think—an `arguments` array, like a DOM node list, doesn't inherit methods from `Array`. We can use `call` to get around this issue by stealing methods from `Array.prototype`:

```
function takesVariableArgsWithOptionalHash() {
  var options = {};
  var otherArgs = arguments;
  // steal slice from Array.prototype
  var slice = Array.prototype.slice;
  if (typeof arguments[arguments.length-1] == 'object') {
    options = arguments[arguments.length-1];
    otherArgs = slice.call(arguments, 1);
  }
  ⋮
}
takesVariableArgsWithOptionalHash(1, { option : 'thing' });
takesVariableArgsWithOptionalHash(1,3,5, { option : 'thing' });
takesVariableArgsWithOptionalHash(1,3,5);
```

Another useful property of the `arguments` array is `callee`, which contains a reference to the function itself:

```
function returnMe() {
  return arguments.callee;
}
console.log(returnMe()); //=> returnMe()
```

Stealing Methods from Other Objects

In JavaScript, as we discovered earlier in the chapter, an object's methods are merely functions that are attached as properties to that object. So to "steal" a method from one object and give it to another, all we need to do is change the object that the `this` property points to from the "victim" to the "thief." The example above, in which we steal the `slice` method from `Array`, is a perfect illustration of JavaScript's malleability.

Using `callee` to Store Properties Between Function Calls

The `callee` property may not immediately seem useful, but in fact it's quite a handy tool for storing values across function calls. Traditionally, if you'd wanted this functionality, you might have used a global variable to store the values:

```
var uid = 0;

function newId() {
  return ++uid;
}

newId(); //=> 1
newId(); //=> 2
```

This approach is a little messy, as it involves the use of a global variable, and pollutes the `window` object. Wouldn't it be nice if a function could store its own values between calls? This should be possible, after all, as functions are objects and objects can have expando properties. But how do we get a reference to the function from inside that function? The answer to that question is … `arguments.callee`! Take a look:

```
function newId() {
  var thisFunction = arguments.callee
  // if the uid property is not there yet, make it
  if (!thisFunction.uid) thisFunction.uid = 0;
  return ++thisFunction.uid;
}

newId(); //=> 1
newId(); //=> 2
newId.uid; //=> 2
```

Comprehending Closures

The concept of closures often eludes many programmers—largely because the usage of closures is notoriously difficult to explain. However, once you've grasped the concept, you'll realize that the closure is an incredibly powerful language feature—one that forms the backbone of many metaprogramming techniques. As such, it's worth spending some time to get some … er … closure on closures! The best way to do this is to experiment with the code examples in this section, and have a play on your own. There's also a wealth of information about JavaScript closures on the Web, but of course you won't need to go trawling for further explanations after reading my perfectly clear and easy-to-understand explanation over the next couple of pages (ahem!). Here we go.

What is a Closure?

The concept of a closure is actually very simple: a **closure** is the combination of a function and the environment (the set of available variables) in which it was defined.

That's it. See, it wasn't complicated, was it?

In JavaScript, a closure is created when a function is defined within another function. If the inner function is accessed from outside of its containing function, it still has access to the scope in which it was originally defined—even though the variables in that scope are not accessible to any other functions or variables. Call me a romantic, but I like to think of a closure as a kind of magical, forgotten world. Even though the outer function has completed executing, the closure allows us to tap into the past and access variables that would normally be unavailable.

Here's an example:

```
function createFunc() {
  var aValue = 15;   ❶
  // The following is assigned without var, so it's in the global
  // scope (and therefore equivalent to window.returnAValue = ...)
  returnAValue = function() {   ❷
    return aValue;
  }
}
createFunc();               //   creates returnAValue
console.log(aValue);        //=> undefined because its in the
                            //   scope of createFunc
console.log(returnAValue()); //=> 15 because it was created in   ❸
                            //   the scope of createFunc and still
                            //   has access to that scope.
```

Let's step though this code together.

 Inside the `createFunc` function, we define a local variable, `aValue`.

 We also create a global function called `returnAValue`, which refers to `aValue`, thus creating a closure.

❸ When we call `returnAValue` *outside* of the scope of the function that created it, `returnAValue` still has access to the local variable in the scope in which it was created.

This seems like unusual behavior at first. Take the time to experiment at this point and get a handle on exactly what's happening here.

To illustrate why closures are so useful, let's take a look at couple of uses for them.

Partial Function Application

Closures are useful for creating functions that prefill some of their own arguments. The use of closures for this purpose is called **partial function application**. Let's see it in action:

```
function joinWords(a, b) {
  return[a, b].join(' ');
}
console.log(joinWords('Love', 'JavaScript')); //=> 'Love JavaScript'
function prefixer(word) {
  return function(b) {
    return joinWords(word, b);
  }
}
var prefixWithHate = prefixer('Hate'); //=> returns a function that
                                       // adds 'Hate' to the front
                                       // of its argument,
                                       // essentially prefilling
                                       // the first argument of
                                       // join words for you
console.log(prefixWithHate('Java'));   //=> 'Hate Java'
console.log(prefixWithHate('PHP'));    //=> 'Hate PHP'
```

In this example, we've created a simple function, joinWords, which takes two strings and joins them together. We then create another function, prefixer, which returns partially applied versions of joinWords.

prefixer takes a word as its argument, and returns a function that prefills the first argument with that word. This is possible because word is still available to the inner function via the closure. The final function that we created, prefixWithHate, takes only one argument and appends it to the word "Hate."

As we'll see later in the chapter, partial function application is a means by which we can create dynamic functions.

The Self-executing Function Pattern

Limiting the number of global variables your script creates is an important step in creating portable code: the fewer variables there are, the less likely it is that another script will clobber those variables, or, of course, that your variables will clobber another script's variables. One handy technique for addressing this issue is the **self-executing function pattern**, which is a syntax for creating scripts that have no impact at all on the global scope. Let's take a look:

```
(function() {
  var google = 'http://google.com';

  open(google);
```

```
})();

console.log(google); //=> returns undefined, as it's now
                     //    out of scope
```

The syntax isn't pretty—to say the least!—but the idea is simple. We define an anonymous function, then execute it immediately (the parentheses around the function definition are needed to ensure that the interpreter evaluates things in the correct order). All of the code inside the function definition is local to the anonymous function, which executes straight away; then, being anonymous, the function evaporates into the ether, leaving no global variables at all.

But how do we go about defining functions that are called *after* the anonymous function has executed—for instance, if we've assigned those functions as event handlers? All of the local variables and functions to which the anonymous function refers will have disappeared into the ether, right?

Well, no, actually—they're still accessible via the closure:

```
(function() {
  var windowRef;

  var openWindow = function() {
    windowRef = open(this.href, 'mywin');
  };

  var closeWindow = function() {
    if (windowRef) windowRef.close();
  };

  window.onload = function() {
    document.getElementById('open_help').onclick = openWindow;
    document.getElementById('close_help').onclick = closeWindow;
  };
})();
```

Here, we use the self-executing function pattern to create a script that opens and closes a help window. When the user clicks on certain elements of the page, this window launches—without leaving any global variables behind at all. We define the open and close functions—both of which refer to the variable `windowRef`, which is local to the anonymous function—before setting an `onload` handler that will attach these functions as event handlers to the relevant elements.

The `onload` function knows about the local open and close functions because it was defined in the same scope as they were, and therefore shares that scope with them. The same concept applies to the case when a user clicks an **open** or **close** link—the event handlers still have access to the `windowRef` variable, even though the function that defined them finished executing some time ago.

Applications of the Self-executing Function Pattern

The self-executing function pattern is very useful for working with libraries that have lengthy namespace prefixes, such as the Yahoo User Interface (YUI) library.[5] YUI manages its namespaces very strictly, leaving only a single variable—YAHOO—in the global scope. Inside this scope, properties are separated (mostly by functional area: Event, Dom, etc.) using nested objects. This means that, to gain access to a particular function in YUI, we end up writing quite lengthy statements:

```
YAHOO.util.Event.addListener('an_element', "click", callback);
var opacity = YAHOO.util.Dom.getStyle('test2', 'opacity');
```

If we were, for example, using the Event and Dom utilities heavily within our script, it would make sense to shortcut them in some way, to make our script smaller and more readable. Here's how we might use the self-executing function pattern to achieve this:

```
(function(event, dom) {
    event.addListener('an_element', "click", callback);
    var opacity = dom.getStyle('test2', 'opacity');
})(YAHOO.util.Event, YAHOO.util.Dom);
```

This little trick specifies to your anonymous function two arguments that will be your shortcuts; it then executes the function, passing in the long names as the arguments. This is as close as you can get to a Java-style import statement in JavaScript at the moment!

The Module Pattern

Speaking of YUI, another interesting use of closures (and a useful pattern in itself) is the **module pattern** that the YUI team developed as a means to arrange code into independent modules, and to manage method and property visibility. It is, in fact, a close cousin of the self-executing function, and works in exactly the same way. We'll cover it briefly here, but be sure the read the full article on the YUI Blog if you want to know more.[6]

Let's dig into some example code:

```
Menu = (function() {
    // a private method
    var active = false;

    // a private method
    var reset = function() {
        ⋮
    }
```

---

[5] http://developer.yahoo.com/yui/
[6] http://yuiblog.com/blog/2007/06/12/module-pattern/

```
    return {
      // a public property accessible via Menu.instances
      instances: [],

      // a public method accessible via Menu.create()
      create: function(element) {
        ⋮
      }
    }
})();
```

As you can see, this example is almost the same as the self-executing function pattern, although it returns an object with public properties and methods that, in this case, are assigned to Menu, our module. The interesting thing about this solution is that the public methods have access to all of the private functions and properties through the closure. That peculiarity aside, the private methods are truly private—there's no way to access them from outside the module at all.

Be Wary of `eval`

The built-in `eval` function simply takes a string of JavaScript and evaluates it in the current scope. You can evaluate any string with `eval`, so it's generally considered unsafe practice to use it in many circumstances, since it can be used by attackers to inject malicious JavaScript into your pages. Such attacks are referred to as **cross-site scripting (XSS)** attacks, and are among the most commonly used methods of hacking a web site.

Most JavaScript programmers have come across `eval` in their travels—it's often used incorrectly to achieve some of the tasks that I've described above. However, in 99.9% of cases, using `eval` is simply not necessary, and it's worth avoiding if possible. Of course, if you really do need it, it's always there in the toolbox.

Metaprogramming Techniques

Now that we've explored the language features that represent our metaprogramming building blocks, let's see how we can combine these features into several useful techniques.

Just the Beginning ...

These techniques are just starting points for your own experiments—they by no means represent an exhaustive list of metaprogramming techniques in JavaScript.

Creating Functions with Default Arguments

To start off gently, let's look at an example that, though it's more of a convention than a metaprogramming technique, is a useful example of how we can use JavaScript to mimic features that are built into in other languages.

Consider that in Ruby we might specify a method that has default arguments like this:

```
# Ruby code

def send(url, options={})
  # options could be passed; if not, they default to an empty hash
end
```

When we call the `send` function above, the `options` parameter is optional; if we choose to omit this argument, it will be assigned a default value (in this case, the empty hash `{}`).

Wouldn't it be convenient if we could take a similar approach with JavaScript? Well, we can, but not by using any built-in language features! Instead, we can employ a little trick to achieve (nearly) the same effect:

```
function send(url, options) {
  options = options || {}
}
```

You can use this approach to simulate any number of optional arguments with defaults, but heed this word of warning: in order to use this technique effectively, you'll need to know a certain amount about the types of values that might be passed to the argument. In JavaScript, many unexpected values will evaluate to `false`, including `0`, `undefined`, `null`, and—most scarily—empty strings. In the case above, we expect an `options` object or nothing at all, so we're safe. But if you want defaults for arguments that may either be numbers or strings, you'll need to use a slightly more convoluted, though safer, method:

```
function repeat(func, times) {
  times = (typeof times == 'undefined') ? 1 : times;
  for (var i=0; i<times; i++) func();
}
```

Working with Built-ins

JavaScript has a relatively small set of built-in functions and objects that vary from implementation to implementation, but fortunately we have the ability to extend most of these functions dynamically with our scripts. To add extra methods to a built-in object, you just need to add them to the object's prototype. Suppose we wanted to add a `strip` method to remove preceding and trailing spaces from a `String`, for example:

```
String.prototype.strip = function() {
  return this.replace(/^\s+|\s+$/g, '');
}
'  some text  '.strip(); //=> "some text"
```

Another common situation in which we might want to add a method to a built-in object is when we want to smooth over incompatibilities or unsupported language features across browsers (or other implementations).

For example, IE versions 5 and earlier failed to implement the useful `push` method for `Array` objects. Let's add this method manually—but only in cases in which it doesn't exist (it's generally not a good idea to overwrite existing native methods with your own versions).

Here's how we'd go about it:

array_methods.js *(excerpt)*

```
if (!Array.prototype.push) {
  Array.prototype.push = function(item) {
    return this[this.length] = item;
  }
}
```

That's all there is to it! We can now make use of the `push` function in IE 5:

```
[1,2,3,4].push(5); //=> 5 in IE 5 now too!
```

 Be Careful When Adding Methods to Built-in Objects

Be very careful when you're adding methods to built-in objects. The more you add, the greater will be the chance that your script will collide badly with others and fail to work. The Prototype library, for example, adds many objects to built-ins. While the library is convenient, the fact that Prototype doesn't work well with other libraries and scripts has drawn some criticism.

One thing that's definitely a no-no is adding methods to the prototype of `Object`. This will break `for-in` loops and bring many scripts to a grinding halt!

As a final example, let's see how we can implement JavaScript 1.6's new iteration methods across all browsers,[7] so we can use them not only in Firefox, but also in IE, Safari, and other environments.

The methods in question are `forEach`, `map`, and `filter`. In the following code, we check to see whether these methods are already defined. If they're not, we add them to the `Array` object's prototype, ensuring that they work identically to the versions of these methods in JavaScript 1.6:

---

[7] http://developer.mozilla.org/en/docs/Core_JavaScript_1.5_Reference:Objects:Array

array_methods.js *(excerpt)*

```
if (!Array.prototype.forEach) {
  Array.prototype.forEach = function(func, scope) {
    scope = scope || this;
    for (var i = 0, l = this.length; i < l; i++)
      func.call(scope, this[i], i, this);
  }
}
if (!Array.prototype.map) {
  Array.prototype.map = function(func, scope) {
    scope = scope || this;
    var list = [];
    for (var i = 0, l = this.length; i < l; i++)
       list.push(func.call(scope, this[i], i, this));
    return list;
  }
}
if (!Array.prototype.filter) {
  Array.prototype.filter = function(func, scope) {
    scope = scope || this;
    var list = [];
    for (var i = 0, l = this.length; i < l; i++)
      if (func.call(scope, this[i], i, this)) list.push(this[i]);
    return list;
  }
}
```

JavaScript 1.6 also implements "generic" versions of these functions that we can use on any object. It's useful to emulate these too—once we've done so, we can use them on node lists and the arguments array. In the following code, we'll use `apply` to create a function that, when called, sets the value of this to be equal to the argument that was passed in; we'll do this for each of the iteration functions that we'd like to implement (as well as `slice` and `concat`, as they're useful too):

array_methods.js *(excerpt)*

```
// loop through each method we want to genericise
['forEach', 'map', 'filter', 'slice', 'concat'].forEach(
  function(func) {

      // test if the method exists already, and only create
      // it if it doesn't
      if (!Array[func]) Array[func] = function(object) {

          // use the call trick to slice() the first argument off the
          // argument list, as that is going to be the object we
          // operate on
          var newArgs = Array.prototype.slice.call(arguments, 1);
```

```
        // call the array function with object as this with
        // the arguments we just created
        return this.prototype[func].apply(object, newArgs);
    }
});
```

The result is that we now have access to these methods, and can use them as if they were part of the language. Here's an example of them in use:

```
var lis = document.getElementsByTagName('li');
Array.forEach(lis, function(li) {
  li.style.display = 'none';
});
```

In this discussion, we've used several of the building blocks we defined in the first section of this chapter. It's worth taking some time at this point to review this code—reread the comments and break it down until you understand how the building blocks fit together to create the desired result before moving on.

Creating Self-optimizing Functions

Because of the myriad differences between browser implementations, many functions still require **branching**—a technique whereby the function is written to contain different logic depending on the language features supported by the browser. The best-practice approach to doing this is to test for the objects and properties we need and, if they exist, to use those methods and properties. If you look into many libraries or other pieces of JavaScript, you'll notice this pattern:

```
function addEvent(element, type, func) {
  if (document.addEventListener)
    element.addEventListener(type, func);
  else
    element.attachEvent(type, func);
}
```

This simple (although admittedly quite contrived) function checks to see if the addEventListener method exists, and uses it to attach an event. If addEventListener doesn't exist, the function falls back to IE's proprietary attachEvent. This code does the job perfectly well (although I should temper this by pointing out that it ignores a whole heap of other cross-browser event handling problems—for the moment!). However, we can do a little bit better with a dash of metaprogramming.

The function above tests for addEventListener every single time we call the method. However, ideally we should only perform that test once—on the first execution of the function. Once that's done, we can use the result of that method from that point forward. To achieve this outcome, we can use a pattern similar to the one documented by Peter Michaux and known as **lazy function evaluation.**[8] In the following code, when the function is called for the first time, it rewrites itself with a version of the function that's specific to that browser:

```
function addEvent(element, type, func) {
    if (document.addEventListener) {
        addEvent = function(element, type, func) {
            element.addEventListener(type, func)
        };
    } else {
        addEvent = function(element, type, func) {
            element.attachEvent( type, func)
        };
    }
    addEvent(element, type, func);
}
```

Here, the initial function call performs the method detection, but then uses the appropriate method to overwrite `addEvent` with a new function. Finally, the new version of the function is called.

While this example is very simple, the same pattern can be used on much more complex functions, saving hundreds, or even thousands, of object lookups and method calls. In a large JavaScript application or, for instance, in a library, these speed gains can make a real difference.

Now that we've covered the basic concept, let's look at a more complex problem.

Functions that collect page elements that have a certain class name have taken many forms over the past year or two. These functions tend to be used very heavily, which makes them ideal candidates for a little performance enhancement. The slowest approach to collecting elements is to retrieve all elements on the page, then to loop through them, checking the `className` property of each with a regular expression. Some browsers, however, support XPath, which is a much faster and more powerful way to select nodes.

We can tell if a browser offers XPath support by checking whether the `document.evaluate` method exists. With this in mind, here's a first stab at the problem:

```
document.getElementsByClassName = function(className, context) {
    context = context || document;
    var els = [];
        if (typeof document.evaluate == 'function') {
            var xpath = document.evaluate(
                ".//*[ contains(concat(' ', @class, ' '), ' "
                + className + " ')]", context, null,
                XPathResult.ORDERED_NODE_SNAPSHOT_TYPE, null);
```

---

[8] http://peter.michaux.ca/article/3556/

```
      for (var i = 0, l = xpath.snapshotLength; i < l; i++)
          els.push(xpath.snapshotItem(i));
  } else {
    nodeList = context.getElementsByTagName('*');
    var re = new RegExp('(^|\\s)' + className + '(\\s|$)');
    els = Array.filter(nodeList, function(node) {
      return node.className.match(re)
    });
  }
  return els;
}
```

As you might have noticed, there's clearly scope for us to use our pattern to optimize this function. However, in this case, the process is a little more complex than the last example we saw. Essentially, we only need to check once to see if document.evaluate exists. Once we've confirmed that it does exist, we can have the function rewrite itself with the optimized version of the method.

The main problem here is that we have a lot of code that needs to run in both cases. So how can we apply our pattern? Try this:

get_elements_by_class_name.js

```
document.getElementsByClassName = function(className, context) {
  var getEls;
  if (typeof document.evaluate == 'function') {
    getEls = function(className, context) {   ❶
      var els = [];
      var xpath =
        document.evaluate(
            ".//*[contains(concat(' ', @class, ' '), ' "
            + className + " ')]", context, null,
            XPathResult.ORDERED_NODE_SNAPSHOT_TYPE, null);
      for (var i = 0, l = xpath.snapshotLength; i < l; i++)
        els.push(xpath.snapshotItem(i));
      return els;
    }
  } else {
    getEls = function(className, content) {
      var nodeList = context.getElementsByTagName('*');
      var re = new RegExp('(^|\\s)' + className + '(\\s|$)');
      return Array.filter(nodeList, function(node) {
        return node.className.match(re) });
    }
  }
  document.getElementsByClassName =   ❷
    function(className, context) {
      context = context || document;
      return getEls(className, context);
```

```
  }
  return document.getElementsByClassName(className, context);
}
```

❶ First, we check for the existence of the document.evaluate function, as we did in the previous example. But this time, instead of just executing the code to select the nodes, we set getEls to the most optimized version of the function that that browser supports: Firefox et al use the fast XPath version, while IE and the older browsers use the RegExp-based version.

❷ Once getEls is set, we can write the function document.getElementsByClassName to use getEls (which is available via the closure). We then call getElementsByClassName in order to return the selected nodes.

Aspect-oriented Programming on a Shoestring

Like closures, the field of **aspect-oriented programming (AOP)** is often viewed as being enormously confusing and complex, though it's really quite simple.

Aspect-oriented programming refers to the practice of augmenting a function by defining code to be executed before or after the function, rather than using inheritance to extend the code. In AOP, we manipulate the arguments or the return value of the original function, and sometimes prevent the original function from executing altogether.

It turns out that this technique is quite an effective one within the realm of JavaScript—as we discovered earlier, inheritance is not as easy to achieve in JavaScript as it is in other object oriented languages, where the concept is built into the language. The lightweight technique of augmenting existing code to meet our own needs, however, can result in much cleaner solutions to browser scripting problems than more traditional approaches. We can conduct this mysterious function augmentation by utilizing a relatively simple function that comes bundled in Prototype as of version 1.6.0: Function.wrap.

Let's start by looking at an example of Function.wrap in action. Imagine we're debugging some code, and we need to write to the log every time a certain function (let's call it Doggle.ping) is called. The log entry will contain the arguments passed to our function. We can replace that function with a wrapped version that logs the arguments, then executes the function as normal. And, just for the heck of it, we'll also log the return value:

```
Doggle = {
  ping: function() { … }
};

Doggle.ping = Doggle.ping.wrap(function(original, arg, arg2) {
  console.log(arg, arg2);
```

```
   var result = original(arg, arg2);
   console.log(result);
   return result;
});
```

The wrapper function receives the original function as the first argument, and any other arguments that are passed to the function subsequently. You can do as you wish with this wrapper function, using the original function argument to call the wrapped function as you see fit. In this example, we're overwriting the original method, but you could save the wrapped function to another variable if you prefer.

As you can see, `Function.wrap` is a very useful little piece of metaprogramming magic. Better still, it's really simple to implement! Here's the code for `Function.wrap` in its entirety (adapted from the original version in Prototype):

function_wrapping.js

```
Function.prototype.wrap = function(wrapper) {
 var __method = this;  ❶

 return function() {
  var args = [];

  // We need to copy arguments into a new array so that
  // concat works below.
  for (var i=0; i<arguments.length; i++) args.push(arguments[i]);  ❷
  return wrapper.apply(this, [__method.bind(this)].concat(args));  ❸
 }
};
```

You have to admire the conciseness of that code, given the huge amount of utility it offers:

❶   Firstly, it saves a reference to the original method.

❷   It then returns a function that collects the arguments passed to it, and places that function into a *real* array (remember, the `arguments` array is a sort of annoying mutant array, as we found out earlier).

❸   Finally, it executes the original function (spot the closure in action here!) using `apply`, and constructs the array of arguments with `concat`.

Better APIs through Dynamic Functions

The task of creating functions dynamically has been covered in some detail already in this chapter. In this section, we're going to use partial function application to construct an API that's more compact and user-friendly than the default API provided by the browser. The DOM Builder,[9] a helper object that I wrote as part of the Low Pro extensions to Prototype,[10] is a great example for demonstrating this principle (if I do say so myself). We'll only be looking at certain parts of the code so, if you need to, refer to the full source in the book's code archive.

The purpose of DOM Builder is simple: to make the programmatic creation of HTML elements as easy and compact as possible. The API provided to us by browsers for accessing and manipulating the DOM is functional, but it's not very pleasant to work with. I'm sure you've seen (or written) code like this before:

```
var ul = document.createElement('ul');
ul.setAttribute('id', 'my_list');
var li = document.createElement('li');
var text = document.createTextNode('Some text');
li.appendChild(text);
ul.appendChild(li);
```

For all but the most trivial DOM structures, this approach quickly gets nasty—the code is long-winded and repetitive. Fortunately, we can wrap a much nicer API around these functions to remove some of the repetition.

We'll start by creating a function called `DOMBuilder.create` (we'll use the `DOMBuilder` object to prevent our methods clashing with other `create` methods). Here's how we want this function to work:

```
var ul = DOMBuilder.create('ul', { id : 'my_list' }, [
  DOMBuilder.create('li', null, 'Some text')
]);
```

Here, `DOMBuilder.create` takes the tag name, an object containing the attributes to be set, and an array of child nodes. Here's how that function might look (with some of the details omitted for clarity):

dom_builder.js *(excerpt)*

```
DOMBuilder = {
  create : function(tag, attrs, children) {
    // the attrs object and children array are optional
    attrs = attrs || {};
    children = children || [];
    // create the element
    var el = document.createElement(tag);
```

---

[9] http://svn.danwebb.net/external/DomBuilder/trunk/dombuilder.js
[10] http://svn.danwebb.net/external/lowpro/

```
      // set each attribute
      for (var attr in attrs) {
        el.setAttribute(attr, attrs[attr].toString());
      }
      // append each child converting to a text node
      // if the child is a string
      for (var i=0; i < children.length; i++) {
        if (typeof children[i] == 'string')
          children[i] = document.createTextNode(children[i]);
        el.appendChild(children[i]);
      }
      // return the element
      return el;
    }
}
```

Now that we have this basic function, we can go a little further and see how we can use metaprogramming to further polish the API. Taking inspiration from Ruby's XML builder, we'd like to add an extra layer to the API so that our code looks similar to the resulting HTML structure. This example shows what we're aiming for, using normal JavaScript syntax:

```
var ul = $ul(
  { id : 'my_list' },
  $li('Some text')
);
```

To achieve this, we need to dynamically generate a function for every conceivable HTML element; the name of the function should be equal to the name of the element—for example, $div, $span, $h1, and so on.

Here's how we go about that:

dom_builder.js *(excerpt)*

```
// use the self-calling function syntax to ensure that
// nothing is left in the global scope
(function() {
    var els = ("p|div|span|strong|em|img|table|tr|td|th|thead|" +
"tbody|tfoot|pre|code|h1|h2|h3|h4|h5|h6|ul|ol|li|form|input|" +
"textarea|legend|fieldset|select|option|blockquote|cite|br|hr|" +
"dd|dl|dt|address|a|button|abbr|acronym|script|link|style|bdo|" +
"ins|del|object|param|col|colgroup|optgroup|caption|label|dfn|" +
"kbd|samp|var").split("|");
    var el, i=0;
    // create functions on the window object (which, in a browser
```

```
      // implementation of JavaScript, is the global scope)
      while (el = els[i++]) window['$' + el] = DOMBuilder.tagFunc(el);
 })();
```

As you can see in the code above, we're calling the method `DOMBuilder.tagFunc` for each element. `tagFunc` is the method that's responsible for building each dynamic function:

dom_builder.js *(excerpt)*

```
tagFunc : function(tag) {
  // notice that tagFunc returns this function
    return function() {
      var attrs, children;
      // if some are arguments passed, we need to sort the
      // arguments into attributes and children
      if (arguments.length > 0) {
        // if the first argument is a node or a string
        // then we don't have an attribute hash
        if (arguments[0].nodeName
            || typeof arguments[0] == "string")
          children = arguments;
        // otherwise we do have an attribute hash
        else {
          attrs = arguments[0];
          children = Array.prototype.slice.call(arguments, 1);
        };
      }
    // once we have sorted out the arguments, call create normally
    return DOMBuilder.create(tag, attrs, children);
  };
}
```

You'll notice that, in this function, we're examining the `arguments` array in order to determine whether or not the `attributes` hash exists. If it doesn't, we no longer need to pass an array to these functions—we can simply pass the `arguments` array as the `children` argument to the `create` method.

Let's take a look once more at the difference that our enhanced API makes when adding page elements to our document. Here's the original code for adding an unordered list with one list item:

```
var ul = document.createElement('ul');
ul.setAttribute('id', 'my_list');
var li = document.createElement('li');
var text = document.createTextNode('Some text');
li.appendChild(text);
ul.appendChild(li);
```

And here's the equivalent code that utilizes the modified API provided by the DOM Builder object:

```
var ul = $ul({ id : 'my_list' }, $li('Some text'));
```

I'm sure you'll agree that the convenience associated with utilizing the above syntax, both in terms of lines of code and readability, is enormous—especially if you're creating multiple elements.

Creating Dynamic Constructors

Since object constructors are just regular functions, we can use all of the techniques that we employed to create dynamic functions in the creation of dynamic constructors. We can also dynamically add functions and properties to the prototype of the constructor function. Once we've done this, we can use the new keyword to create instances of these dynamic constructors.

"Why would we want to do all of this?" I hear you ask. Well, being able to create instances of dynamic constructors gives us the JavaScript equivalent of a **dynamic class creation** event, which is an event that will allow us to recreate traditional classes and inheritance.

But I'm getting ahead of myself. To examine the first, much simpler case of creating an instance of a dynamic constructor, we turn again to the Low Pro extension to the Prototype framework, and its implementation of behavior classes.

A **behavior class** is a class that controls the life cycle of an element in an object oriented way. To implement a behavior class, we must first define the class, then bind an instance of that class to each desired element. A behavior class defines various methods that are called when an event is triggered on the element to which the class is bound. Since each element is bound to its own instance of the behavior, we can easily maintain state throughout the element's lifespan.

When you're building a class like this, it's worth considering the API before you begin to explore ways in which the class might actually be implemented. In this case, I wanted an API that looked like this:

draggable.js (excerpt)

```
var Draggable = Behavior.create({
  initialize : function(options) {
    // gets called when the element is loaded or the
    // behavior is bound to it.
  },
  onclick : function(event) {
    // any onxxx method is attached to the bound element
    // as a event handler
  },
  anotherMethod : function(x, y) {
    // any other methods can be called normally from within
    // the event handlers
```

```
    }
});
// Draggable is now created as a constructor.
// The first argument must be the element to bind
// any other arguments are passed to the initialize() method
var myEl = document.getElementsById('my_element');
var dragger = new Draggable(myEl, { revert : true });
// Each behavior class has an apply() method that can be used to
// bind instances of itself to lists of elements.
var lis = document.getElementsByTagName('li');
Draggable.apply(lis);
```

You can see above that the Behavior.create function will need to return an object constructor that can be instantiated as normal with new. The attach method will need to be added to each of these constructors so we can use functions like Draggable.attach. Here's a simplified view of Behavior.create:

lowpro.js *(excerpt)*

```
Behavior = {
  create : function(members) {
    // define the constructor function
    var behavior = function() {
      // store reference to the bound element
      this.element = $(arguments[0]);
      // run initialize method if one is specified
      if (members.initialize)
          members.initialize.apply(this,
              Array.prototype.slice(arguments, 1));
      // bind onxxx methods to event handlers
      for (var method in this)
        if (method.match(/^on(.+)/)
            && typeof this[method] == 'function')
          this.element.observe(RegExp.$1,
              this[method].bindAsEventListener(this));
    };
    // attach the given methods to the prototype
    Object.extend(behavior.prototype, members);
    // attach any singleton methods to the constructor
    Object.extend(behavior, Behavior.ClassMethods);
    // return the constructor
    return behavior;
  },
  ClassMethods : {
    apply : function(elements) {
      // body omitted for clarity
```

```
      }
    }
  }
}
```

This example illustrates that to dynamically create a constructor, we simply create a function, then attach methods and properties to its prototype. Here, Prototype's `Object.extend` method is used to copy properties from one object to another in order to "mix in" all the necessary methods to the object's prototype. We'll talk more about mix ins in the next section.

Simulating Traditional Object Orientation

In the previous example, we saw how we can use methods like the Prototype framework's `Object.extend` method to copy a group of methods to an object—a task that's known as **mixing in** the methods.

However, this feature does not represent the limit of JavaScript's extensibility. In fact, we can use JavaScript itself to implement programming constructs, such as class-based object orientation and inheritance, from other languages. One library that attempts to do this is Prototype. So, to investigate some of these concepts, let's take a closer look at the evolution of Prototype's class-based object orientation, inheritance, and other features.

In the Beginning ...

The first versions of Prototype started along the road to class-based inheritance with two methods: `Object.extend` (which we've already encountered) and `Class.create`. As we've seen, `Object.extend` simply copies properties from one object to another. The implementation is simple:

```
Object.extend = function(destination, source) {
  for (var property in source)
    destination[property] = source[property];
  return destination;
};
```

This function is extremely helpful for performing all kinds of tasks, such as cloning objects:

```
Var newObj = Object.extend({}, oldObject);
```

You can also use it to provide defaults to an `options` hash:

```
function sendRequest(url, options) {
  options =
    Object.extend({ method: 'post', async: false }, options);
  // code omitted
}
```

`Object.extend` is also useful for emulating **mix ins**. A mix in is a language construct that's found in Ruby and several other languages. A mix in is a class that defines a group of methods and properties that can be added (or "mixed in") to other objects to provide new functionality. A mix in is not intended to be used as a standalone class. Prototype employs this concept to add useful iteration methods to several built-in types. Here's an example:

```javascript
var Enumerable = {
  each: function(iterator, context) {
    var index = 0;
    iterator = iterator.bind(context);
    try {
      this._each(function(value) {
          iterator(value, index++);
      });
    } catch (e) {
      if (e != $break) throw e;
    }
    return this;
  },
  // more methods here
}

Object.extend(Array.prototype, Enumerable);
```

Here, the `Enumerable` object is defined to contain a number of useful methods. Using `Object.extend`, we can mix these methods into other objects or, as in the above example, into the prototype of a constructor. Mixing in a method to a constructor causes the method to be added to all the objects that are created with that constructor.

The second Prototype method that's worthy of discussion is `Class.create`. Here's the code for this method, as of Prototype 1.5.1.1:

prototype-1.5.1.1.js *(excerpt)*

```javascript
var Class = {
  create: function() {
    return function() {
      this.initialize.apply(this, arguments);
    }
  }
}
```

All this method does is create a dynamic constructor function. This allows us to define an `initialize` function in which we can place our constructor code, rather than putting that code into the object's constructor function. This is ultimately an aesthetic enhancement, but it's a starting point. The `Class.create` method allows you to create "classes" like so:

```
var TreeView = Class.create();
Object.extend(TreeList.prototype,
    { initialize: function(element) {}, open: function() {} }
);

// create a new instance normally
var treeview = new TreeView('my_element');
```

This approach does have its limitations, however. While these utilities help us to build things that *look* like classes—complete with an `initialize` method—they take us very close to the bone of JavaScript's crude, prototype-based inheritance. This can make tasks that you might take for granted in a truly class-based object oriented language, such as gaining access to the superclass's methods, extremely difficult to achieve. `Class.create` could definitely be improved upon.

Classes in Prototype 1.6

Prototype 1.6.0 has brought with it, among other things, a beefed-up version of `Class.create` that actually comes close to providing real class-based object orientation. It's a great example of meta-programming in action, and brings together all of the concepts that we've covered in this chapter.

Before we dive under the hood, though, let's see exactly what benefits these improvements give us. For one, the new `Class.create` syntax provides a more extensive syntax for defining classes:

```
// example from the post:
// www.prototypejs.org/2007/8/15/prototype-1-6-0-release-candidate/
var Animal = Class.create({
  initialize: function(name) {
    this.name = name;
  },
  eat: function() {
    return this.say("Yum!");
  },
  say: function(message) {
    return this.name + ": " + message;
  }
});
// subclass that augments a method
var Cat = Class.create(Animal, {
  eat: function($super, food) {
    if (food instanceof Mouse) return $super();
    else return this.say("Yuk! I only eat mice.");
  }
});
```

As you can see, `Class.create` has been turned from a simple function that lets you use an `initialize` method into a full-grown, class-making beast. Most importantly, you can now pass arguments to it—either a class to inherit from, an object literal of properties to add the class's prototype, or both. As illustrated in the `eat` method of the class `Cat`, you can now call the super class's version of an overridden method using the special `$super` argument.

On top of this, each class has the `extend` method, which allows you to mix methods into the class's prototype whenever you need to:

```
Attack = {
  bite: function(enemy) {
    return this.say('rargh!');
  },

  scratch: function(enemy) {
    return this.say('grr!');
  }
};

Cat.extend(Attack);

var henry = new Cat('henry');
henry.scratch(owner); //=> 'grr!'
```

That's right—we've got a fully functioning class implementation here!

Now it's time for us to peek under the hood to examine the `Class.create` function. I've heavily annotated this code, so read through it carefully and bear in mind the concepts we covered in the first part of the chapter. If you've skipped any sections, or you didn't quite grasp some of the concepts, go back, reread them, and experiment with the code until they sink in. To understand the following discussion, you'll need to have a firm grasp on dynamic constructors, prototype inheritance, and closures. Trust me, it'll be worth the effort![11]

Here's the code:

prototype-1.6.0_rc1.js (excerpt)

```
var Class = {
  // use the self-executing function pattern so we can have access
  // to the local variable named "extending"
  create: (function() {
    // we use this later on to determine if we are in the process
    // of extending (ie. copying properties onto the prototype)
    // in the constructor
    var extending = { };

    // return the actual create function
```

---

[11] In fact, the final release of Prototype 1.6.0 uses a slightly different technique to achieve the same result, and avoids the use of closures. However, the code here brings so many concepts together that it's worth exploring nonetheless.

```
    return function(parent, properties) {
      // both parent and properties are optional so work
      // out which is which and rearrange them if need be
      if (arguments.length == 1 && !Object.isFunction(parent))
        properties = parent, parent = null;

      // define the actual constructor function
      function klass() {
        // if we aren't in the process of constructing the class
        // do a normal object intialization
        if (arguments[0] !== extending)
          this.initialize.apply(this, arguments);
      }

      // create properties useful for performing introspection
      klass.superclass = parent;
      klass.subclasses = [];

      // if we are inheriting from another class
      if (Object.isFunction(parent)) {
        // Assign a new instance of the parent object to the new
        // classes prototype. Note that extending object is used
        // to tell the constructor not to call initialize
        klass.prototype = new parent(extending);

        // add this to the parents subclasses
        parent.subclasses.push(klass);
      }
      // copy all the given properties onto the new
      // classes prototype
      if (properties)
        Class.extend(klass, properties);
      klass.prototype.constructor = klass;
      // return that new classes constructor function!
      return klass;
    };
  })()
}
```

One of the most interesting features of this code is the way that a new object is created in the closure and assigned to the extending object. This occurs for the specific purpose of letting the constructor know whether to call initialize (something we want to happen when we create a new instance using new) or to do nothing (which is what we want to happen when we create a subclass).

But how does it work?

When a new object is created, the value that's actually stored in the variable is a reference—a pointer to the location in memory where that new object lives. Because of the closure created by the self-executing function, both the main code block and the new constructor know about the `extending` variable. So, when `new parent(extending)` is called, the constructor function takes the object reference it's received as an argument, and compares it to the `extending` object. Since they're the same object, the constructor doesn't run `initialize`.

When the same constructor is called via `new`, however, no argument that's passed to it will ever be equal to the `extending` object, because `extending` only exists in that particular closure.

Got that? Excellent! Take a deep breath, and we'll move on to our final application of metaprogramming: the domain-specific language.

Implementing Domain-specific Languages

Wikipedia defines a **domain-specific language**, or DSL, as "a programming language designed for, and intended to be useful for, a specific kind of task."[12]

We find DSLs all over the computing world: configuration files; build files; even HTML and CSS could be considered to be DSLs, as they are languages built for specific tasks.

Each of these is an example of an external DSL—a brand new language invented to solve a specific problem. But wouldn't it be nice if we could build our DSL out of a general-purpose programming language? This way, we could create constructs that were specific to our problem using an existing language whose features could then be used to solve other problems as required. We'd benefit from both the convenience of a specialized language and the power of a general-purpose language.

To illustrate the power of this approach, let's take a brief look at one of Ruby's most successful DSLs: Builder.[13]

Builder allows you to create XML (and other types of markup) documents in Ruby without having to deal with all the nasty string processing that's normally required to create and process XML. Builder has essentially extended Ruby for this specific task. Here's an example:

```
xml = Builder::XmlMarkup.new

puts xml.people do
    xml.person do
        xml.name("Dan Webb")
        xml.age("30")
    end
end

# prints:
# <people>
```

---

[12] http://en.wikipedia.org/wiki/Domain-specific_language/
[13] http://builder.rubyforge.org/

```
#     <person>
#        <name>Dan Webb</name>
#        <age>30</age>
#     </person>
# </people>
```

If you're thinking that the code above looks similar to DOMBuilder from earlier in the chapter, you're right—DOMBuilder took inspiration from Ruby's Builder and is a DSL, of sorts, in itself.

Now that we have an idea of what we're aiming for, let's examine how we might go about building a DSL in JavaScript. The example I'm going to use is from my microformat parsing library, Sumo.[14]

Microformats give us the opportunity to add more machine-readable semantic value to HTML documents using structures with standardized class names. At the time of writing, several micro-formats were available (hCard, hCalendar, and hReview for contact information, events, and reviews, respectively) but many more are on the way.[15] Each has its own specification and particular structure. In writing Sumo, I wanted to create a parser that wasn't just specific to one microformat, or even all of the currently known microformats. I wanted to create a parser that could parse *any* microformat that might be specified in the future, as well.

So I first set out to create a specification format that could be used to define the class name structures for a given microformat. The parser would then be able to use this specification to find and parse all instances of that microformat in an HTML document.

Parsing microformats is difficult—while they're reasonably standard (for example, an element with class name A can contain one or more elements with class name B; an element with class C can contain one class D element), there's always an exception to the rule.

The hCard specification, for instance, uses an **implied n** optimization: if a person's full name is provided in the document as two words (separated by a space and marked up with a class named fn), but separate given and family names are not provided, then we can imply values for the contact's given name and family name by splitting the full name into two fields. So, for an fn of Dan Webb, we imply that the values of the given name and family names are Dan and Webb, respectively. You can see how the compounding of several of these small exceptions could result in our parser code becoming impossibly complex.

So, how can we create a standard specification language *and* retain the flexibility to cope with all these exceptions? The answer is, of course, to build the parsing instructions from JavaScript, as a DSL.

Let's look at an example hCalendar microformat:

---

[14] http://www.danwebb.net/2007/2/9/sumo-a-generic-microformats-parser-for-javascript/

[15] http://microformats.org/

```
<div class="vevent">
  <h5 class="summary">Pub Standards 100</h5>
  <div>posted on <abbr class="dtstamp"
      title="20070901T1300Z">September 1, 2007</abbr></div>
  <div>Dates: <abbr class="dtstart"
      title="20140313T190000Z">March 13, 2014, 19:00</abbr> -
      <abbr class="dtend" title="20140313T233000Z">23:30 UTC</abbr>
  </div>
  <p class="description">Celebrate the 100th Pub Standards! Put the
      date in your Filofax NOW!</p>
</div>
```

And here's the Sumo specification we'd use to parse it:

```
HCalendar = Microformat.define('vevent', {
  one : ['class', 'description', 'dtend', 'dtstamp', 'dtstart',
    'duration', 'location', 'status', 'summary', 'uid',
    'last-modified', { 'url' : 'url' }],
  many : ['category']
});
```

This code indicates that an `HCalendar` is enclosed by an element of class `vevent`. Within that element, we're allowing one of each element that has a class value of `class`, `description`, `dtend`, and so on. We've also specified that the `HCalendar` can contain many elements with the class name `category`. The function `Microformat.define`, when called with this specification, builds a specialized parser object.

So now that we have a specification that our parser can use for hCalendar microformats, let's attempt to locate and parse some hCalendars on a page. Here's how we'd go about it:

```
var events = HCalendar.discover();

event[0].name; //=> '@media Ajax 2007'
```

Easy, isn't it? But what about the exceptions to the rule I mentioned before?

Well, take a look at these parsing instructions for an hCard. You'll notice that the code is chock-full of such exceptions:

hcard.js (excerpt)

```
var HCard = Microformat.define('vcard', {
  one : ['bday', 'tz', 'sort-string', 'uid', 'class', {
    'n' : {
      one : ['family-name', 'given-name', 'additional-name'],
      many : ['honorific-prefix', 'honorific-suffix']
```

```javascript
    },
    'geo' : function(node) {
      var m;
      if ((node.nodeName.toLowerCase() == 'abbr')
        && (m = node.title.match(/^([\-\d\.]+);([\-\d\.]+)$/))) {
          return { latitude : m[1], longitude : m[2] };
        }

      return this._extractData(node,
          { one : ['latitude', 'longitude'] }
      );
    },
    // implied n
    'fn' : function(node, data) {
      var m, fn = this._extractData(node, 'simple');
      if (m = fn.match(/^(\w+) (\w+)$/)) {
        data.n = data.n || {};
        data.n.givenName = data.n.givenName || m[1];
        data.n.familyName = data.n.familyName || m[2];
      }
      if (m = fn.match(/^(\w+),? (\w+)\.?$/)) {
       data.n = data.n || {};
       data.n.givenName = data.n.givenName || m[2];
       data.n.familyName = data.n.familyName || m[1];
      }
      return fn;
    }
}],
many : ['label', 'sound', 'title', 'role', 'key', 'mailer',
  'rev', 'nickname', 'category', 'note', 'tel', {
    'url' : 'url', 'logo' : 'url', 'photo' : 'url',
        'email' : 'url' }, {
    'adr' : {
      one : ['post-office-box', 'extended-address',
          'street-address', 'locality', 'region', 'postal-code',
          'country-name']
},
    // implied org
    'org' : function(node) {
      var org = this._extractData(node, {
        one : ['organization-name'],
        many : ['organization-unit']
      });

      if (!org.organizationName) {
        org.organizationName = this._extractData(node, 'simple');
        return org;
      }
```

```
    }
  }]
});
```

Without going into too much detail on the specifics of these exceptions, you can see that wherever some custom processing needs to be done, we can specify a custom function right inside the definition. So when the parser spots a function in the definition, it will execute the function, passing the node and other arguments to it rather than just reading the value from the node as it would normally. The ability to break out into regular JavaScript when required makes these specifications living programs that are capable of accommodating any exceptions, while still retaining an elegant simplicity in all other cases.

Bear this technique in mind as you create similar scripts. If you accept some static data as an argument, for example, would it be useful to also accept a function for that argument, so that you can perform custom processing?

Here's the snippet of code from Sumo that achieves this aim:

microformat.js (excerpt)

```javascript
_extractData = function(node, dataType, data) {
  // Check if the data type provided is actually a function.
  // If it is then call that function.
  if (typeof dataType == 'function')
    return dataType.call(this, node, data);
  // otherwise just extract the value from the document normally
  var values = Microformat.$$('value', node);
  if (values.length > 0)
    return this._extractClassValues(node, values);
  switch (dataType) {
    case 'simple': return this._extractSimple(node);
    case 'url': return this._extractURL(node);
  }
  return this._parse(dataType, node);
}
```

If you'd like to examine the full source code, it's available online.[16]

Summary

Hopefully, you should now have a good overview of the hows and whys of metaprogramming, and a solid understanding of what it takes to write code using these techniques.

---

[16] http://svn.danwebb.net/external/microformat/microformat.js

In mastering some of the techniques we've discussed in these pages, you'll not only end up writing cleaner, more flexible, and more optimized code, but you'll hopefully have learned some important facts about the deeper workings of the Web's most widely deployed—and underrated—language. At least you'll have no reason to brand it as "dumb" anymore!

Building a 3D Maze with CSS and JavaScript

In this chapter we'll look at a technique for using CSS and JavaScript to build a first-person-perspective maze, in homage to old-school adventure games like Dungeon Master[1] and Doom.[2]

In truth, the scripting involved is fairly complex, and it won't be possible for me to spell out every nuance of the code in this single chapter. In fact, I won't even list every method used in the script, as some of them are quite long. What I can do, though, is introduce you to the principles of creating shapes and perspective with CSS, and the task of using JavaScript to generate those shapes on demand to create a dynamic, three-dimensional perspective from a static, two-dimensional map.

The script, and all of its components, are included in the book's code archive. All the code is robustly commented, so you should find it easy to follow. I recommend that you have it available to view as you read, so that you can refer to it as we go along.

Before we dive into a discussion of how it's built, let's take a look at the final result—it's shown in Figure 6.1.

---

[1] http://en.wikipedia.org/wiki/Dungeon_Master_(computer_game)
[2] http://en.wikipedia.org/wiki/Doom

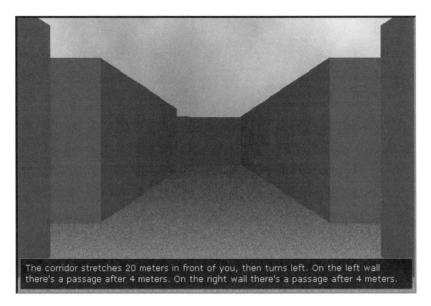

Figure 6.1. A view inside the finished maze

That screenshot was taken with Opera, in which this script was originally developed, and it also works as intended in Firefox, Safari, and Internet Explorer 7. IE 6, however, is not fully supported: the game works, but it looks poor because IE 6 doesn't have all the CSS support we need (most notably, it lacks support for transparent borders).

I should also point out, in case it crosses your mind, that what we're doing here has no practical use. In fact, it could be argued that we're not really using the right technology for the job. I made this maze because I wanted to see if it was possible—to push the envelope a little in terms of what can be done with JavaScript and CSS. But we're right at the edge of what's reasonable, and maybe Flash or SVG would be better suited to building a game like this.

But hey—why climb a mountain? Because it's there!

Basic Principles

In 2001, Tantek Çelik published a technique for creating shapes using the interactions between CSS borders.[3] We're going to use that technique to make a bunch of right-angle triangles.

Why triangles, I hear you ask? Well, because once you can render a triangle, you can render any polygon that you like. By combining triangles with the rectangles that we've always been able to render (using a good old `div` and the `background-color` property), we can create the walls of our maze and contribute to the sense of perspective. As you'll see, we'll draw these walls by slicing the player's view up into a number of columns.

---

[3] http://tantek.com/CSS/Examples/polygons.html

We'll also need a floor plan for our maze, and a handful of methods for dynamically converting that floor plan into the polygons that represent the walls of our maze.

Making Triangles

If an element has a very thick border (say 50px), and adjacent borders have different colors, the intersection of those borders creates a diagonal line, as Figure 6.2 illustrates.

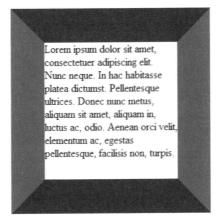

Figure 6.2. Making diagonal lines from CSS borders

That example is simply a `div` element to which the following CSS rules are applied:

```
width: 200px;
height: 200px;
border: 50px solid #900;
border-color: #009 #900;
```

To render a triangle, we don't actually need the contents of that `div`—we only need its borders. So let's remove the text, and reduce the `width` and `height` values to zero. What we're left with is the image shown in Figure 6.3.

Figure 6.3. Making triangles from CSS borders

Here's the CSS that achieves that effect:

```
width: 0;
border: 50px solid #900;
border-color: #009 #900;
```

If we were to vary the relative border widths (applying, say, 50px on the left border and 25px on the top), we could create triangles with various angles. By setting the color of one of the borders to `transparent`, the diagonal line from the solid border stands alone, as Figure 6.4 reveals.

Figure 6.4. Creating diagonal lines using transparent adjacent borders

Now, if we wrap a second `div` element around the first, we'll be able to extract a single, discreet triangle. We can achieve this by:

1. applying `position: relative` to the outer container
2. applying `position: absolute` to the inner element
3. clipping the inner element

Clipped elements are required to have absolute positioning,[4] so the relative positioning on the container provides a positioning context for the inner element, as Figure 6.5 shows.

Figure 6.5. Extracting a single triangle using CSS `clip`

The code that produces Figure 6.5 is still very simple. Here's the HTML:

```
<div id="triangle">
<div></div>
</div>
```

And here's the CSS:

```
#triangle
{
  border: 2px solid #999;
  position: relative;
  width: 50px;
  height: 25px;
}
#triangle > div
{
  border-style: solid;
  border-color: transparent #900;
  border-width: 25px 50px;
  position: absolute;
  left: 0;
```

---

[4] http://www.w3.org/TR/CSS21/visufx.html#propdef-clip

```
  top: 0;
  clip: rect(0, 50px, 25px 0);
}
```

Clipping and positioning is the crux of our ability to create discreet shapes using CSS. If we removed the `clip`, we'd get the result shown in Figure 6.6.

Figure 6.6. The unclipped element hangs outside its parent

You can see that by varying the `clip` and `position` properties on the inner element, we control which part of it is shown, and hence which of the triangles will be visible. If we wanted the bottom-right triangle, we would apply these values:

```
left: -50px;
top: -25px;
clip: rect(25px, 100px, 50px, 50px);
```

And we'd get the result depicted in Figure 6.7.

Figure 6.7. Extracting a different triangle

Defining the Floor Plan

The essence of our maze script lies in our ability to create a three-dimensional perspective from a two-dimensional map. But before we can make sense of how the perspective works, we must look at the map—or, as I'll refer to it from now on, the **floor plan**.

The floor plan is a matrix that defines a grid with rows and columns. Each square in the floor plan contains a four-digit value that describes the space *around that square*—whether it has a wall or floor on each of its four sides. As we'll see in a moment, we'll use a 1 or a 0 for each of the four digits.

Understanding `clip`

`clip` totally confuses me—every time I use it, I have to think about how it works all over again. To help jog your memory, Figure 6.8 illustrates what the values in that clipping rectangle mean.

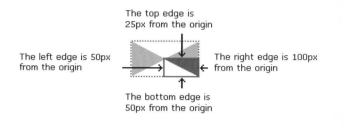

Figure 6.8. How CSS `clip` works

The main element in this example (indicated by the dotted line) is 100px wide and 50px high. The four values in the clipping rectangle are (in order): top offset, right offset, bottom offset, and left offset. Each of these values defines the offset of that edge from the main element's origin (its top-left corner).

These values are specified in the same order (top, right, bottom, left) as they are for other CSS properties, such as `border`, `padding`, and `margin`. Thinking of the word *trouble* (TRBL) should help you remember the correct order.

Figure 6.9 shows how each of these squares is constructed.

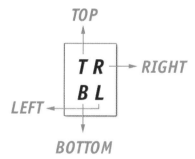

Figure 6.9. A single square describes the space around that square

Figure 6.10 shows a simple floor plan that uses four of these squares.

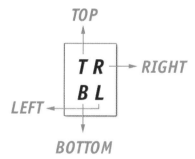

Figure 6.10. A simple floor plan example

In Figure 6.10:

- A dark gray block represents a square of solid wall.
- The borders at the edge of the diagram also represent solid wall.
- A light gray block represents a square of open floor.

For each square in the diagram:

- The digit 0 means "there's solid wall in this direction." Think of the number 0 as being shaped like a big brick, which means "Nope, you can't walk here."
- The digit 1 means "there's open floor space in this direction." Think of the number 1, being a positive value, as "Yes, you may walk on this square."
- Each of the four digits in a square represents a direction when the floor plan is viewed from above. The numbers should be read left-to-right, top-to-bottom, and they should appear in the same clockwise order as CSS values: top, right, bottom, left (or, when considered from the point of view of someone within the maze: forward, right, backwards, left).

A square like the one in the top-right of Figure 6.10 therefore represents the following information:

- The four-digit number represented is 0010.
- There are solid walls above, to the right, and to the left of the square.
- There is open floor space below the square.

As you can see, the concept is rather similar to the classic Windows game, Minesweeper!

The floor plan in Figure 6.10 would be represented in JavaScript by the following matrix:

```
this.floorplan = [['0110','0010'], ['0100','1001']];
```

Note that these values are strings, not numbers; with numbers, leading zeros are not preserved, but in this case those leading zeros are an important part of the data.

So far, we've only seen very small examples of floor plan data. To make our maze really useful, we'll want something much larger—the floor plan included in the code archive is 20 by 40 squares, and even that is comparatively small.

Just for kicks, Figure 6.11 shows what that floor plan looks like—you can refer to this plan if you get lost wandering around! As before, the light squares represent floor space and the dark squares depict solid wall, while the red cross-marks show positions where the person navigating our maze (from here on referred to as the **player**) can stand.

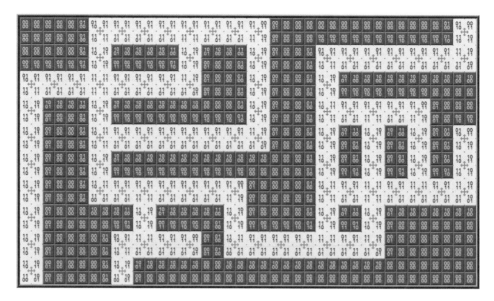

Figure 6.11. A complete maze floor plan

I don't expect you to be able to read those numbers! But later on, when we talk about the floor plan designer that goes with the game, you can look at this plan in its original context. The floor plan designer is also included in the code archive.

There are Many Ways to Skin a Cat!

There are, of course, numerous ways to approach a problem like this, each with its own pros and cons. For example, instead of binary digits, we could have used letters like WFFW to indicate wall and floor space. We could have made use of nested arrays, like [[0,1,1,0],[0,0,1,0]]. We could even have represented each square using only a single digit, which would certainly have made creating and modifying a floor plan easier.

The reason I chose to use four digits is because, this way, each square is able to represent *what's around it*, rather than *what the square itself is*. If we had a floor plan that used single digits, and we wanted to represent the view from the middle square, we'd need not only that square's data, but also the data from the four squares that surrounded it.

With the approach I've taken, we only need the data from the middle square to know what those surrounding squares are. Granted, we end up with some duplicate data in our floor plan. However, in terms of pure computational efficiency, the two are equivalent, and using four digits makes more sense to me as each square is much more self-contained.

Creating Perspective

Now that we understand how the floor plan works, and we've seen how to make triangles, we have all the data—and the building blocks—we need to create a 3D view.

Take a look at Figure 6.12. What this diagram shows is a breakdown of all of the elements that create the illusion of perspective in our maze. The walls on each side of the long hallway are composed of 16 columns. Each of the columns contains four inner elements which, for the rest of this chapter, we'll refer to as **bricks**. I've labeled the bricks, and highlighted them in a different color so that they're easier to distinguish. In each column, the **top brick** is highlighted as a gray rectangle; the **upper brick** is a rectangle comprising a red and blue triangle, as is the **lower brick**; and the **middle brick** is a green rectangle.

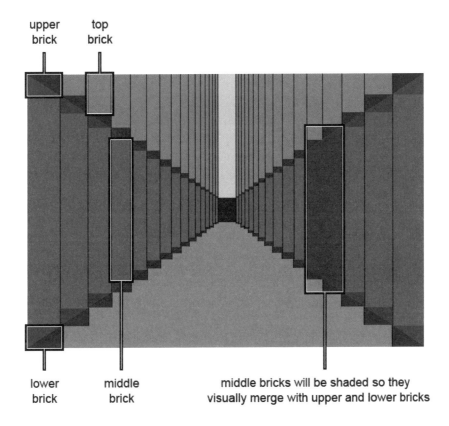

Figure 6.12. Combining the building blocks to create perspective

The upper and lower bricks are implementations of the triangles we saw earlier, clipped differently for each of the four orientations we need, thus creating diagonal lines in four directions. The red parts of these bricks will always be visible, whereas the blue parts are only blue for demonstration purposes—in practice, they'll be transparent. The top bricks will also be transparent, to expose a sky-patterned background.[5] The middle bricks will be shaded the same dark red color as the triangles in the upper and lower bricks, so that the bricks merge together and create the appearance of part of a wall.

---

[5] It isn't strictly necessary to use top bricks—we could have applied a top margin to the upper bricks—however, it was easier for me to visualize this way.

This Is Not a True Perspective!

What we're dealing with here is not actually a true perspective—it's skewed slightly so that the vanishing point is a short vertical line, rather than a point.

I originally created this maze using a true perspective with a single vanishing point, but it just didn't look right. The ceiling appeared too low relative to the distance between the walls (or the walls were too far apart, depending on how you looked at it). Changing the aspect ratio (that is, making the viewport square instead of the widescreen ratio that it has) would have made a difference, but I didn't want to do that—I wanted the game to look more cinematic!

The view is also limited as the columns get smaller, rather than stretching all the way to the vanishing point, because the resolution that we can achieve at such a distance is limited. The view ends at the point where we no longer have enough pixels to draw effectively, which restricts the maximum length of corridor we can represent. We'll talk about this issue again, along with the other limitations of this approach, towards the end of the chapter.

If you look carefully, you'll see in Figure 6.12 that each of the triangles has the same angle—it's just the size of the brick itself that's progressively reducing. This makes the illusion of perspective nice and easy to create, as we don't have any complex math to worry about. Still, it's not something that we'd want to code by hand. Let's use JavaScript to calculate the size of each brick, so that it can be generated on the fly …

Making a Dynamic View

One of the beautiful things about using a programming language to generate complex visual patterns is that it's not necessary for us to work out every line and angle manually—we only need to worry about the math that represents the pattern.

There are times when I really wish I'd paid more attention in school math classes. But computer games were in their infancy then, and none of my teachers knew much, if anything, about them. So when I asked in class, "What use is any of this?", they didn't have a good answer!

It's just as well, then, that the math involved here is not complicated—we don't even need trigonometry, because the angles have already been determined for us. All we need to calculate is the size of the bricks and the clipping regions that are used to create our triangles; the browser's rendering engine will do the rest.

Core Methods

Let's take a look at the scripting now. We'll start with the main script, **underground.js**, which is located in the **scripts** folder of the code archive. The entire script would be too large to list in its entirety in this book; instead I've just listed the signature of each method to give you a high-level appreciation for what's going on:

```javascript
// DungeonView object constructor
function DungeonView(floorplan, start, lang, viewcallback)
{ … };

// Create the dungeon view.
DungeonView.prototype.createDungeonView = function()
{ … };

// Reset the dungeon view by applying all of the necessary
// default style properties.
DungeonView.prototype.resetDungeonView = function()
{ … };

// Apply a floorplan view to the dungeon
// from a given x,y coordinate and view direction.
DungeonView.prototype.applyDungeonView = function(x, y, dir)
{ … };

// Create the map view.
DungeonView.prototype.createMapView = function()
{ … };

// Reset the map view.
DungeonView.prototype.resetMapView = function()
{ … };

// Apply a position to the map view.
DungeonView.prototype.applyMapView = function()
{ … };

// Clear the view caption.
DungeonView.prototype.clearViewCaption = function()
{ … };

// Generate the caption for a view.
DungeonView.prototype.generateViewCaption = function(end)
{ … };

// Shift the characters in a string by n characters to the left,
// carrying over residual characters to the end,
// so shiftCharacters('test', 2) becomes 'stte'
DungeonView.prototype.shiftCharacters = function(str, shift)
{ … };

// Bind events to the controller form.
DungeonView.prototype.bindControllerEvents = function()
{ … };
```

Rather than examine every method here, I'll explain the three core methods that do most of the work for our script, and leave you to fill in the gaps by following the code from the code archive yourself. Throughout this section I'll use the word **view** to mean "a 3D representation of a position on the floor plan" (that is, the player's point of view, looking north, east, south, or west).

The `createDungeonView` Method

The `createDungeonView` method takes an empty container, populates it with all the elements we need (the columns are `div`s, and the bricks are nested `span`s), and saves a matrix of references to those elements for later use:

underground.js *(excerpt)*

```
// Create the dungeon view.
DungeonView.prototype.createDungeonView = function()
{
  var strip = this.tools.createElement('div',
              { 'class' : 'column C' }
           );
  this.grid['C'] = this.dungeon.appendChild(strip);

  for(var k=0; k<2; k++)
  {
    // the column classid direction token is "L" or "R"
    var classid = k == 0 ? 'L' : 'R';
    for(var i=0; i<this.config.gridsize[0]; i++)
    {
      var div = this.tools.createElement('div',
          { 'class' : 'column ' + classid + ' ' + classid + i }
      );
      this.grid[classid + i] = {
          'column' : this.dungeon.appendChild(div)
      };
      for(var j=0; j<this.config.gridsize[1]; j++)
      {
        // create the main span
        var span = this.tools.createElement('span',
            { 'class' : 'brick ' + this.bricknames[j] }
        );
        if (j == 1 || j == 3)
        {
          var innerspan =
              span.appendChild(this.tools.createElement('span'));
        }
        this.grid[classid + i][this.bricknames[j]] =
            div.appendChild(span);
      }
    }
  }
```

```
  }
  this.resetDungeonView();
};
```

As you can see if you scroll through the code, there isn't much more to this method: its sole responsibility is to create a group of elements, and assign `class` names to each of them so that they can be distinguished from one another. The values I've used are reasonably intuitive—`upper` identifies an upper brick, for example.

I've made use of CSS `floats` in order to line the columns up (left `floats` for a column on the left wall, and right `floats` for one on the right). To create the columns, we iterate on each side from the edge inwards (in other words, the left-most column is the first of the columns that comprise the left wall, and the right-most column is the first for the right wall).

The `resetDungeonView` Method

The `resetDungeonView` method applies style properties (`size`, `position`, `clip`, `background`, and `border-color`) to the elements that form the most basic view—that shown when our user is looking straight down a corridor that stretches the maximum distance that our script can support, as depicted in Figure 6.13.

Figure 6.13. The `resetDungeonView` method rendering a basic view, without floor plan data

This method can be called whenever we need to reset the view, which we'll do at initialization, and again before applying each new view. It works by iterating through the matrix of element references we created in `createDungeonView`; it calculates the width of each column and the height of each of the bricks inside it.

To perform this calculation, we need to define some structural constants. These constants can be found in the configuration script, **config.js**, which is also in the code archive's **scripts** directory:

config.js (excerpt)

```
this.viewsize = [600, 400]; ❶
this.gridsize = [16, 4]; ❷
this.bricksize = [50, 31]; ❸
this.multiplier = 0.84; ❹
```

These constants represent the following values:

❶ The `viewsize` represents the total width and height of the view container.

❷ The `gridsize` represents the number of columns from the edge of the `viewsize` to the center, and the number of bricks from top to bottom.

❸ The `bricksize` is the size of the upper and lower (triangle-creating) bricks.

❹ Finally, the `multiplier` controls the factor by which the brick size is reduced for each column as we move towards the center of the view.

Figure 6.14 shows the same perspective diagram that we saw in Figure 6.13, this time with captions indicating how each of these structural constants applies.

 Working Out the Values

I'd love to say I had a clever mathematical algorithm for calculating the values I've used here (and there probably is one), but I can't. I just used trial and error until I arrived at something that looked about right. Note, however, that the values are *very closely* interrelated, so be extremely careful when adjusting them!

The choice of correct values is also dependent upon the overall performance of the script—it would be possible to create a higher resolution maze with a larger number of smaller bricks. However, that would mean we had more objects to render, which would result in lower overall performance. Even with the default values that I've set above, you need a fairly decent computer to render this maze effectively.

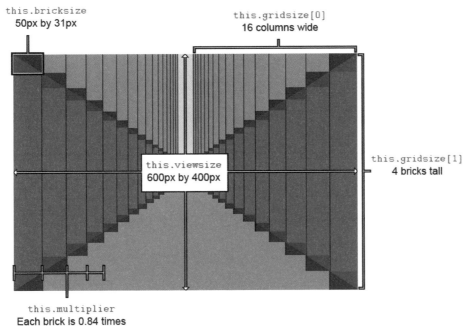

Figure 6.14. Structural constants defining the maze's perspective

If you have a look at Figure 6.14 again, you'll notice that the bricks line up perfectly—in each column, the upper brick is exactly below and to the side of the upper brick in the previous column; likewise, each lower brick lines up below and to the side of its neighbor. The clip and position values of the inner elements of those bricks decrease proportionally as the brick size decreases, while the height of the top and middle bricks changes as necessary to complete the wall.

Finally, in order to improve the appearance of perspective, we want each column to be slightly darker than the previous one. To achieve that goal, I've introduced constants that define the base color of our bricks and the darkening proportion that's applied to them. We'll define the wallcolor using RGB values—they're easier to work with, as the values are decimal rather than hexadecimal. We'll name the constant that controls the darkness of each column the darkener. Both of these constants are defined in the **config.js** file:

```
this.wallcolor = [127, 0, 0];
this.darkener = 0.95;
```

On each iteration of our code, we render a single column on each side, moving towards the center of the view; the base color is darkened by the amount specified in the darkener constant. I chose a dark red for the main demo (dark colors generally work best), but as Figure 6.15 shows, you can use any color you like—even pink!

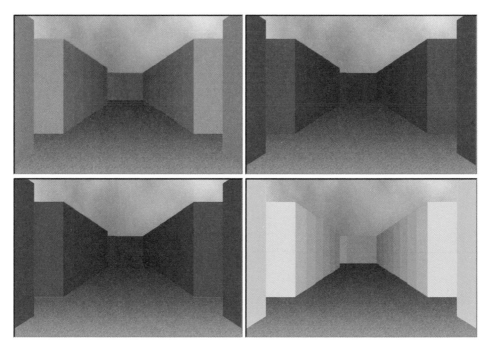

Figure 6.15. Rendering the walls of the maze with different base colors

The `applyDungeonView` Method

The `applyDungeonView` method applies style variations to the basic view, creating passageways off to either side of our main passage. To do this, it first compiles a matrix, stored in the variable `this.squares`, which is a subset of the complete floor plan. This matrix consists of only those floor plan squares that are necessary for us to render the player's view from the current location in the maze.

Figure 6.16 shows an excerpt of a floor plan. The green square highlights the spot where the player is currently standing, while the blue border surrounds what the player can see. It's the region inside this blue border that defines the part of the plan required to draw the view for the player.

In this example we're looking north, and each of the floor squares provides us with information about the surrounding squares. However, for any direction of movement, the player is always looking "forwards," and it's the player's view that we render. So the first thing we must do is translate the data contained within each square into data that's accurate for the direction in which the player is facing. Let me explain this with an example …

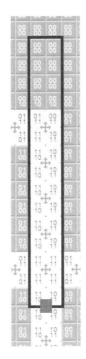

Figure 6.16. An extract from a floor plan showing the data for a single view

Remember that the digits in a square indicate the presence of wall or floor surrounding that square, in clockwise order, starting from the top. Well, we want those four digits always to indicate that information clockwise from the top, regardless of the direction in which the player is actually facing. Should we have the value 1110 when facing north, then, when the player was facing east, that same square would be represented by the value 1101. When the player faced south, the value would be 1011, as shown in Figure 6.17.

Figure 6.17. The floor plan data varying when the player looks in different directions

So, as we compile the `this.squares` matrix, we need to translate each square's value to the direction in which the player is facing. A small utility method named `shiftCharacters` performs this translation: `str` is the four-digit string, and `shift` is the number of times the square must be rotated in a counterclockwise manner when the player turns in a clockwise direction. Each turn corresponds to each of the four digits that represent that square moving to the left by one position (with the leftmost digit jumping to the end of the string).

To continue with the example in Figure 6.17, if the player's view was to change from north (with floor plan data of 1110) to west (0111), the `shift` value would be 3.

The `shiftCharacters` method looks like this:

underground.js *(excerpt)*

```
DungeonView.prototype.shiftCharacters = function(str, shift)
{
  var saved = str.substr(0, shift);
  str = str.substring(shift);
  str += saved;
  return str;
};
```

Once we have the data we need, we can iterate through it and create the actual view. This is where things get rather tricky.

First of all, we need to iterate forwards through the squares, starting from the player's current location. With each iteration, we test the first digit of each square (which tells us what's in front of it) until we find the end wall. The end wall marks the limit of what the player can see—every column from that point onwards should be assigned the same height and color. These columns will create the illusion of a facing wall, as shown in Figure 6.18.

Figure 6.18. Columns combining to form a facing wall

Once we know the limit of the player's view, we iterate from that point *backwards* through the floor plan data towards the player's location, looking for adjoining passageways. We need to iterate backwards because the height of a passageway's facing wall is the height of the furthest column that defines it.

To illustrate, Figure 6.19 shows another excerpt from the perspective diagram, this time with lines and shading overlaid to show a corridor with a passageway off to the left.

Figure 6.19. Constructing perspective to create a passageway off to the left

If we want those second and third columns to create that passage to the left, we need to remove the upper and lower bricks from those columns, leaving only the middle bricks, which then must be resized as necessary. But our passage is two columns across, and it's the furthest column (or what we might call the **corner column**) that determines the height of the wall—not the nearest. So we need to modify that corner column first, so that we know how tall to make the adjacent columns.

Iterating forwards would require us to jump two steps ahead to find the corner, then move one square back to make a further adjustment. And that's why we iterate backwards, rather than forwards. (I told you it was tricky!)

When we create those passageways, we also lighten the facing walls slightly, to improve the visual appearance and make the wall look more realistic. As we did when we darkened the walls, we use a single constant value (I've called it the `lightener`) to determine the amount of lightening required:

```
this.lightener = 1.25;
```

As with the height value, the lightening is applied to the corner column first, then copied onto the nearer column (for the same reasons). And once again, as with all of the constants used in this script, I have no magic formula to share for how these values were obtained—they're just what looked right after trial and error.

Figure 6.20 shows the same view excerpt again—this time without the exposed construction—looking as it does in the final game.

Figure 6.20. A passageway off to the left

Applying the Finishing Touches

Now, I hope, you should have a fairly concrete sense of how the script generates perspective views, with walls and passages created as necessary. From the diagrams we've seen so far, you can understand that any given view is simply a combination of rectangles and triangles.

One final touch we'll need to make is to shift the entire view up inside the container in order to raise the horizon slightly. This is just another visual tweak that I included because I think it produces a better-looking and more realistic result, as Figure 6.21 shows.

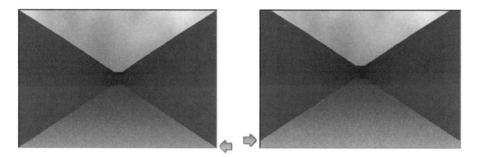

Figure 6.21. Adding a slight horizon shift to the overall view

You'll notice I've used images for the sky and floor patterns. These images provide some texture to add to the realism of my maze; they also contain a slight gradient, growing darker as they approach the horizon, which again reinforces the sense of perspective.

The end result is not perfect, though: unavoidable rounding errors occur in the final output figures, and these errors give rise to an occasional discrepancy of one or two pixels between adjacent columns. The shading computation is not exact either—sometimes, on close walls, you can see a slight color difference between two columns that should be exactly the same.

All things considered, however, what we've created here is a reasonably convincing 3D maze.

Limitations of This Approach

The approach we've taken to build this maze imposes some limitations on the design of a maze floor plan, thus restricting the kind of layout we can draw:

- Corridors must always be two squares wide—we can't create wider spaces because we don't have the pieces with which to draw them.

- No single corridor can be longer than 16 squares, as this is the maximum number of pairs of columns that we can draw.

- Walls must also consist of an even number of squares—every block must comprise a block of at least two squares by two squares.

It may help to think of four squares on the floor plan as one single square; those smaller squares only exist so that we have more elements to apply progressive shading to, and hence achieve a better-looking and more realistic 3D view.

Creating the Map View

To the right of the maze view, we'll add a map that shows the floor plan in the player's immediate location. I originally added this feature to display a top-down view of the same view that the player can actually see … but then I realized—what's the point of such a map, if it provides no extra advantage?

Instead, we'll add a map that shows a little more of the surrounding area, as an aid to orientation. In the view shown in Figure 6.22, you can see that the player can only move a short distance forwards before reaching a wall, but the map to the right shows further corridors beyond that wall.

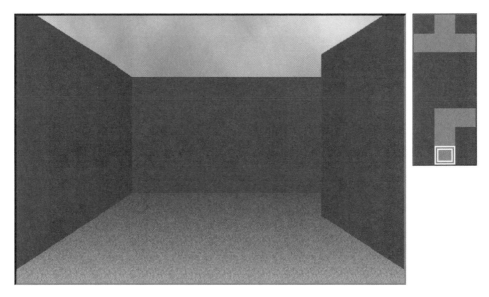

Figure 6.22. Showing extra information in the player's map

The construction of the map itself is very simple—it's just a bunch of `spans` floated in a container. I've applied a solid background where there's wall, and transparency where there's floor. This allows the green background of the container to show through, as Figure 6.23 reveals.

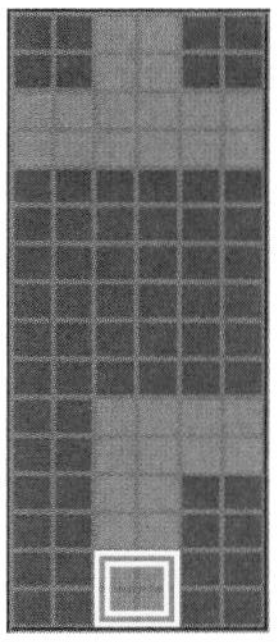

Figure 6.23. How the player's map is constructed

Generating the map is equally simple, since it's just a two-dimensional representation of data that is itself a 2D matrix.

Remember that when we generated the maze view, we created a matrix called `this.squares`. This matrix contained as much of the floor plan as was required to generate the current view, with the data transposed so that it represented a forwards view for the player. Well, we can use that same data matrix to generate this 2D map.

To create the map, we begin by coloring every square (using the base `wallcolor` property). Then we iterate through the matrix of squares, and apply transparency to every square in the map that represents open floor space—including the space directly beneath the spot where the player is standing. The `applyMapView` method in the file **underground.js** takes care of this for us:

```javascript
DungeonView.prototype.applyMapView = function()
{
  this.resetMapView();
  for(var i=0; i<this.squares.L.length; i++)
  {
    var n = this.mapsquares.length - 2 - i;
    if(this.mapsquares[n])
    {
      if(this.squares.L[i].charAt(3) == '1')
      {
        this.mapsquares[n][0].style.background = 'transparent';
        this.mapsquares[n][1].style.background = 'transparent';
        if(i == 0)
        {
          this.mapsquares[n+1][0].style.background = 'transparent';
          this.mapsquares[n+1][1].style.background = 'transparent';
        }
      }

      if(this.squares.R[i].charAt(1) == '1')
      {
        this.mapsquares[n][4].style.background = 'transparent';
        this.mapsquares[n][5].style.background = 'transparent';
        if(i == 0)
        {
          this.mapsquares[n+1][4].style.background = 'transparent';
          this.mapsquares[n+1][5].style.background = 'transparent';
        }
      }

      if(this.squares.L[i].charAt(1) == '1')
      {
        this.mapsquares[n][2].style.background = 'transparent';
        this.mapsquares[n][3].style.background = 'transparent';
        if(i == 0)
        {
          this.mapsquares[n+1][2].style.background = 'transparent';
          this.mapsquares[n+1][3].style.background = 'transparent';
        }
      }
    }
  }
};
```

Adding Captions

One of the things that excites me most about web programming is its potential for improving accessibility. Although we're making a visual game here, we have data in a format that can easily be translated into other kinds of output, such as plain text. We can use the same information that we used for making the map to generate a live text description of each maze view, of the kind shown in Figure 6.24.

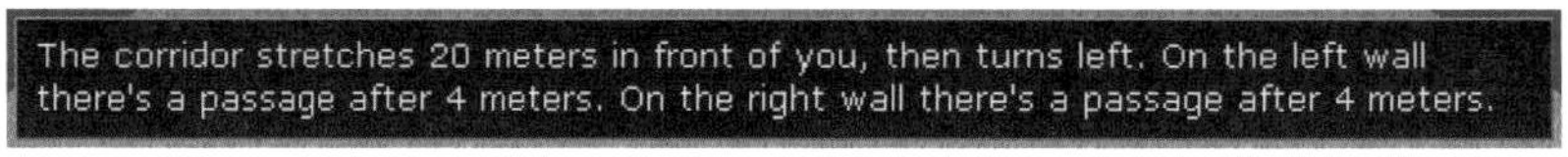

The corridor stretches 20 meters in front of you, then turns left. On the left wall there's a passage after 4 meters. On the right wall there's a passage after 4 meters.

Figure 6.24. A generated caption that describes a maze view

Not only does captioning potentially aid comprehension for players who have a cognitive or visual disability, it also extends the basic game play to people who are completely blind—suddenly we can navigate around the maze without any visuals at all! Admittedly, and unfortunately, the game will be much harder to play like this—not just because you have to hold orientation information in your head, but because you don't have the map to refer to in order to gain clues about what's behind the next wall.

Still, it's a start. Try viewing the game with CSS disabled, and you'll get a basic sense of the experience of what it would be like to play the game if you were blind. I've also confirmed that the game is playable in the JAWS 8 screen reader.

Generating the core data for the captions is straightforward—we simply need to know how many passageways there are to the left and right, and how far away they are. We can work this out by:

- iterating once again through the `this.squares` matrix
- building arrays to store the index of each opening

These openings will be converted to a perceived distance. As we navigate our maze, one square looks to be roughly two meters in length, so we'll adopt this as the scale for our map. We can stop iterating once we reach the end of the player's view—we've created an `end` variable in the `applyDungeonView` method, which is the index of `this.squares` at the point that the view ends. Therefore, we can simply pass this value to the `generateViewCaption` method when we call it.

In the code, I've used `len` to represent the total length of the corridor in front, and arrays called `passages.left` and `passages.right` to store the distance of each passage from the player. The result of our iterations might produce data like this:

```
var len = 16;
var passages = {
  'left' : [8, 16],
  'right' : [4]
};
```

This looks simple enough to interpret, right? Well, yes … however, turning this data structure into coherent English is still a little tricky. The *basic* conversion is easy. Using the data we have, we can describe the view in coarse terms:

"The corridor stretches 16 meters in front of you. To the left there are passages after 8 meters and 16 meters. To the right there are passages after 4 meters."

However, this language is fairly obtuse. For one thing, we wouldn't want to say "there are passages" if there was only one. Instead, we'd want to say "there's a passage." Additionally, the last passage to the left is at the far end, so it would be nicer to describe that by saying "The corridor stretches 16 meters in front of you, then turns left."

We also need to deal with exceptions. For example, if the player is standing directly in front of a wall, we don't want to say "… stretches 0 meters in front …" Likewise, if the player has just turned right into a passage, we don't want to say "to the right there's a passage after 0 meters."

To cater for all these exceptions, the script accepts a dictionary of sentence fragments with replacement tokens, which are then compiled and parsed as necessary, in order to obtain a result that approaches decent prose. If you have a look in **init.js**, you'll notice that the DungeonView object is instantiated with this data as an argument. Each of the language properties is a sentence fragment with replacement tokens; for example, %dir is a direction token that will be replaced with the word for "left" or "right," as applicable.

I'd encourage you now to scroll through the generateViewCaption method in **underground.js**, and read the comments there that explain each situation. As it is, there's still room for improvement, but this is one of those things that you could refine to the nth degree, and it would still never be perfect.[6] That said, I believe that the end result is fairly good—the captions are verbose enough to get the information across, they're succinct enough not to be arduous to read, and they flow well enough that they don't sound too much like they were generated by a machine (even though they were!).

Designing a Floor Plan

In the code archive for this book, you'll find a **floor plan designer**, which is a separate JavaScript application that generates the floorplan matrix used by this game. It's a table of squares, and you

---

[6] Read more about the problems associated with constructing natural-sounding sentences in English in the Wikipedia entry on natural language processing at http://en.wikipedia.org/wiki/Natural_language_processing/.

can click a square to toggle it between floor and wall. The script will work out the numbers for each square that relate to that view, using the TRBL syntax I introduced earlier in the chapter to denote whether a square has wall or floor on each of its four sides.

Hovering over a square in the floor plan designer will also display a tooltip containing the x,y position of that square in the grid. This information is useful for defining a start position (the first two values of the `start` array in **init.js**).

To use the floor plan designer, first create your plan by clicking on the squares. When you're happy with your maze, click the **Generate output matrix** button and a `floorplan` matrix will be generated for you. You can then copy and paste this data directly into your **init.js** file—the next time you run the maze application, your new floor plan data will be passed to the script.

Alternatively, you can begin your floor plan editing session by pasting existing floor plan data into the `textarea` field. Click **Display input matrix**, and the floor plan designer will display the map representation of the data that you pasted into the field, which you can then edit further as required. Try pasting in the original `floorplan` matrix from **init.js**, and you'll see the plan that I showed you near the start of this chapter, in all its glory!

Simple as it is, without this tool, making the maze floor plan would be a very painful process! In fact, I created this tool before I wrote the main script.

Further Developments

Before we close this chapter, I'd like to take a couple of moments to discuss some general possibilities for further development of the maze. More specifically, we'll look at the **callback** facility that's available for hooking additional code into each view change.

Using the Callback

Have a look in **init.js** and you'll notice that, in addition to the floor plan, start position, and language parameters, there's an optional fourth argument specifying a `viewchange` callback function. This function will be called every time a new view is drawn, and can be used to add logic to the game.

The `viewchange` function referred to in this example can be found in the script called **demogame.js**, which is located in the **addons** directory of the code archive. This script and its associated style sheet are both included in **underground.html**, at the very end of the `head` section (after the core style sheets and scripts).

As you'll see, the callback accepts the following arguments:

x   the current *x* position of the player

y   the current *y* position of the player

dir   the direction that the player is currently facing

inst   a reference to this instance of the `DungeonView` object

By defining conditions based on the first three arguments, you could add logic that applies only at specific locations in the maze. And because the callback function will always be called when the player begins navigating the maze at the start position, you could also use the callback function for initialization code. For example, a flag could be set to indicate that a location-specific action has occurred, so that it occurs only once.

The fourth argument, *inst*, is a reference to this instance of DungeonView, and can be used for tasks like adding a new element to the view (such as objects for the player to find), or modifying the configuration properties (in order to change the wall color in certain areas of the maze).

In the demo game example, I've made use of the callback function at one specific position in the floor plan—at this point in the maze you can see a simple object in front of you, and at another position you're standing directly above that object (that is, picking it up). That's all there is to the demo game—there's nothing ground-breaking—but at least it adds an end purpose to an otherwise aimless meander through the maze! It should also serve to illustrate the principle of extending the maze, and will hopefully inspire you to try something more ambitious and creative.

At sitepoint.com, you can find a more sophisticated example in which a hidden surprise is located within a larger maze, and your mission is to find it.[7]

Blue-sky Possibilities

It would be quite simple to use Ajax to relay a player's position to a server—other players could read that data, thus facilitating the creation of an online multiplayer environment. It should also be possible to implement a server-side program that generates floor plan data and sends it back to the game, effectively creating multiple "levels" in the maze. Taking this idea one step further, players could potentially receive and transmit floor plan data between themselves, thereby allowing individuals to host maze levels.

However, it would be quite tricky to represent other players in the view—we would need a graphic for every additional player, as well as versions of that graphic at each of eight different distances, facing in four directions. Short of generating the players as simple shapes, there's no pure-CSS way to create these graphics. They would have to be a collection of specially drawn images, and I don't have the artistry to design those characters!

But if you do, be my guest. If you had those images, adding them to the game would be most simply achieved with absolutely positioned overlays—placing the image so that its center is in the center of the maze. Then, for each view, it would be a case of working out which was the correct image to

---

[7] Visit http://maze.sitepoint.com/ to play this game.

show, based on the locations of that player relative to the main player. This might also be quite tricky, especially when you had three or more players sharing the same corridor, but I have no doubt that it's doable.

Who knows—maybe you could add combat too!

Summary

In this chapter, we took the languages of CSS and JavaScript well beyond the tasks for which they were intended—the presentation and basic behavior of HTML documents—and used them to create an interactive 3D maze.

First, we looked at the basic principles by which triangles can be displayed using only CSS. We then extended that concept to render a perspective view, creating the illusion of three dimensions. Next, we established a convention for specifying floor plan data, and for dynamically translating that data into a perspective view. By adding listeners for user events, we successfully created an interactive maze that can be completely customized and extended. To top things off, we added some usability aids, such as a top-down map, and accessibility aids including keyboard navigation and captions.

While I haven't delved into the details of every method that comprises the game script (there are plenty of comments, so I'll leave that for you to pursue in your own time), I hope this chapter has convinced you to look at JavaScript in a new light. The possibilities really are only limited by your imagination!

Chapter  7

Flickr and Google Maps Mashups

The API revolution started with two key sites: Flickr and Google Maps. In this chapter, we'll combine the two to create a handy widget that displays a Google Map of your recent Flickr photos—all without writing a single line of server-side code. Our finished widget will produce something like the display shown in Figure 7.1.

Figure 7.1. The final widget that combines data from Flickr and Google Maps

Along the way, we'll discuss mapping hacks, JavaScript optimization tricks, JSON data feeds, cross-browser event handling, and more.

APIs, Mashups, and Widgets! Oh, My!

Buzzwords are unavoidable in web development. The most useful are the ones like Ajax that introduce vocabulary for a concept that was previously difficult to discuss. The techniques around Ajax had existed for years before the term was coined, but it was only after it was given a name that the Ajax revolution kicked off and made JavaScript a hot skill again.

This chapter is fairly heavy on buzzwords. We're going to use APIs to build a mashup that can be embedded as a widget on our site. Before we get started, let's define what we actually mean by those terms.

- An **API (Application Programming Interface)** is a documented interface that allows third-party developers to access a product's functionality.
- **Mashups** are services that combine functionality from two or more distinct APIs.
- **Widgets** are self-contained mini-applications that can be embedded in a site.

Two APIs that were available early (and are therefore the most prominent) are those provided by Flickr and Google Maps.

Flickr and Google Maps

Flickr is a photo sharing service.[1] The site offered an API from a point very early in its life, based on the recognition that users should own not just their photos, but the data surrounding them, and that they should be free to do what they want with them. The API proved tremendously successful, as hundreds of applications emerged that made use of Flickr photos in some way; of course, many of these apps drove extra users and traffic to the Flickr site. One popular example is fd's Flickr Toys,[2] an impressive collection of fun tools and effects that can be applied to photos hosted on Flickr. Another is moo.com, a printing company that produces business cards from a user's Flickr photos.

The Google Maps API had slightly different origins. Google launched its drag-and-drop mapping service in February, 2005, to great critical acclaim. It didn't take long for smart programmers to reverse-engineer the application to find out how it worked, and developers quickly figured out ways of including a Google-powered map in their own applications. Two notable early examples of these unofficial mashups were housingmaps.com and chicagocrime.org.

 API Documentation

Flickr's full API documentation can be found at http://www.flickr.com/services/api/. The Google Maps reference is located at http://www.google.com/apis/maps/.

---

[1] http://flickr.com/
[2] http://bighugelabs.com/flickr/

This developer excitement didn't go unnoticed, and a few months later Google announced an official API for embedding its maps in third-party applications. Today, the Google Maps API powers over 1,000 mashups listed on programmableweb.com, making it the most popular API on the site. By comparison, over 250 external sites use the Flickr API, which comes second on that list.

In this chapter, we're going to combine these two APIs. We'll create a widget that pulls in our most recently geotagged photos from Flickr, and displays them on a Google Map. The widget will also include thumbnail-based navigation to let users quickly move around the map—and all without writing a single line of server-side code.

Drawing a Map

The first step in using the Google Maps API is to obtain a free API key. An API key is a string of characters that identifies your application; Google uses these keys to keep track of who's using the API, and for what purpose.

To obtain an API key, visit http://www.google.com/apis/maps/. You'll need a free Google account; if you already use another Google service, such as Gmail, you can use that account; otherwise, you'll need to create one. You'll also need to provide the URL that you intend to use for the page that contains the map; if you plan to develop locally, you can enter http://localhost/, but this means that you'll need to run a web server on your local machine.

Once you've obtained an API key, the "Hello world!" of Google Maps looks like this:

helloworld.html

```
<!DOCTYPE HTML PUBLIC "-//W3C//DTD HTML 4.01//EN"
    "http://www.w3.org/TR/html4/strict.dtd">
<html>
<head>
<title>Hello World!</title></head>
<script src="http://www.google.com/jsapi?key=[YOUR API KEY]"   ❶
  type="text/javascript">
</script>
<script type="text/javascript">
  google.load('maps', '2'); // Load version 2 of the Maps API   ❷

  function showMap() {
   var gmap = new google.maps.Map2(document.getElementById('gmap'));   ❸
   // Center on England, zoom level 5
   var uk = new google.maps.LatLng(53.6967, -3.2080);   ❹
   gmap.setCenter(uk, 5);
   // Show an info window attached to Brighton
   var brighton = new google.maps.LatLng(50.8268, -0.1394);   ❺
   gmap.openInfoWindow(brighton, document.createTextNode("Brighton"));
  }
  google.setOnLoadCallback(showMap);   ❻
```

```
</script>
</head>
<body>
  <div id="gmap" style="width: 500px; height: 300px"></div>
</body>
</html>
```

Remember to replace *[YOUR API KEY]* with the API key you obtained from the Google Maps site.

The above code example creates a 500×300 pixel map centered on the UK, and opens an **info window** (a box with an arrow) pointing at Brighton, as shown in Figure 7.2.

Figure 7.2. An info window pointing to Brighton

Let's go through this code line by line:

❶ This line includes Google's API loader script. This is a small piece of JavaScript that provides two functions: `google.load` and `google.setOnLoadCallback`. We begin proceedings by calling the first of these functions.

❷ The `google.load` function knows how to load additional components from Google's collection of JavaScript APIs. In this case, we're asking for version 2 of the `maps` component.

❸ Next, we define our `showMap` function, which includes the following line:

```
var gmap = new google.maps.Map2(document.getElementById('gmap'));
```

This code creates a new Google Map object, called `gmap`. The map is created using the `div` that has `gmap` as its ID. It will automatically pick up the width and height of that `div`; for brevity, we've set those values using inline styles in this example, but they could also be set using an external style sheet.

④ Next, we create a new `LatLng` object representing the center of the UK. The coordinates you'll use here can be found using an online tool like Get Lat Lon.[3] We call `setCenter` to set the center of the map to that point, at zoom level 5 (higher numbers zoom further in).

⑤ Next, we create another `LatLng` object representing the position of Brighton (my home town, on the south coast of England). We then open an info window at that point, passing in a brand new DOM text node that will be displayed within that window.

⑥ Finally, we use `google.setOnLoadCallback` to set the `showMap` function to run once the page has loaded. This is important: if `showMap` ran too early, it wouldn't be able to find the `gmap` `div`, and the page would fail to render.

We'll return to Google Maps later on, once we have some photos to display.

Geotagging Photos

Before we can show our photos on a map, we need to know where they were taken. The process of adding this information is called **geotagging**, and Flickr provides us with a number of different tools to assign a location to a photograph.

If your camera (or camera phone) is ridiculously fancy it might have GPS built in, in which case GPS locations would be embedded in the EXIF metadata associated with your images, and Flickr would pick up the location as soon as you uploaded them.

For those of us who aren't living in the satellite-enabled future, Flickr provides a more pedestrian but equally effective mechanism for assigning locations to our photos: we can drag them on to a map using Flickr Organizr. Sign in to Flickr and navigate to http://www.flickr.com/photos/organizr/, then click on the **Map** tab. The interface is illustrated in Figure 7.3.

With the Organizr, it's the work of moments to assign locations to a group of photos; just drag them from the bar at the bottom of the page on to the map. Behind the scenes, Flickr will associate latitude and longitude values with each photo. We'll use these latitude and longitude points later on to plot the images on our own map.

---

[3] http://www.getlatlon.com/

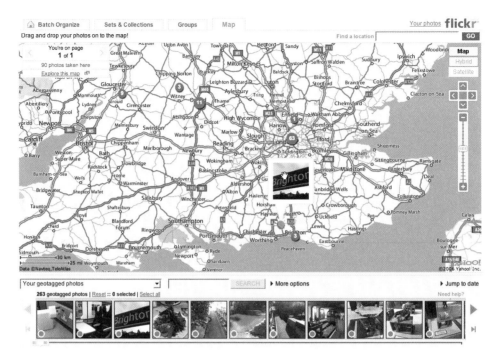

Figure 7.3. The Flickr Organizr's geotagging interface

Getting at the Data

Flickr has a very friendly policy around what you can do with the data associated with your own photos. The policy is this: you created the photos, so they belong to you, and you should be able to do whatever you want with them. This philosophy translates into a bewildering array of practical options for pulling data out of the service.

The Flickr API

If you're building server-side or desktop applications, Flickr's Web Services API gives you the ability to do almost anything that's possible on the site itself. In fact, Flickr's Ajax code actually uses the API when you rename a photo, add tags to it, or drag it on to a map. Fire up the Firebug[4] or LiveHTTPHeaders[5] Firefox extensions while using Flickr to watch the Ajax in action.

Our simple map application doesn't need access to private data, nor does it need to make any changes to the data stored on the site. As a result, we can skip the API entirely and use a powerful but less well-known alternative: the feeds.

---

[4] http://getfirebug.com/
[5] http://livehttpheaders.mozdev.org/

Flickr Feeds

RSS and Atom have become well established as ways to monitor different blogs and news sites without visiting them directly in a browser. But these common syndication feeds can be used for other purposes as well—any document that contains a list of items is a potential source for a feed.

Flickr provides RSS and Atom feeds for much of its data. You can subscribe to a feed of your own photos, someone else's photos, your friends' photos, or all of the photos matching a certain "tag." You can even subscribe to a feed containing every single photo uploaded to Flickr, although this would likely overwhelm your feed reader in just a few seconds!

While the Flickr API requires an API key (as does Google Maps, as we'll see soon), a Flickr feed is available to anyone—no registration step is required. In this chapter's project, we'll be using Flickr's feeds to pull out a list of the photos that we want to display on the map.

JSON

The final ingredient in our technology cocktail is **JSON (JavaScript Object Notation)**. JSON is a simple data format that's often used as a lightweight alternative to XML, and is particularly well suited to JavaScript development.

JSON was "discovered" by Douglas Crockford, a senior engineer at Yahoo. Douglas recognized that most modern programming languages share the same simple core set of data structures: numbers, strings, booleans, arrays, and collections of name/value pairs (known variously as records, structs, dictionaries, hash tables, hashes, or associative arrays). JavaScript provides an elegant literal syntax for all of these data structures, and the JSON standard reuses that syntax to define a mini-language for representing those data structures in a language-agnostic fashion.

Libraries for generating and parsing JSON exist for dozens of different languages, but JavaScript itself has a particularly easy time of it: it can evaluate JSON strings directly by passing them to the built-in eval function.

Here's a simple example that shows a JSON structure representing a collection of photos:

```
{
  "items": [{
    "title": "Foiled!",
    "link": "http://www.flickr.com/photos/simon/1345617936/",
    "media": {
     "m":"http://farm2.static.flickr.com/…/35c319c9a5_m.jpg"
    },
    "date_taken": "2007-09-08T08:11:14-08:00",
    "description": "[ … ]",
    "published": "2007-09-08T07:12:15Z",
    "author": "nobody@flickr.com (Simon Willison)",
```

```
      "tags": "cameraphone england london train [ … ]"
  }, {
    "title": "Arriving in Brighton",
    "link": "http://www.flickr.com/photos/simon/1345607350/",
    "media": {
      "m":"http://farm2.static.flickr.com/…/c11ac6973f_m.jpg"
    },
    "date_taken": "2007-09-01T13:31:12-08:00",
    "description": "[ … ]",
    "published": "2007-09-08T07:08:47Z",
    "author": "nobody@flickr.com (Simon Willison)",
    "tags": "cameraphone celltagged [ … ]"}]
}
```

If we were given a string s containing JSON, here's how we'd convert it into a JavaScript object:

```
var obj = eval('(' + s + ')');
```

 The Security of `eval`

The `eval` function is the fastest way to parse a JSON string into a JavaScript object, but it should only be used on JSON from a trusted source. If the JSON string came from an untrusted source (for example, user input or an untrusted third-party site), it may contain malicious JavaScript code. A safe alternative to directly calling `eval` is the `parseJSON` method from http://www.json.org/js.html. `parseJSON` uses regular expressions to check that a JSON string is safe before passing it to `eval`.

The JSON string must be wrapped in parentheses before evaluation, or JavaScript will confuse it with a malformed `for` loop or function definition, and throw a syntax error. Once evaluated in this way, the data within the JSON structure can be accessed using dot and array notation:

```
var photos = obj.items;
var photo = photos[0]; // The first photo structure
var title = photo.title;
var link = photo.link;
var url = photo.media.m;
```

The Same-origin Restriction

Traditional Ajax calls (using the `XMLHttpRequest` object) suffer from an important limitation: they're only allowed to communicate with the domain that served up the original script. For example, if your code is running on http://example.com/mypage.html, your `XMLHttpRequest` objects can only communicate with other pages or services running under http://example.com/.

There's a very good reason for this—many people surf the Web from a network that belongs to their company. This network may provide private intranet sites that aren't available to the wider Web—for example, there might be a top-secret wiki full of confidential information running at the address http://examplecorp.intranet/wiki/.

Without the same-origin restriction, malicious pages running on the public Internet could use XMLHttpRequest to steal information from the private wiki whenever a user on that company's network visited the malicious site. If browsers didn't enforce the same-origin policy, many private sites would be open to having their data stolen.

While it's essential for security, the same-origin restriction is a real nuisance if you're trying to create applications—such as our map—that have a legitimate need to pull data from different domains.

Luckily, JSON enables a workaround for this restriction that relies on the cooperation of the external domain. The workaround has various names, including **cross-domain JSON** and JSON-P (short for "JSON with Padding").

Enabling Cross-domain JSON

To enable cross-domain JSON, a site just needs to serve up a regular JSON object wrapped in a call to a named function. Flickr produces cross-domain JSON feeds that look like this:

```
jsonFlickrFeed({
  "title": "Photos from Simon Willison, with geodata",
  "link": "http://www.flickr.com/photos/simon/",
  "description": "",
  "modified": "2007-09-08T07:12:15Z",
  "generator": "http://www.flickr.com/",
  "items": [{
    "title": "Foiled!",
    "link": "http://www.flickr.com/photos/simon/1345617936/",
    "media": {
      "m":"http://farm2.static.flickr.com/…/35c319c9a5_m.jpg"
    },
    "date_taken": "2007-09-08T08:11:14-08:00",
    "description": "[ … ]",
    "published": "2007-09-08T07:12:15Z",
    "author": "nobody@flickr.com (Simon Willison)",
    "tags": "cameraphone england london train [ … ]"
    },
    :
  ]
});
```

By defining our own jsonFlickrFeed function, and using a regular HTML <script> tag to include the JSON feed, we can grab data from the flickr.com domain while bypassing the cross-domain restriction completely.

Trust Your Source

JSON-P is a deliberate workaround for the same-origin restriction—a restriction that's designed to protect your application's security. You should never load a JSON-P document from a site that you don't trust—doing so could leave you vulnerable to malicious cross-site scripting attacks.[6]

Let's look at a simple example: a page that shows thumbnails of a user's last 20 Flickr photos. For this example, all code points to my own Flickr account, but you'll find that it's easy enough to adapt it to your own account.

First, we need the URL for the JSON feed. At the bottom of my photos page,[7] there's a link to the RSS feed that looks like this:

http://api.flickr.com/services/feeds/photos_public.gne?id=35034346572@N01&lang=en-us&forma
➥t=rss_200

We can turn this into a JSON feed by modifying the last argument in the URL—changing `rss_200` to `json`—as follows:

http://api.flickr.com/services/feeds/photos_public.gne?id=35034346572@N01&lang=en-us&forma
➥t=json

That URL gives us the JSON format we're looking for. Note that `35034346572@N01` is my Flickr user ID; to obtain a feed of your own photos, you'll need to determine your own feed URL by visiting the link on your photo page.

The next step is to write the `jsonFlickrFeed` function that's called when the feed has loaded. For this simple example, we're just going to assign the returned JSON object to a global variable:

showphotos.html (excerpt)

```
function jsonFlickrFeed(json) {
  // Assign to a global variable
  window.jsonFromFlickr = json;
}
```

We also need functionality to display the thumbnails of the photos. We'll split this functionality into two separate functions: one that creates the DOM node to display a single photo, and one that loops through all of the photos and attaches a representation of each photo to the DOM:

---

[6] http://en.wikipedia.org/wiki/Cross-site_scripting/
[7] http://www.flickr.com/photos/simon/

showphotos.html *(excerpt)*

```
function makePhoto(photo) {
  var li = document.createElement('li');
  var a = document.createElement('a');
  a.href = photo.link;
  var img = document.createElement('img');
  img.src = photo.media.m;
  img.title = photo.title;
  img.alt = photo.alt;
  a.appendChild(img);
  li.appendChild(a);
  return li;
}

function showPhotos() {
  if (!jsonFromFlickr) {
    alert('Flickr photos failed to load');
  }
  // Remove the only list item from the photos <ul>
  var ul = document.getElementById('photos');
  ul.removeChild(ul.getElementsByTagName('li')[0]);
  // Loop over the photos and display them all
  for (var i = 0, photo; photo = jsonFromFlickr.items[i]; i++) {
    ul.appendChild(makePhoto(photo));
  }
}
```

The initial HTML for the page body is very simple:

showphotos.html *(excerpt)*

```
<ul id="photos">
  <li><a href="http://www.flickr.com/photos/simon/">My Flickr
  photos</a></li>
</ul>
```

Graceful Degradation Guaranteed!

Our code removes the simple link from our HTML document and replaces it with the list of photos. By taking this approach, we ensure that users without JavaScript will still be able to access our photographs by clicking on the link.

Let's combine the code above in to a working page. We'll set the showPhotos function to run as soon as the page has finished loading:

```
                                                              showphotos.html
<!DOCTYPE HTML PUBLIC "-//W3C//DTD HTML 4.01//EN"
"http://www.w3.org/TR/html4/strict.dtd">
<html>
<head>
  <title>Hello World!</title></head>
  <script type="text/javascript">
    function jsonFlickrFeed(json) {
      // Assign to a global variable
    window.jsonFromFlickr = json;
  }
  </script>
  <script type="text/javascript" src="http://api.flickr.com/services/feeds/photos
    ➥_public.gne?id=35034346572@N01&amp;format=json">
  </script>
  <script type="text/javascript">
    function makePhoto(photo) {
      var li = document.createElement('li');
      var a = document.createElement('a');
      a.href = photo.link;
      var img = document.createElement('img');
      img.src = photo.media.m;
      img.title = photo.title;
      img.alt = photo.alt;
      a.appendChild(img);
      li.appendChild(a);
      return li;
    }

    function showPhotos() {
      if (!jsonFromFlickr) {
        alert('Flickr photos failed to load');
      }
      // 'Empty' the ul by removing all of its children
      var ul = document.getElementById('photos');
      while (ul.hasChildNodes()) {
        ul.removeChild(ul.firstChild);
      }
      // Loop over the photos and display them all
      for (var i = 0, photo; photo = jsonFromFlickr.items[i]; i++) {
        ul.appendChild(makePhoto(photo));
      }
    }
    window.onload = showPhotos;
  </script>
</head>
```

```
<body>
  <ul id="photos">
    <li><a href="http://www.flickr.com/photos/simon/">My Flickr photos</a></li>
  </ul>
</body>
</html>
```

This works exactly as we intended, as Figure 7.4 shows. However, the photos are a little large; it would be nice if they were smaller and square, rather than displaying as different sized rectangles.

Notice how the photo URLs all look something like this:

http://farm2.static.flickr.com/1033/1345617936_35c319c9a5_m.jpg

If we replace the _m near the end of the URL with a _s, we get a cropped, 75×75 pixel thumbnail of the image.[8] Let's update our makePhoto function to use that URL instead:

showphotos-grid.html (excerpt)

```
function makePhoto(photo) {
  ⋮
  img.src = photo.media.m.replace('_m', '_s');
  ⋮
  return li;
}
```

That's much nicer. Now if we add a little bit of CSS, we can create a neat-looking grid effect:

showphotos-grid.html (excerpt)

```
<style type="text/css">
ul#photos, ul#photos li, ul#photos img {
  display: block;
  margin: 0;
  padding: 0;
  border: none;
  float: left;
}
ul#photos {
  width: 375px; /* 75 * 5 */
}
</style>
```

The resulting grid is shown in Figure 7.5.

---

[8] Other Flickr photo sizes are documented at http://www.flickr.com/services/api/misc.urls.html.

Figure 7.4. A basic list of full-size photos retrieved via a Flickr feed

Figure 7.5. A feed of Flickr photos, arranged as a grid of squares

Cross-domain JSON on Demand

So far, we've hard-coded the JSON feed directly into our HTML. It's also possible to load external JSON files dynamically, in a similar way to traditional Ajax requests. We can do this by constructing a new script element using the DOM, and appending it to the head section of our document:

tagsearch.html *(excerpt)*

```
function loadJSON(url) {
  var script = document.createElement('script');
  script.type = 'text/javascript';
  script.src = url;
  document.getElementsByTagName('head')[0].appendChild(script);
}
```

We can modify our previous example to allow users to enter a tag, and then view the 20 most recent photos that include that tag. We'll use the following URL (*[TAG]* will be replaced with the tag entered by the user) to retrieve our tagged photos:

http://api.flickr.com/services/feeds/photos_public.gne?tags=*[TAG]*

Here's the revised code:

tagsearch.html

```
<!DOCTYPE HTML PUBLIC "-//W3C//DTD HTML 4.01//EN"
    "http://www.w3.org/TR/html4/strict.dtd">
<html>
<head>
  <title>View photos by tag</title></head>
  <style type="text/css">
    ul#photos, ul#photos li, ul#photos img {
    display: block;
    margin: 0;
    padding: 0;
    border: none;
    float: left;
  }
  ul#photos {
    width: 375px; /* 75 * 5 */
  }
</style>
<script type="text/javascript">
  function loadJSON(url) {
    var script = document.createElement('script');
    script.type = 'text/javascript';
    script.src = url;
    document.getElementsByTagName('head')[0].appendChild(script);
  }
  function makePhoto(photo) {
    var li = document.createElement('li');
    var a = document.createElement('a');
    a.href = photo.link;
    var img = document.createElement('img');
    img.src = photo.media.m.replace('_m', '_s');
```

```
      img.title = photo.title;
      img.alt = photo.alt;
      a.appendChild(img);
      li.appendChild(a);
      return li;
    }
    function jsonFlickrFeed(json) {
      // 'Empty' the ul by removing all of its children
      var ul = document.getElementById('photos');
      while (ul.hasChildNodes()) {
        ul.removeChild(ul.firstChild);
      }
      // Loop over the photos and display them all
      for (var i = 0, photo; photo = json.items[i]; i++) {
        ul.appendChild(makePhoto(photo));
      }
    }
    function loadTag(tag) {
      loadJSON(
        "http://api.flickr.com/services/feeds/photos_public.gne?" +
        "format=json&tags=" + tag
      );
    }
  </script>
  </head>
  <body>
    <p>
      <label>Enter tag: <input type="text" id="t"></label>
      <input type="submit"
        onclick="loadTag(document.getElementById('t').value); return false;">
    </p>

    <ul id="photos">
      <li><a href="http://www.flickr.com/photos/simon/">My Flickr photos</a></li>
    </ul>
  </body>
</html>
```

We could improve the code above by adding an Ajax loading indicator and avoiding the inline event handler on the **Submit** button, but it demonstrates the cross-domain JSON technique nicely, so we'll leave it at that. Figure 7.6 shows the resulting application.

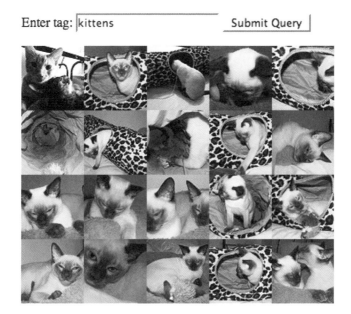

Figure 7.6. A feed of Flickr photos matching the tag "kittens"

Pulling it All Together

We now have all of the raw materials we'll need to create a Google map from our Flickr photos: we know how to draw a map, and we know how to selectively pull and display photos from Flickr using JSON. Let's combine this knowledge to create a map displaying the locations of our photos.

The first step is to find the appropriate JSON feed. We don't just want our recently added photos; we want the photos that we've geotagged. Luckily, Flickr offers a feed for doing exactly that, at the following URL:

http://api.flickr.com/services/feeds/geo/?id=35034346572@N01&format=json

As before, 35034346572@N01 is my Flickr User ID (also known as an NSID).

Our map code is going to build on our earlier JSON example, but as well as displaying the photo in a list of thumbnails, we're going to plot a marker on a map. Later, we'll set up the markers to display more information about each photo when either the marker or the thumbnail for that photo is clicked.

We'll reuse the map initialization code from the previous example in this project. First up, we need to rewrite the function that shows the photos so that it plots them on the map as well as displaying them in the thumbnail grid:

```
function showPhotos() {
  if (!window.jsonFromFlickr) {
    alert('Flickr photos failed to load');
  }
  // 'Empty' the ul by removing all of its children
  var ul = document.getElementById('photos');
  while (ul.hasChildNodes()) {
    ul.removeChild(ul.firstChild);
  }
  // Loop over the photos and display them all
  for (var i = 0, photo; photo = jsonFromFlickr.items[i]; i++) {
    ul.appendChild(makePhoto(photo));
    // Add a marker to the map at the correct point
    var point = new google.maps.LatLng(photo.latitude, photo.longitude);
    var marker = new google.maps.Marker(point);
    gmap.addOverlay(marker);
  }
}
```

When we combine this with our map's initialization code, we get the following:

```
<!DOCTYPE HTML PUBLIC "-//W3C//DTD HTML 4.01//EN"
"http://www.w3.org/TR/html4/strict.dtd">
<html>
<head>
  <title>Hello World!</title></head>
<script src="http://www.google.com/jsapi?key=[YOUR API KEY]"
    type="text/javascript">
</script>
<script type="text/javascript">
  google.load('maps', '2'); // Load version 2 of the Maps API
  function showMap() {
    window.gmap = new google.maps.Map2(document.getElementById('gmap'))
    // Center on England, zoom level 5
    gmap.setCenter(new google.maps.LatLng(53.6967, -3.2080), 5)
  }
  google.setOnLoadCallback(showMap);

  function jsonFlickrFeed(json) {
    // Assign to a global variable
    window.jsonFromFlickr = json;
  }
</script>
<script type="text/javascript" src="http://api.flickr.com/services/feeds/geo/?id=
  ➡35034346572@N01&amp;format=json">
```

```
</script>
<script type="text/javascript">
  function makePhoto(photo) {
    var li = document.createElement('li');
    var a = document.createElement('a');
    a.href = photo.link;
    var img = document.createElement('img');
    img.src = photo.media.m.replace('_m', '_s');
    img.title = photo.title;
    img.alt = photo.alt;
    a.appendChild(img);
    li.appendChild(a);
    return li;
  }

  function showPhotos() {
    if (!jsonFromFlickr) {
      alert('Flickr photos failed to load');
    }
    // 'Empty' the ul by removing all of its children
    var ul = document.getElementById('photos');
    while (ul.hasChildNodes()) {
      ul.removeChild(ul.firstChild);
    }
    // Loop over the photos and display them all
    for (var i = 0, photo; photo = jsonFromFlickr.items[i]; i++) {
      ul.appendChild(makePhoto(photo));
      // Add a marker to the map at the correct point
      var point = new google.maps.LatLng(photo.latitude, photo.longitude);
      var marker = new google.maps.Marker(point);
      gmap.addOverlay(marker);
    }
  }

  window.onload = function() {
    showMap();
    showPhotos();
  };
</script>
<style type="text/css">
ul#photos li, ul#photos img {
  display: block;
  margin: 0;
  padding: 0;
  border: none;
  float: left;
}
ul#photos {
  width: 375px; /* 75 * 5 */
  position: absolute;
```

```
    top: 0;
    left: 375px;
    margin: 0;
    padding: 0;
  }
  div#gmap {
    width: 375px;
    height: 300px;
    position: absolute;
    top: 0;
    left: 0;
  }
  </style>
  </head>
  <body>
    <div id="gmap"></div>
      <ul id="photos">
        <li><a href="http://www.flickr.com/photos/simon/">My Flickr photos</a></li>
      </ul>
  </body>
  </html>
```

We've made a couple of important changes here. In the `showMap` function, we're creating `gmap` as an explicit global variable:

simplemap.html *(excerpt)*

```
window.gmap = new google.maps.Map2(document.getElementById('gmap'));
```

`window` is the global object, so assigning properties to `window` creates a global variable. We can also create global variables simply by omitting the `var` keyword from a variable declaration, but doing so makes it hard to distinguish deliberate global variables from accidental ones.

Why Use a Global Variable?

It's good JavaScript style to avoid global variables as much as possible. In this case, we create a global `gmap` variable for the sake of convenience: every one of our functions that manipulates the map needs access to Google Map instance, so making them global is a handy shortcut. It also means that we can interactively explore the Google Maps API using Firebug's interactive console.

Our `window.onload` function now needs to call two separate functions: one to create the map, and one to show the photos. We've upgraded to an anonymous function that calls the two setup functions in turn:

simplemap.html (excerpt)

```
window.onload = function() {
  showMap();
  showPhotos();
};
```

Order is important here, as `showPhotos` relies on a global variable that's created in `showMap`.

Finally, we've added a sprinkle of CSS. Our photos and maps are of known pixel sizes, which makes it nice and easy to lay things out—the map is set to 375×300px, which is the same size as a grid of 20 photographs. You can see what it looks like in Figure 7.7.

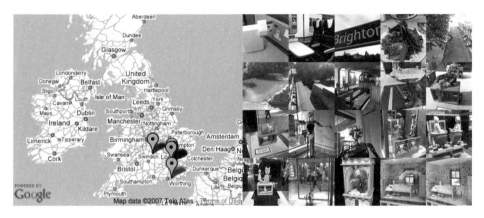

Figure 7.7. The first incarnation of our widget, combining Flickr photos with a map from the Google Maps API

Now we have a map with some markers, but it's not really a very interactive way to browse our photos. Let's add the following features:

- controls for zooming in and out on the map, and switching to satellite view
- clickable thumbnails: when an image is clicked, we'll highlight the thumbnail and show an info window next to the marker
- a "Zoom in" button in the map window, to quickly zoom in on the map
- the ability to recenter the map once the photos have loaded, to display all of the markers at the most appropriate zoom level

We'll address these features in turn.

Enhancing Our Widget

By further exploiting the Google Maps API—and flexing our JavaScript muscle a little—we can easily add the features that we listed in the previous section.

Adding Map Controls

The Google Maps API comes with a number of useful controls that can be added to a map. Adding a zoom control is easy:

```
gmap.addControl(new google.maps.LargeMapControl());
```

This code adds the large zooming and panning interface shown in Figure 7.8.

Figure 7.8. The large version of the Google Maps zoom control

Since our mashup deals with photographs, it makes sense to allow users to access a satellite photo view in addition to the regular map. We can add a control that lets them do that using `MapTypeControl`:

```
gmap.addControl(new google.maps.MapTypeControl());
```

 Smaller Controls Are Available

If we were to decide that that control was too big, we could use the `SmallMapControl`, which takes up less screen real estate, instead:

```
gmap.addControl(new google.maps.SmallMapControl());
```

Let's default the map to the satellite view using the `setMapType` method:

```
gmap.setMapType(google.maps.SATELLITE_MAP);
```

Try experimenting with `SmallZoomControl`, `ScaleControl`, and `OverviewMapControl` as well.

Creating Clickable Thumbnails

When a user clicks on a thumbnail in the grid, we want our widget to perform a specific action: we want to highlight that thumbnail and display the info window attached to the corresponding map marker.

We'll do this using a callback function attached to the `click` event on the thumbnail … but there's a catch! We don't need just one callback function, we need 20—one for each thumbnail.

JavaScript supports a language feature called **closures**, which you may remember from Chapter 5. While I won't describe closures in detail here, they allow us to create functions that capture one or more of the variables that are required for their operation. This concept is best illustrated with an example:

finishedwidget.html *(excerpt)*

```
function makeClickCallback(photo) {
  return function(ev) {
    stopEvent(ev);
    photo.marker.openInfoWindow(buildInfoWindow(photo));
    highlightPhoto(photo);
  }
}
```

`makeClickCallback` is an example of what I call a **function factory**—a function that creates and returns another function. We pass a photo object to `makeClickCallback`, and it returns a function which, when called, shows the info window for that photo and highlights it on the thumbnail grid.

We can call the function factory as many times as we like, passing in a different photo object each time. Each time we call it we get back a brand new function object that "remembers" which photo it was created with.

Using this technique, we can easily create the callback functions we need to add interactivity to the thumbnails and markers in our application.

Our callback function is passed a single argument, `ev`, which is the event object created by the browser. We can use it to prevent the browser's default action from occurring; in the case of a link, the action would be navigating to another page entirely. Unfortunately, the way in which event information is stored—and, therefore, the way in which we prevent the default action from occurring—differs wildly between IE and other browsers. The good news is that our `stopEvent` function handles those differences for us:

```
function stopEvent(ev) {
  ev = ev || window.event; // IE provides window.event instead
  if (ev) {
    if (ev.preventDefault) {
      ev.preventDefault(); // Other browsers
    } else {
      ev.returnValue = false; // IE
    }
  }
}
```

Highlighting the Current Thumbnail

To make the page a little more interesting, we're going to highlight the currently displayed photo in the thumbnail grid to the right of the map. One simple way to highlight an image is to "fade out" all of the others. We can do this using CSS opacity:

```
function highlightPhoto(photo) {
  var ul = document.getElementById('photos');
  var links = ul.getElementsByTagName('a');
  for (var i = 0, a; a = links[i]; i++) {
    var img = a.getElementsByTagName('img')[0];
    if (a.href == photo.link) {
      img.style.opacity = 1;
    } else {
      img.style.opacity = 0.4;
    }
  }
}
```

Our input here is a photo object. We know that the `ul` with the `id` of `photos` contains a collection of links. Each of these links is a thumbnail image, and the link points to that image's photo page on Flickr (stored in `photo.link`). We cycle through the links, looking for one with a URL that matches that of our current photo. When we find it, we set the contained image's opacity to 1 (making it completely visible). The opacity of all the other images is set to 0.4, which makes them partially see-through.

The result of this work is shown in Figure 7.9.

Figure 7.9. Fading out all thumbnails except the current photo

This approach works fine in every browser except IE 6, which doesn't provide support for the CSS opacity property.[9] To ensure compatibility with that browser, we need to add an extra line that uses IE's proprietary filters:

finishedwidget.html *(excerpt)*

```
if (a.href == photo.link) {
  img.style.opacity = 1;
  img.style.filter = 'alpha(opacity=100)';
} else {
  img.style.opacity = 0.4;
  img.style.filter = 'alpha(opacity=40)';
}
```

Whereas opacity is a value between 0 and 1, IE's alpha filter expects a value between 0 and 100. Multiplying our regular value by 100 does the trick. Browsers other than IE ignore the `filter` property entirely.

Displaying an Info Window

The info window is a versatile component of the Google Maps API that allows information to be displayed in a floating window attached to a point or marker on the map. There are a number of different ways to create an info window, but the approach we'll use is to call the `openInfoWindow` method on the marker object.

---

[9] This is a perfectly reasonable omission; opacity is not defined as part of CSS 2, but instead has been back-ported by the other browsers from the draft CSS 3 specification.

openInfoWindow takes a single argument: a DOM node that we can use for the info window's content. We therefore need a method that can create this DOM node for us. The finished info window will look like Figure 7.10.

Figure 7.10. The completed info window for one of our geotagged photos

Thankfully, we only need to provide the HTML for the text and image that goes inside the window; the close button, or **x**, at top-right, rounded corners, and drop shadow effect are all provided for us. Here's the HTML we'll need:

finishedwidget.html (excerpt)

```
<div class="infoBox">
  <h4>The end of the Piccadilly line</h4>
  <img alt="The end of the Piccadilly line" src="http://farm1.static.flickr...">
  <a href="#">zoom in</a><br>
  <a href="http://www.flickr.com/.../">photo page</a>
</div>
```

We need to assemble the HTML dynamically to fill in the correct details for the given photo. There are a number of ways we can do this: we can construct a string of HTML and use innerHTML, or we can use the more verbose DOM methods (appendChild, createElement, and friends) directly.

Surprisingly, innerHTML performs better than explicit DOM methods in most browsers. It also results in less verbose, slightly more maintainable code. We'll create our info window using a combination of innerHTML and DOM manipulation methods:

finishedwidget.html (excerpt)

```
function buildInfoWindow(photo) {
  var div = document.createElement('div');
  div.className = 'infoBox';
```

```
div.innerHTML = [
  '<h4>', photo.title, '</h4>',
  '<img src="', photo.media.m.replace('_m', '_t'),
  '" alt="', photo.title, '">',
  '<a href="#">zoom in</a><br>',
  '<a href="', photo.link, '">photo page</a>'
].join('');
```

This code illustrates a couple of useful optimization tricks. It's inefficient to incrementally modify the `innerHTML` of an element that's "live" on a page, since the browser has to constantly rerender the page as the changes are being made. Instead, the best practice is to create an element and assign content to its `innerHTML` before displaying it.

It's also a good idea to avoid gluing large strings together with the + operator, as this approach causes many temporary strings to be created in memory. Instead, we construct an array of strings, then use the `join` method to concatenate the array together in a single operation.

Having constructed our info box, we have one remaining task to complete: we need to assign an event handler to the "zoom in" link. For that, we'll switch back to using DOM methods:

finishedwidget.html *(excerpt)*

```
  // Add event listener
  var link = div.getElementsByTagName('a')[0];
  google.maps.Event.addDomListener(link, 'click', makeZoomCallback(photo));
  return div;
}
```

`makeZoomCallback` is another function factory; it looks like this:

finishedwidget.html *(excerpt)*

```
function makeZoomCallback(photo) {
  // Creates a callback function that zooms the map to that photo
  return function(ev) {
    stopEvent(ev);
    gmap.setCenter(new google.maps.LatLng(photo.latitude, photo.longitude), 14);
    photo.marker.openInfoWindow(buildInfoWindow(photo));
    highlightPhoto(photo);
  }
}
```

This function uses `photo.marker` to correspond to the marker that represents a given photo; we'll need to set that relationship up in our initialization code.

Note that we zoom and recenter the map, and then redisplay the info window. Google's code for displaying an info window includes an algorithm that shifts the map slightly to make sure the info window is fully displayed—it's important that we recenter the map before triggering that code, or the info window may display half off the map.

Finally, we need to style our info window using CSS. It's important that we provide a sensible height and width: Flickr thumbnail images can be up to 100 pixels high, but we don't know a thumbnail's exact size until the image has loaded, as it may be in either landscape or portrait orientation. The image's explicit width is needed to work around an issue in IE that sees info windows without an explicit width expand to the width of the entire map. Here's the CSS we'll use:

finishedwidget.html *(excerpt)*

```
div.infoBox {
  height: 130px; /* Ensure room for 100px high thumbnail + h4 */
  width: 230px; /* Needs a width to avoid issues with IE */
  font-family: helvetica, arial, sans-serif;
}
div.infoBox img {
  float: left;
  margin-right: 5px;
}
div.infoBox h4 {
  margin: 0 0 5px 0;
}
div.infoBox a {
  font-size: 0.9em;
  color: #666;
}
```

Recentering the Map

We've already seen the `centerAndZoom` method, which recenters the map on a particular point. If we want to center the map so that all of our photos are visible, we'll need to calculate a zoom level and the coordinates of the map's center point. Google provides a method called `getBoundsLevel` to help deal with exactly this situation.

`getBoundsZoomLevel` takes a single argument: a `bounds` instance, which represents an area on the map defined by that map's maximum and minimum latitude and longitude. We can create this `bounds` instance by finding the extreme latitudes and longitudes ourselves, but an easier approach is to take advantage of that object's `extend` method, which takes a point and extends the bounds to include that point (if it isn't included already).

If we call `bounds.extend` on every point in a collection of points, the resulting `bounds` object will include all of those points:

finishedwidget.html (excerpt)

```
var bounds = new google.maps.LatLngBounds();
for (var i = 0, point; point = points[i]; i++) {
  bounds.extend(point);
}
```

We can then find the optimum zoom level using the `getBoundsZoomLevel` method:

finishedwidget.html (excerpt)

```
var zoomLevel = gmap.getBoundsZoomLevel(bounds);
```

We find the optimum center point using `getCenter`:

finishedwidget.html (excerpt)

```
var center = bounds.getCenter();
```

A final call to `gmap.setCenter` can center and zoom the map to the correct level:

finishedwidget.html (excerpt)

```
gmap.setCenter(center, zoomLevel);
```

Putting it All Together

We now have all of the components we need to assemble a final map that satisfies all of our additional feature requests. Here's the complete code:

finishedwidget.html

```
<!DOCTYPE HTML PUBLIC "-//W3C//DTD HTML 4.01//EN"
    "http://www.w3.org/TR/html4/strict.dtd">
<html>
<head>
<title>My Flickr photos, on a map!</title>
<script
  src="http://www.google.com/jsapi?key=[YOUR API KEY]"
  type="text/javascript">
</script>
<script type="text/javascript">
google.load('maps', '2'); // Load version 2 of the Maps API
function showMap() {
  window.gmap =
```

```
        new google.maps.Map2(document.getElementById('gmap'));
    // Center on England, zoom level 5
    gmap.setCenter(new google.maps.LatLng(53.6967, -3.2080), 5);
    gmap.setMapType(google.maps.SATELLITE_MAP);
    // Add controls
    gmap.addControl(new google.maps.LargeMapControl());
    gmap.addControl(new google.maps.MapTypeControl());
}


function jsonFlickrFeed(json) {
    // Assign to a global variable
    window.jsonFromFlickr = json;
}
</script>
<script type="text/javascript" src="http://api.flickr.com/services/feeds/geo/?id=
➥35034346572@N01&amp;format=json"></script>
<script type="text/javascript">
function showPhotos() {
    if (!jsonFromFlickr) {
        alert('Flickr photos failed to load');
        return;
    }
    // 'Empty' the ul by removing all of its children
    var ul = document.getElementById('photos');
    while (ul.hasChildNodes()) {
        ul.removeChild(ul.firstChild);
    }
    // For calculating center of all points later
    var bounds = new google.maps.LatLngBounds();
    // Loop over the photos and display them all
    for (var i = 0, photo; photo = jsonFromFlickr.items[i]; i++) {
        var li = document.createElement('li');
        var a = document.createElement('a');
        a.href = photo.link;
        var img = document.createElement('img');
        img.src = photo.media.m.replace('_m', '_s');
        img.title = photo.title;
        img.alt = photo.title;
        a.appendChild(img);
        li.appendChild(a);
        // Add to the ul
        ul.appendChild(li);
        // Add a marker to the map at the correct point
        var point = new google.maps.LatLng(photo.latitude, photo.longitude);
        bounds.extend(point);
        photo.marker = new google.maps.Marker(point);
        gmap.addOverlay(photo.marker);
        // Hook up the link click event
        google.maps.Event.addDomListener(a, 'click', makeClickCallback(photo));
        // Hook up the marker click event
```

```
      google.maps.Event.addListener(
        photo.marker, 'click', makeClickCallback(photo)
      );
    }
    // Center the map to show our points
    gmap.setZoom(gmap.getBoundsZoomLevel(bounds));
    gmap.setCenter(bounds.getCenter());
}

function buildInfoWindow(photo) {
    var div = document.createElement('div');
    div.className = 'infoBox';
    div.innerHTML = [
      '<h4>', photo.title, '</h4>',
      '<img src="', photo.media.m.replace('_m', '_t'),
      '" alt="', photo.title, '">',
      '<a href="#">zoom in</a><br>',
      '<a href="', photo.link, '">photo page</a>'
    ].join('');
    // Add event listener
    var link = div.getElementsByTagName('a')[0];
    google.maps.Event.addDomListener(link, 'click', makeZoomCallback(photo));
    return div;
}

function stopEvent(ev) {
    ev = ev || window.event;
    if (ev) {
      if (ev.preventDefault) {
        ev.preventDefault();
      } else {
        ev.returnValue = false;
      }
    }
}

function makeClickCallback(photo) {
  return function(ev) {
    stopEvent(ev);
    photo.marker.openInfoWindow(buildInfoWindow(photo));
    highlightPhoto(photo);
  }
}

function makeZoomCallback(photo) {
  // Creates a callback function that zooms the map to that photo
  return function(ev) {
    stopEvent(ev);
    gmap.setCenter(new google.maps.LatLng(photo.latitude, photo.longitude), 14);
    photo.marker.openInfoWindow(buildInfoWindow(photo));
```

```
      highlightPhoto(photo);
    }
}

function highlightPhoto(photo) {
  var ul = document.getElementById('photos');
  var links = ul.getElementsByTagName('a');
  for (var i = 0, a; a = links[i]; i++) {
    var img = a.getElementsByTagName('img')[0];
    if (a.href == photo.link) {
      img.style.opacity = 1;
      img.style.filter = 'alpha(opacity=100)';
    } else {
      img.style.opacity = 0.4;
      img.style.filter = 'alpha(opacity=40)';
    }
  }
}

google.setOnLoadCallback(function() {
  showMap();
  showPhotos();
});
</script>
<style type="text/css">
ul#photos li, ul#photos img {
  display: block;
  margin: 0;
  padding: 0;
  border: none;
  float: left;
  width: 75px;
  height: 75px;
}
ul#photos {
  width: 375px; /* 75 * 5 */
  position: absolute;
  top: 0;
  left: 375px;
  margin: 0;
  padding: 0;
}
div#gmap {
  width: 375px;
  height: 300px;
  position: absolute;
  top: 0;
  left: 0;
}
div.infoBox {
```

```
    height: 130px; /* Ensure room for 100px high
                      thumbnail + h4 title */
    width: 230px; /* Needs a width or IE breaks */
    font-family: helvetica, arial, sans-serif;
}
div.infoBox img {
    float: left;
    margin-right: 5px;
}
div.infoBox h4 {
    margin: 0 0 5px 0;
}
div.infoBox a {
    font-size: 0.9em;
    color: #666;
}
</style>
</head>
<body>
<div id="gmap"></div>
<ul id="photos">
  <li><a href="http://www.flickr.com/photos/simon/">My Flickr photos</a></li>
</ul>
</body>
</html>
```

At last, the finished widget is shown in Figure 7.11!

Figure 7.11. Our final widget, incorporating all the additional features

Taking Things Further

This chapter has barely scratched the surface of what's possible with these two powerful APIs. If I've piqued your interest, the following sites should help further your exploration:

Flickr Services, at http://www.flickr.com/services/
> the official guide to the Flickr API, complete with dozens of interesting examples

Google Maps API, at http://www.google.com/apis/maps/
> the official documentation, with plenty of code samples

The Google Maps API blog, at http://googlemapsapi.blogspot.com/
> important to watch for news on Google's frequent updates to the API

Google Lat Long Blog, http://google-latlong.blogspot.com/
> news from the teams at Google behind Google Maps and Google Earth

ProgrammableWeb, http://programmableweb.com/
> lists of APIs and mashups from all over the Web

Summary

Mashups are a powerful new category of application that take full advantage of the distributed nature of the Web. JSON and JSON-P have brought mashups to the browser, enabling client-side developers to participate in this exciting new form of development.

In this chapter, we've seen how two popular services can be combined to create a useful widget, constructed entirely using client-side JavaScript and CSS. The tools and techniques we used provide a useful basis for other mashups, and you're encouraged to use them in your own applications.

Flickr and Google Maps are both excellent examples of JavaScript-friendly APIs, but they represent the tip of an iceberg: many other services also offer APIs, and the number is growing all the time. Since mashups result from the combination of two or more APIs, every new API opens up a multitude of possibilities for new combinations. Your only constraint is your imagination.

Index

THE PRINCIPLES OF
BEAUTIFUL
WEB DESIGN

BY JASON BEAIRD

DESIGN BEAUTIFUL WEB SITES USING THIS SIMPLE STEP-BY-STEP GUIDE

THE ART & SCIENCE OF CSS

BY CAMERON ADAMS
JINA BOLTON
DAVID JOHNSON
STEVE SMITH
JONATHAN SNOOK

INSPIRATIONAL STANDARDS-BASED WEB DESIGN

THE PHP
ANTHOLOGY
101 ESSENTIAL TIPS, TRICKS & HACKS

BY **DAVEY SHAFIK**
MATTHEW WEIER O'PHINNEY
LIGAYA TURMELLE
HARRY FUECKS
BEN BALBO
2ND EDITION

SOLUTIONS TO THE MOST COMMON PROGRAMMING PROBLEMS

THE ASP.NET 2.0 ANTHOLOGY

101 ESSENTIAL TIPS, TRICKS & HACKS

BY **SCOTT ALLEN**
JEFF ATWOOD
WYATT BARNETT
JON GALLOWAY
PHIL HAACK